MW00717164

THE HERMENEUTICS OF THE
BAN ON IMAGES

The Hermeneutics of the Ban on Images

Exegetical and Systematic Theological Approaches

Friedhelm Hartenstein and *Michael Moxter*
Translated by *Linda Maloney*

Paulist Press
New York / Mahwah, NJ

Unless otherwise stated, the Scripture quotations contained herein are from the New Revised Standard Version: Catholic Edition, Copyright © 1989 and 1993, by the Division of Christian Education of the National Council of the Churches of Christ in the United States of America. Used by permission. All rights reserved.

Cover image: Anselm Kiefer, Bilderstreit (1977). Oil on canvas, 211.3 x 272 cm, Van Abbe Museum, Netherlands. © Atelier Anselm Kiefer.
Cover design by Sharyn Banks
Book design by Lynn Else

Originally published as *Hermeneutik des Bilderverbots. Exegetische und systematisch-theologische Annäherungen. Forum Theologische Literaturzeitung (ThLZ.F)* 26, copyright © 2016 negotiated by Evangelische Verlagsanstalt GmbH, 04155 Leipzig, Deutschland.

English translation copyright © 2021 by Paulist Press, Inc.

The translation of this work was funded by Geisteswissenschaften International – Translation Funding for Work in the Humanities and Social Sciences from Germany, a joint initiative of the Fritz Thyssen Foundation, the German Federal Foreign Office, the collecting society VG WORT and the Börsenverein des Deutschen Buchhandels (German Publishers & Booksellers Association).

All rights reserved. No part of this publication may be reproduced, stored in a retrieval system, or transmitted in any form or by any means, electronic, mechanical, photocopying, recording, scanning, or otherwise, without either the prior written permission of the Publisher, or authorization through payment of the appropriate per-copy fee to the Copyright Clearance Center, Inc., www.copyright.com. Requests to the Publisher for permission should be addressed to the Permissions Department, Paulist Press, permissions@paulistpress.com.

Library of Congress Cataloging-in-Publication Data
Names: Hartenstein, Friedhelm, 1960– author. | Moxter, Michael, 1956– author.
Title: The Hermeneutics of the ban on images : exegetical and systematic theological approaches / Friedhelm Hartenstein and Michael Moxter ; translated by Linda Maloney.
Other titles: Hermeneutik des Bilderverbots. English
Description: New York / Mahwah, NJ : Paulist Press, [2021] | "Originally published as Hermeneutik des Bilderverbots. Exegetische und systematisch-theologische Annäherungen. Forum Theologische Literaturzeitung, copyright 2016." | Summary: "Recognizing both the potential of biblical prohibition of images for causing religious conflict and the promise of a more nuanced appreciation of the role of images in human experience, this book constructs a framework for understanding the place of images, and their prohibition, within the biblical text and Christian religious practice"— Provided by publisher.
Identifiers: LCCN 2020040282 (print) | LCCN 2020040283 (ebook) | ISBN 9780809154548 (paperback) | ISBN 9781587688461 (ebook)
Subjects: LCSH: Image of God. | Idols and images. | Image (Theology) | God—In art.
Classification: LCC BL205 .H36713 2021 (print) | LCC BL205 (ebook) | DDC 203/.7—dc23
LC record available at https://lccn.loc.gov/2020040282
LC ebook record available at https://lccn.loc.gov/2020040283

ISBN 978-0-8091-5454-8 (paperback)
ISBN 978-1-58768-846-1 (e-book)

Published by Paulist Press
997 Macarthur Boulevard
Mahwah, New Jersey 07430
www.paulistpress.com

Printed and bound in the
United States of America

Contents

Contents

Contents

Contents

Plates 1 through 15 are inserted between pages 144 and 145.

Illustrations and Acknowledgments

Illustrations and Acknowledgments

Plate 2—Page I.2. Istanbul, Aya Irini Kilisesi—Hagia Eirene. © Photo: akg-images/Andrea Jemolo

Plate 3—Page I.3. *Saint Veronica with the Sudarium*, Master of Saint Veronica, shroud, ca. 1420. © Photo: akg-images

Plate 4—Page I.4. Altarpiece of the Lutheran Hospital Church of the Holy Ghost (Spitalkirche zum Heiligen Geist) at Dinkelsbühl, Franconia, Germany, central nave with altar and crucifix, 1537. © Photo: Foto Marburg/Art Resource, NY

Plate 5—Page I.5. Rabanus Maurus (ca. 825/26), *In honorem sanctae crucis (De laudibus sanctae crucis).* © Bibliothèque nationale de France

Plate 6—Page I.6. Klaus Kröger *Schriftbild* (1974). © 2018 Artists Rights Society (ARS), New York/VG Bild-Kunst, Bonn; Digital Image © The Museum of Modern Art/Licensed by SCALA/Art Resource, NY

Plate 7—Page I.7. Rémy Zaugg, *I, the picture, see* [*Ich, das Bild, sehe*] (1998). © Rémy Zaugg

Plate 8a—Page I.8. Kazimir Severinovich Malevich, *Black Square* (Suprematist composition, 1915) © Photo: akg-images

Plate 8b—Page I.9. Kazimir Severinovich Malevich, *White on White* (Suprematist composition, 1918) © Photo: akg-images/Album/ Fine Art Images

Plate 9—Page I.10. Ad Reinhardt, *Abstract Painting* (1966). The Museum of Modern Art, New York, NY, U.S.A. © 2018 Estate of Ad Reinhardt/Artists Rights Society (ARS), New York. Digital Image © The Museum of Modern Art/Licensed by SCALA/ Art Resource, NY

Plate 10—Page I.11. Piet Mondrian, Composition no. 10 in Black and White (1915) © Photo: akg-images

Plate 11—Page I.12–13 (double sided). John Hilliard, *Black Depths* (1974). © 2018 Artists Rights Society (ARS), New York DACS, London

Plate 12a—Page I.14. Anselm Kiefer, *Bilderstreit* (1980) (artist book) © Atelier Anselm Kiefer

Plate 12b—Page I.15. Anselm Kiefer, *Bilderstreit* (1977) , oil on canvas © Atelier Anselm Kiefer

Preface

THIS BOOK IS the outcome of a cooperation between (Old Testament) exegesis and systematic theology focusing on a current and—we think—theologically and anthropologically fundamental topic. It began with joint seminars in Hamburg, which means that the roots of the undertaking and our agreement about the methods of procedure go back some years. The current brisance of the subject in culture and politics underscores its importance, but it did not prevent us from focusing our own work and our attention primarily on the issues surrounding the biblical prohibition of images. Our main concern was and is about separating and sorting historical and contemporary layers of interpretation of one exemplary case around which implicit or explicit concepts of image and image theories have clustered. *Hermeneutics* here serves primarily as a pragmatic code word for a common effort at understanding that encompasses text and image, bridging disciplines and subject fields.

A few "unevennesses" are due to the genesis of the volume. (Some sections and parts have existed for quite a while; others were written only shortly before the book was completed.) The authors would be happy if the book were to be received as a "dialogical" project. One may and should read as well as consider its two differently situated main sections (II and III) in terms of each other. (Cross-references are provided as an aid to such reading.) The introduction (I) and prospect (IV) are the responsibility of the two authors working in tandem; the basic form of section I was shaped by Moxter, that of section IV by Hartenstein. The process of creating such a book project *à deux* is clearly more complex, but it offers an extra degree of perspective and argumentation that the authors and—we hope—the readers would not want to do without.

The volume would never have been completed without the assistance of many people. We are very grateful for numerous suggestions, discussions, notes, and corrections to (in Hamburg) Nina Heinsohn, Markus

Firchow, and Olivia Brown (who was responsible for the editorial work) and to (in Munich) Ann-Cathrin Fiss and Elisabeth Kühn, Mathias Litzenburger and Susanne Schleeger (these two having read the final corrected copy of sections II and IV). The DFG-Project "Bild und Zeit. Exegetische, hermeneutische und systematisch-theologische Untersuchungen zur Bildlichkeit religiöser Repräsentationsformen" (Image and time: Exegetical, hermeneutical, and systematic-theological studies in the imagery of religious representational forms) gave us an important forum for discussion. Finally, we are grateful to the editors of the series ThLZ.F (Theologische Literaturzeitung. Forum), especially Ingolf U. Dalferth, who encouraged the writing of the book, as well as to the Evangelische Verlagsanstalt Leipzig, above all Dr. Annette Weidhas, for her active support and for her patience during the long period of incubation.

Friedhelm Hartenstein
Michael Moxter
February 2016

I

Introduction

"DO YOU UNDERSTAND what you are reading?" Philip asks the chamberlain from the East as he bends over a scroll of the Prophet Isaiah (see Acts 8:26–40). Practitioners of theological hermeneutics love to cite that passage because the question names an elementary field of their inquiry: eliminating misunderstandings that arise between text and reception and that not only impede communication but dampen any desire to go on reading. From some points of view the sketch of a hermeneutics of the ban on images presented here can be readily linked to Philip's question. It is true that another text from the Torah (whether in the form of Exod 20:4–6 or Deut 5:8–10) would seem more relevant, but in fact we only need to expand the text used in Luke's scene, because when the chamberlain is faced with the question of whom the prophet means, exactly, when he speaks of the suffering servant of God, the answer presupposes a reading of Isaiah 53, in which context, shortly before, he must have found the prophetic ridicule of the ineffective idols of the pagans (Isa 44). Could he have succeeded in linking the critique of the statues of gods, of other cults and religions, with the ban on images, or did he recognize it as a unique characteristic of monotheistic religion?

So it is not a mere conjecture that one may read the Lukan story in this variant as well, and consequently assign to a hermeneutics of the prohibition of images the task of clarifying the meaning of biblical passages, their influence on other parts of Scripture, and their significance for cultic conflicts, iconoclasm, and religiously motivated violence. We could also take up the question, important for a hermeneutical theology, of the relationship between understanding a text and understanding oneself. After all, few things are more irritating to believers' awareness than the confusing twilight that has fallen upon monotheism and the ban on images, on rigorism and exclusivism. As has often happened throughout the history of church and theology, so in the present time: decisions about one's own religious orientation are made in terms of biblical texts. Are a ban on images and a critique of them the expression of a particularly rational stance (intellectualism) and a sense of freedom typical of monotheistic religions—because they no longer move within the frame of sensuality and unshielded concreteness of polytheistic cults—or is such a conception the seedbed of feelings of superiority and religious intolerance? But above all: Are we really understanding the text correctly if we read it in that sense?

The present studies adopt a position on these and related questions, but they cannot and will not avoid the other question: "Do you understand what you see?" That reminds us that the biblical ban on making and worshiping statues of gods also calls attention to the power of images. The way we understand the ban on images implies a position with regard to the question of what is really so problematic and objectionable about the image, or, more precisely, what is or ought to be so incompatible with the God of Israel. The history of interpretation shows that there are varied and very different answers to that question and that these have silently— that is, often without methodological clarity and explicit reflection— imposed themselves on the interpretation of the text. Specific theories about images exercise scarcely less influence on our understanding of texts than does the way in which we conceive of God.

The question whether one understands what one sees evokes the additional question of how concept and opinion are related, whether thought and perception can exhaustively encompass what appears to be given. And still more: what is the status of imagery in terms of human dealing with the world? Are images enhanced forms of visual perception that not only present something to our sight but exclude other things from view and make them invisible? Then established images, far from simply reproducing and reflecting reality, are themselves boundaries between what is visible and what is hidden.

A hermeneutics of the prohibition of images therefore expands our methods of working toward an understanding of the text. It lets itself be drawn from Scripture (and the history of its influence and interpretation) toward an overall hermeneutics of the image. Protestant theology has been focused on the connections between understanding texts, things, and self; its new tasks must be related to the insights of the study of imagery.

2

Introduction

The assessment of the ban on images has changed, especially in Old Testament exegesis. Historical observations on ancient Near Eastern religious history as well as the worlds of imagery within which ancient cultures articulated themselves have called into question the idea of an incommensurable special role for Israel, and above all have shown the terse formula of the ban on images to be a late development within the history of Old Testament theology. There is debate over the time when the ban on images made a virtue of necessity: perhaps it was the loss of a once-existing cultic image of Yhwh, compensated for by the fiction that a divine statue had never been compatible with the God of Israel. The majority of exegetes believe that the cult in the Jerusalem temple always de facto dispensed with an anthropomorphic cultic image and so was in that respect "imageless," but for contingent reasons. Then, our thesis proposes, the nonexistence of a Yhwh image as a mark of identification imposed itself in connection with explicit monotheism in order to mark the difference in principle between this God and all other gods. The authenticity and sovereignty of the Creator God demanded the exclusion of everything not appropriate to such a God, and instead an adherence to what could be discerned from God's (self-)revelation. Thus the prohibition of a cultic image (in human or animal form) appears as a secondary rationalization of a situation that, during the exile, at first seemed to be a deficiency when the exiles compared themselves with Babylonian religion but could be interpreted afterward as an advantage.

Such a derivation warns us to be cautious about drawing excessively broad conclusions from the ban on images with regard to the significance of the visual and of imagery in ancient Israel's worship of God as a whole. The temple cult, ritual, sacrifice, and performative liturgical action were, in any case, always linked to the visual, so that the absence of imagery remains a too-broadly conceived abstract concept for designating the religion of Old Testament texts. Not only the theophany narratives of the Old Testament but still more powerfully its poetic language, above all in the Psalms and the prophetic books, are nourished by mental imagery in which faith in Yhwh expressed itself. May we then say that a specific image of God forbids images of gods? Or does Jewish-Christian belief in God shape what we see in the images?

Thus the historical context also confirms that interpretations of the ban on images are accompanied by a concept of what imagery is. Understanding the text is linked to a *hermeneutics of the image*.

The Hermeneutics of the Ban on Images

Gottfried Boehm introduced that title for the discipline, along with the much-cited concept of an *iconic turn* in cultural studies. Both concepts played a crucial role in the establishment of the so-called science(s) of imagery, but they also contain limitations and biases that we need to address briefly.

The concept of the *iconic turn* is derived from the idea of the *linguistic turn*. When Richard Rorty, in his edited book *The Linguistic Turn*,[1] described the paradigm shift from a speculative metaphysics of consciousness to logic and linguistic philosophy and accelerated it by means of this collection of pertinent essays, his later comparison of philosophy with literary studies was not yet envisioned. The application of thought to the forms of speech and the rules of language games, as well as the primacy of public establishment of meaning over the solipsistic act of assigning meaning, would characterize a new direction in philosophy in both its methods and its orientation. Everything depended on the thesis that our relationship to reality is shaped by language, that the categories of knowledge are intromitted in the forms of communication. The academic public that welcomed the paradigm shift could therefore scarcely understand the later challenge to an *iconic turn* as anything but an invitation to rise again above the previously achieved level of reflection and to deepen the analysis of basic presuppositions. It was not just language but, prior to it, the *image* that was identified as the medium in and through which human access to the world was mediated.

The methodological derivation of the *iconic turn* from linguistic theory and the forms of presentation grounded in it shaped the title that Boehm (at first) chose to designate the discipline that was to assume these complicated tasks: a hermeneutics of imagery. This title for the discipline indicated both the conviction that images constitute knowledge, manifest meaning, and unlock reality and the humanistic methods with which those should be described. The interface between imagery and language therefore also determined the program of the discipline: "The hermeneutics of imagery has its origin at the point where the eye's experience of the image moves to the medium of language."[2] Of course, the fact that Boehm attributed to images a function analogous to what language does signified an implicit methodological accommodation of the new discipline, the study of imagery, to the "logic" of the linguistic sciences, no matter how much the primacy of image over language was emphasized in practice. The tension thus established became more obvious when Boehm wrote that the image is "not a thing among

4

things…but a language of its own"[3] and, moreover, a mute, silent language.[4] Against this background hermeneutics should take into account the reciprocal translatability[5] of word and image, though without pursuing the program of an iconology in the narrower sense (i.e., one that seeks to identify the meanings of individual visual elements).

We should probably ask whether visuality and imagery are adequately presented if our methodological approach is ordered to the sense (meaning) orientation of language and is given priority over the sense orientation and materiality of images. Do images not provoke our reflection precisely because they represent something nonconceptual that resists absorption into the understanding? In that case the *iconic turn* would not really be served by a hermeneutics of imagery.

This problem will not be discounted or trivialized when, in what follows, we speak of a hermeneutics of the ban on images. The cooperation between Old Testament scholarship and systematic theology represented by this publication began with a mutual seminar on hermeneutics at Hamburg, resulting in a study of Gottfried Boehm's programmatic essay on the hermeneutics of imagery. Since the hermeneutical question is a tried and true basis for cooperation between exegesis and systematics, it seemed the appropriate tool for orienting to hermeneutics the common study of the ban on images we had chosen to pursue, and for avoiding labels like "The Ban on Images," which would be too broad and too demanding, or "Forbidden Images," which might rouse false expectations. This problem-oriented sketch is an attempt to understand the text and to achieve an interdisciplinary agreement. But the fact that the authors retain the title *hermeneutics* in this sense does not mean that they are not receptive to concerns or objections.

Disciplining the "drive for understanding"[6] in scholarly (and practical) terms would certainly be one—and not the worst—definition of hermeneutical tasks. Without such disciplining, that drive erupts in an over-hasty grab for the thing it identifies through its interpretation without having thoroughly tested alternatives or adequately weighed the range of possibilities.

Hermeneutics as an aesthetics of understanding is a countermeans intended to decelerate methodological effort in favor of a different way of understanding. It seems to us more important to practice that art than to undertake a programmatic analysis of the concept of hermeneutics. Much of what will be presented below might well be offered in the name of a history of the interpretation and reception of the ban on images.

For us, however, more important than nomenclature for this study is a two-part question: First, can the historical interpretation of biblical texts within the horizon of the questions presented by cultural studies be carried out in such a way that it opens up to the tasks of a theology of the Old Testament? Second, whether and how systematic theology is able to trace its relationship to Scripture not only through an abstract struggle over principles (in the prolegomena section of dogmatics) but also by considering and taking seriously certain biblical texts that present themselves in the process. One of our interests lay in maintaining this connection among exegesis, hermeneutics, and systematics. We need not deny that interdisciplinary work has resulted primarily in mutually critical suspension of previously unconsidered questions. But that exchange is precisely what matters.

We both have let ourselves be guided by Hans Blumenberg's assertion that symbolic forms tend to develop a pregnance that is not by nature contained in the usual forms.[7] The work of reception brings to light meaning that cannot be allocated to any already effective and at the same time a priori existing entelechy. The latter is detrimental to historical experience, which is thus degraded to mere development—the only residual risk being that no one can predict when, exactly, anything has reached its telos. Meanwhile history presents major uncertainties, and its contingencies frequently raise questions of conscience for its subjects. Thus no one would describe the development of Old Testament theology as a natural unfolding of immanent beginnings. Instead, belief in God acquires transformational shapes on the basis of new, often critical experiences; in the face of these, questions about whether what was earlier could have been recognized in what came after must be seen as based on a false premise.

The juxtaposition of the "original" sense of the text and what later times or other cultural contexts understood it to be and made of it helps us to perceive the historical distance, but it should not lead to a positivism of first beginnings. Rather than separating the supposed facts and original situations from the later interpretation, we should note the dictum: "in the beginning was the reinterpretation." It excludes an arrangement of theological disciplines whereby historical exegesis must first complete its work, setting aside all hermeneutical questions and systematic perspectives and producing a finished product, and then, afterward and secondarily, questions of interpretation, significance, and validity may be posed. However, taking seriously the difference between genesis

and validity is something different from trying to cement the boundaries of disciplines by separating facts and interpretation. Because signs
and symbols give us more to think about than a historical positivism can
handle, exegesis is one of the thinking activities, one that poses the questions to be thought about. The history of the ban on images reveals precisely that. Despite its fixed form as a statement of unconditional divine
law, it has been handed down and received in contexts within which its
meaning is considered, refined, and corrected. The multitude of later
exegetical traditions reflects and takes up what has already begun in the
biblical texts. To that extent the reception history of the ban on images
is integral from the beginning and is not external to the ban.

Consequently, the following studies do not fall into a first (exegetical) and a second (systematic) category, which would only exaggerate the
breach between historical identification of the original meaning of the text
and a present responsibility to its truth. Instead, both parts are shaped by
common convictions and questions that each discipline addresses, or con-
fronts, through its own specific methods and that—wherever possible—
have been coordinated. Above all, however, both the exegetical and the
systematic essays in this study look back from a later time to an earlier
one, whether it be starting with the monotheistic redactions and reaching
back to the layers of earlier prophetic tradition, or using the categories
of contemporary image studies to get to the bottom of previous debates.
Using this approach, we decided not to claim to be writing a comprehensive theological history of the ban on images or offering an adequate
overview of the relevant scholarly literature. Besides, that would not be
in accord with the character of this series, which is intended to provide
impulses to current debates and is therefore problem oriented and does
not claim to offer encyclopedic information.

History's judgment on the theological work already achieved by
tradition- and redaction criticism is close to the systematic supposition that the most important things will only be understood afterward.
Luther could say that of the God of the Sinai theophany (Exod 33),
Hegel of the reflective definition of the concept of being, Kierkegaard of
the way in which the subject perceives itself, and finally Lévinas could
summarize it in the question, "The great 'experiences' of our life have
properly speaking never been lived. Are not religions said to come to
us from a past which was never a pure now?"[8] That is not intended to
create disillusion; it gives the work of memory a systematic locus in our
relationship to self as well as in the history of religion.

Finally, we were united in our intention to keep the concept of image as open as possible. We must reckon on the one hand with a multidimensional concept of image that cannot be subsumed within a single definition, but on the other hand with the futility of the command to encounter the attractiveness of the image with refusal. (Nothing can more clearly underscore the anthropological significance of the cult of images than the futility of all efforts to forbid it or channel it in the interest of one power or another.) Certainly there are disgusting images we long to be rid of. But to defend oneself against images, one must trust the power of the counterimages. This imagist-anthropo-theo-logical assessment forbids any sharp break whereby the Old Testament ban on images would apply only to sculpted statues of competing gods and be regarded as a particular cultural development. The assertion that it was only about that does not reckon sufficiently with the symbolic pregnance of imagery, the virulence of the visible, including the imagining of God in biblical texts. The ban on images derives its drama from that of the image itself.

Therefore it was important to take into account the relationships between theology and anthropology, between regulatory power and the power of the image, between imagination and knowledge, but also to ask the biblical texts to tell us what they have to say about YHWH's visibility, appearance, residence in the temple, or about Christ as image of God.

Fascination with the ban on images, a phenomenon that continually calls forth interpretations that go far beyond the texts, the ban's power to organize the contents of different religions, but also the shock and terror it served and serves to justify—all these were clearer to us at the end of our work than they had been when we started. If reading the resulting texts helps others to recognize them, the project will not have been in vain.

II

Exegetical and Religious-Historical Perspectives[1]

THE OLD TESTAMENT ban on images is one of the most important special features of Jewish tradition. Its influence on the history of religion, culture, and philosophy is almost immeasurable (see §III). Throughout its Christian transformations and beyond, it achieved a high degree of relevance, for example, in the Byzantine iconoclasm controversy or the renewed iconoclasm of the Reformation (see §§III.5.2; III.8). Struggles over how to represent God appealed to the ban on images as people tried to give shape to the question of the appropriateness and adequacy of visual forms of expression for God/the divine. But it was also in light of the ban on images that artistic works were both destroyed and created (see §III.9). The following reflections on a thoughtful way of dealing with the ban on images from an exegetical perspective will adopt a twofold approach:

(a) A *religious history of ancient Israel* that combines the perspectives of a historical-critical reconstruction of a *theology of the Old Testament* and the *evaluation of extrabiblical sources*. Here we must give additional consideration in particular to the broader cultural context beyond Palestine (especially ancient Near Eastern temples and their cultic images).

(b) A *hermeneutical reflection on the prohibition of images* from the stance of a Christian (Protestant) theology that considers the exegetical and religious-historical findings.

9

1. Religious-Historical Contexts

In order to work with the challenge of the Old Testament ban on images, we must first sketch the frame within which, and only within which, that ban can be adequately understood: in the religions of the ancient Near East and classical antiquity, the veneration of cultic images played a prominent role. Being the most important media for the divine presence, they stood at the center of sanctuaries and temples. Sacrifices, prayers, and festivals were oriented toward them. Hence in what follows we must first speak of the temple as the primary context for images (§1.1a). Then the images and their most important forms (human, symbolic, and aniconic) and their production and functions will be considered (§1.1b–e). Finally, we will deal with the "mental iconography" associated with the cult, the visual imagination of cult participants regarding the bodies of the gods and their transcendence (§1.2).

1.1 Basics of Ancient Near Eastern Image Cults

a. What is a sanctuary?

When we try to say something about a cultural space that is as sharply different in chronology and region as that of ancient Near Eastern antiquity from a perspective aiming at common and comparable structures, there is always the danger of overgeneralization. Still, it is helpful for dealing with our subject if we keep in mind certain basic features that were common to the cultures of the Middle East and Egypt as a whole.

Beginning with the earliest Neolithic sanctuaries in Anatolia (Göbekli Tepe, Nevali Çori), we find evidence of temple (structures) in the ancient Near East.[2] It is remarkable that this happened so early (ca. 9500 BCE).

There were sanctuaries (outside and inside villages/cities) even before there were enduring settlements, and others were coincident with their establishment. They were architectonic spaces "cut out" from the surrounding landscapes (or localities) (cf. Greek *temenos*, Latin *templum*, "something cut out" for a sacred space). The religious-cultural symbolism of the threshold establishes the elementary spatial distinction between *inside* and *outside*.[3] This was fundamental for everything that will be developed in what follows. Thresholds marked both boundaries/restrictions and overlappings/entries: thus a sanctuary represents a *transitional zone* between the divine and the human, between what is clean/holy and what is unclean/profane.[4] It also includes the meeting of horizontal and vertical symbolic axes or, as the Egyptologist and cultural-studies expert Jan Assmann says, between the "center" and the "way."[5]

The *horizontal* movement leads over the threshold(s) of a temple and moves farther and farther inward, usually following a direct path that can be used in both directions (though it remains an open question whether the subjects of those movements are the same; often the human path leads primarily inward).[6] The axis of the sanctuary ends at a final point: the crucial boundary between outside and inside, which is marked by the strongest presence of the divine. This is the most precarious and important boundary marker in a sanctuary, the spatial point at which "here" and "there," this world and another ("beyond") are most permeable to one another. At this final threshold, usually marked as *naos* or *cella*, it is often the *vertical* dimension that is decisive.

One famous example is the vision of the Prophet Isaiah (Isa 6:1–11), from the second half of the eighth century BCE.[7] Here the dimensions of the earthly temple in Jerusalem become transparent to the cosmic dwelling of Yʜwʜ: a royal throne reaching to heaven from which the earthly realm receives its order and stability (cf. also from the period of the Judean state, Ps 93*). The principal temple in the royal city of Babylon (in the time of Nebuchadnezzar II, 605–562 BCE) had a similar symbolism, divided between two building complexes within the sanctuary area: Esagila, the so-called lower temple, constituted the horizontal axis, with the regulated accessibility of the imperial god Marduk (daily sacrifices and festal worship at various times). The Etemenanki, "house, foundation of heaven and earth," the famous six-story ziggurat, was an artificial mountain that embodied the vertical axis between the layers of the world. On its summit stood a temple, apparently marked by

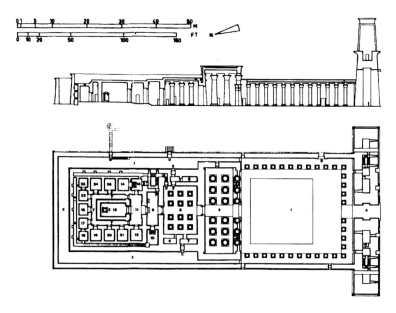

Figure 1: Temple of Horus at Edfu

Side view and layout of the temple edifice: from the entrance pylons the way leads through a number of halls and anterooms to the cultic center itself, the tiny, self-contained *naos*/shrine in which stood the principal cultic image; it was surrounded by a corridor and a wreath of thirteen rooms.

Source: Jan Assmann, *Ägypten. Theologie und Frömmigkeit einer frühen Hochkultur*, UT 366 (Stuttgart et al.: Kohlhammer, 1984), 40, plate 2 (= Serge Sauneron and Henri Stierlin, *Die letzten Tempel Ägyptens: Edfu und Philae* [Zürich: Atlantis, 1975], 36–37).

blue-glazed tiles as belonging to the internal sphere of heaven; this was the so-called towering temple. The temple's tower was regarded as an "image" of the sanctuary of Enlil/Marduk, located cosmologically in the "lower heaven" and named Ešarra, "house of the whole."[8]

Particularly impressive are the Egyptian temples of the Ptolemaic (Hellenistic-Roman) period that have survived to this day. In these, for example the great temple of Horus in Edfu[9] (figure 1), an outer wall first indicated the boundaries between the sphere of the god and the outside world/his city. The entrance to the temple proper was flanked by two gigantic pylons, huge artificial mountains representing the point of the sun's rising between the mountains on the horizon; these bore programmatic images that warded off evil and created order. After passing between them, one proceeded (under a steadily lowering ceiling) through narrower and narrower corridors connecting a system of

13

courts and halls whose size decreased as one proceeded farther toward the interior.[10] With every threshold passed the restriction on access (from a social perspective) increased: the innermost part of the temple could only be entered by the priests acting as representatives of the Pharaoh and simultaneously assuming the roles of gods. At the end of the path was the *naos* (for the cultic image). This was a small building that stood independently within a dark cell/sanctuary, a "temple within the temple."[11] It was equipped with folding doors so that the presence of the deity within appeared accessible but was primarily hidden. In ancient Egypt this hiddenness of the space for the cultic image could be described thus: "It is as unapproachable as what is in heaven, more concealed than the things of the netherworld, more hidden than the inhabitants of the primal ocean."[12]

Because the images were "withdrawn" from this world, (indirect) contact with them was sometimes made possible by means of a so-called countertemple lying opposite to the *cella*, outside the temple, or through a cultic site on the surrounding wall fitted with "ears" (in order that the god might listen).[13]

In short: the basic structure of an ancient Near Eastern temple was that of a threshold. It thereby united within itself the spatial symbolisms of center and way.

It is important again to be clear about the possible lines of sight and action: we think—against the background of Christian church buildings—primarily from outside to inside; thus we imagine the route to the altar/choir. In antiquity this direction for movement or action applied to the many rituals of the *"daily" temple cult* meant to facilitate communication with the deities (sacrifices as audience gifts, petitions to be heard, gestures of veneration). In contrast, the *extraordinary* rituals for feasts often followed the reverse direction. At ancient Near Eastern festivals, collective stagings of a time different from everyday experience, deities appeared (in their cultic images, which were carried in procession), emerging from their temples into the open air, thus presenting "epiphanies." And yet for the most part they remained withdrawn from direct gaze (veiled in transportable shrines and behind curtains). By their emergence in the course of the festival, they sacralized, for a brief time, the landscape/settlement, and what was otherwise "profane" was likewise drawn into their "sacred" presence.[14]

Ultimately determinative for the ancient Near Eastern understanding of a sanctuary was that it was *a place chosen by the gods themselves* for their presence (cf. the *hieroi logoi*, legends of the discovery of these places by human beings, e.g., Gen 28:10–22).[15] The fundamental designation for a temple was thus simply "house of god" (Hebrew *bêt 'ēl*, Akkadian *bīt īli*; cf. Hebrew *hêkāl* from Akkadian *ēkallu(m)*, Sumerian É.GAL, "big house" = palace; Egyptian *ḥwt ntr* [*het-netjer*], "house of God").

Like human lords, the gods lived in "houses." That does not exclude—and in fact it is clearly said of the great cosmic deities (such as those of the sun and moon, or the weather gods)—that at the same time they possessed cryptic "dwelling places" in the depths of the world to which humans had no access. These transcendent spaces (in the heavens, on mountains, in the underworld, and elsewhere) were described, for example, in hymns and prayers, or were simply assumed.[16] Myths of origin and creation tell how, long before the creation of human beings, the gods established their dwellings there.[17] Thus there was a clear awareness of the "oversized" nature and distance of the gods. In that light the "earthly" sanctuaries appeared primarily as points for contact initiated by the deities, who had settled into the world of human beings by means of a "joint venture" (A. S. Kapelrud: "temple building: a task for gods and kings").[18] They thereby deliberately joined themselves with humans. However, in times of crisis (such as catastrophes or the fall of cities)—and this, too, is made clear by the threshold structure of an ancient Near Eastern sanctuary—it was known, and became obvious, that the gods' presence was dicey. In a positive sense the deities were praised in hymns and prayers as generous and superior in power; negatively they were depicted in laments and crisis rituals as wrathful and opaque, averting their faces.[19]

A sanctuary was an asymmetrical place of glory and the circulation of gifts, but also the mark of a presence that could turn into absence. This unbalanced *ambivalence*—in modern terms—characterized an ancient Near Eastern temple; it was a *medium*, a place that from our point of view was as real as it was imaginary, a place of *mediation* between this world and the other. As such it was a gift of the gods but also an enduring responsibility of human beings. Rulers, by building and renovating "houses of god," cultivated their relationship to the gods and thus increased their own prestige (in royal ideology, of course, as representatives of the collective).

To this point we have deliberately avoided an extended discussion of the *images* or *cultic symbols* that were worshiped at the center of sanctuaries. We must now focus on those, for in fact everything we have said thus far about the sanctuary was replicated in nuce in the cultic image. The image of the god was itself the threshold and medium par excellence, the most important embodiment of the divine presence, but at the same time an exciting and tension-filled expression of divine transcendence. What characterized the rituals for the building and maintaining of temples was all the more the case for the central cultic objects around which an ancient Near Eastern cult was staged and a temple erected (cf. the building of the medieval cathedrals, which began with the choir, the architectonic space for the divine presence on the altar, in the sacraments and relics, just as in the ancient Near East the sanctuary was in a sense built from the inside outward).[20]

b. Anthropomorphic cultic images: Production, worship, significance

Cultic images, in the ancient Near East and elsewhere in antiquity, were the primary representations of the presence of the gods.[21] They were at the center of the whole religious symbolic system. Archaeologically speaking, only few cultic images from Mesopotamia (Sumer, Babylon, Assyria) and Syria-Palestine have survived (and there are just a paltry number of examples from Egypt).[22] That is not surprising, given their significance and the expensive materials of which they were made. It may be beneficial to look at the beautifully worked great bronze statue of an enthroned god (height: 36 cm) from the principal temple on the acropolis of the Late Bronze period city of Hazor in Galilee (Bldg 7050), a central image for a temple cult (figure 2).

For the most part, as far as the *external* appearance of central cultic images is concerned, scholarship is dependent on literary descriptions, iconographic representations on cylinder seals and stamp seals, and on information from the ritual texts associated with the images.[23]

> *In summary* we may say that a cultic image was not regarded as being "mimetic" or a "portrait," but as "representational." It only permitted a clear identification of the deity represented when seen in context (its pedestal, *cella*, associated animals) and with its paraphernalia (scepter, symbols, robes, ornaments). These last frequently offered an allusion to the god's specific sphere of action: thus identity and area of responsibility were very closely related.[24]

The first remark in this paragraph aims to show that a "classical" definition of the image in terms of the *similarity* in the relationship of

Figure 2: Bronze statue of a god, from Hazor

The bronze figure is richly detailed. One special feature compared with other examples from the region is the decoration of the headdress with a stylized palmetto tree from which *caprides* (goats or ibexes) are feeding, a very ancient Near Eastern symbol for fullness of life and world order that was also part of the iconography of the Jerusalem temple. The statue from Hazor may represent a weather god (Ba'al, Hadad?).

Source: Sharon Zuckerman, "The Temples of Canaanite Hazor," in *Temple Building and Temple Cult: Architecture and Cultic Paraphernalia of Temples in the Levant (2.–1. Mill. B.C.E.)*, ed. Jens Kamlah and Henrike Micheleau, ADPV 41 (Wiesbaden: Harrassowitz, 2012), 99–125, at 115, fig. 4.1 (= T. Ornan, "'Let Ba'al Be Enthroned': The Date, Identification, and Function of a Bronze Statue from Hazor," *JNES* 70 [2011]: 253–80, figs. 2a–3.)

the image to "what it depicts" is inappropriate for the ancient Near East. Instead, the image is a *place* where the god is present, independent of the question of correspondence with the model/original image.[25] Hence exactly which divine figure was intended by a particular image could not be discerned from its anthropomorphic exterior as such; even when the deities of the ancient Near Eastern pantheons bore individual features in some texts, they were above all *functionally distinct* in their appearance (though sometimes one could replace another or they might be mutually identifiable).

Similarly to the way in which a Mesopotamian sanctuary was marked as belonging to the world of the gods by particular elements of how it was built (such as the layout of niches on the façade and entries or the associated temple towers/ziggurats),[26] the cultic image bore *divine characteristics of a general nature*: it wore (at least usually) a so-called horned crown (simple or multiple pairs of horns) and certain garments reserved for gods (e.g., a flounced robe). The coloration was different from that of ordinary people: the images had blue hair and beards (imitating the sky color of lapis lazuli),[27] and the cladding with precious metals (gold, electrum, silver) gave them a celestial glow. The latter probably applies also to the "terrifying luminosity" of the deities (Sumerian ME.LÁM, Akkadian *melammu, pulḫu*, etc.). This indicated their otherworldly vitality and at the same time the fear-generating alterity—a basic cultural idea in the *mentalité mésopotamienne* to which Elena Cassin has devoted the best study thus far.[28] Angelika Berlejung says of the effect of the images on the beholders,

> There is also an indication of how the images were received by their worshipers: the shining faces were associated with manifestations of light that evoked veneration and inspired awe in humans. The brilliance of the polished stones and precious metals used in the cultic image or applied to it in the form of robes and ornaments blinded and captivated the viewer. The precious nature and rarity of the components of the image revealed its divine quality.[29]

Even if a cultic image could not be identified in terms of an individualizing iconography, its context was decisive, for every major cultic image was made for a particular sanctuary, its rites and festivals, according to a fixed set of rules. For example, "the chief idol of a great sanctuary did not require to be explained…; its position showed what it was"—as W. Robertson Smith wrote with full accuracy in his famous "Lectures on the Religion of the Semites" (1888–1891).[30] If we think, for example, of the Ebabbar, the great sanctuary of the sun at Sippar near Babylon, about whose central cultic image we are very well informed (relief of Nabû-apla-iddina, figure 3) we see that the enthroned sun god Šamaš is readily recognized through a number of "features" present: Šamaš (on the right) sat on a throne of cosmic dimensions in the shape of the door at the horizon through which the sun arises, equipped with bull-men (*kusarikku*)—iconographically a unique mark of identification.[31] To the left, before his shrine, stands a symbol of the sun (a disk with rays of light) toward which a human worshiper is being led (see below at 1.1c).

Figure 3: Relief of the sun god Šamaš from Sippar

The Neo-Babylonian stone tablet (853 BCE) displays not only the relief but a long inscription devoted to the restoration of the cultic image of Šamaš. The image is, on the one hand, deliberately traditional or archaizing (motif of a scene of intro-duction before the enthroned god). On the other hand, it bears some singular features, above all the simultaneous portrayal of the god (or his cultic image) and of a symbol (the sun disk) that embodies him.

Sources: Friedhelm Hartenstein, *Das Angesicht JHWHs. Studien zu seinem höfischen und kultischen Bedeutungshintergrund in den Psalmen und in Exodus 32–34*, FAT 75 (Tübingen: Mohr Siebeck, 2008), 298, plate 4.1 (= Jeremy A. Black, Anthony Green, and Tessa Rickards, eds., *Gods, Demons and Symbols of Ancient Mesopotamia: An Illustrated Dictionary* [Austin: University of Texas Press; London: British Museum, 1992], 94, fig. 73. Drawing by Tessa Rickards).

Crucial for the functionality of a temple's cultic image was its *ability to communicate*, ensured by the frontal orientation of its position and the powerful emphasis on the *facial features* (eyes, mouth, ears, kindly expres-sion) and *gestures* (often a hand open in greeting/blessing; see figure 2). (Late Old Testament criticism of images seized on these characteristics in emphasizing the images' illusory character; see §2.2b below.) A petitioner who advances to the front of the cult image (cf. §1.1a regarding the entry into the temple) enters into relationship with the god. The images are placed within a *context of mutual action*; their manufacture and presen-tation served only that purpose. The *daily temple ritual*, as known to us, for example, from Seleucid Uruk (3rd/2nd c. BCE),[32] included extensive rituals of clothing and feeding the image. Through these (in a reciprocal system of sacrificial gifts), the ruler was seated at the table of the god, and the temple priests were in the "house of god" as representatives of the city/ empire/king, in community with him. (For that reason Leo Oppenheim entitled the corresponding chapter of his history of Mesopotamian culture "The Care and Feeding of the Gods.")[33]

Of course, for the most part the larger public had no direct access to the temple's cultic images (cf. the Assyrian title *erib bīti*, "one who enters the temple").[34] The images were placed in the inaccessible rear portion of the *adyton* (cultic niche), often behind curtains as well.[35] Nevertheless, people were aware, even if they could not view the image directly, of the divine presence, so important for their lives, that connected them to the god, and—thanks to the festivals and the "mass media" (images on seals in particular)—they had a fairly accurate visual idea of the appearance, for example, of the goddess Ishtar (as we can tell, e.g., from the account of a dream vision of the Assyrian king Ashurbanipal in which the goddess made a visual appearance to the ruler).[36] Contact with the images could also be direct or (probably more often) indirect.[37] In any case it was *crucially important for social and cosmic order*, since the loss of a temple's cultic image, something that most often happened during a war (which involved the abduction and sometimes the destruction of the enemy's cultic images), was a catastrophe for the land and its people. Here we find different interpretations in the sources, depending on perspective; in Babylon especially the victors (Elamites, Assyrians) crow over the fact that they have led the disempowered principal god into exile, while the losers (Babylonians) see this, given the circumstances, as Marduk's freely chosen rejection of his people because of their trespasses (see §2.4a below).[38] We can see from this also how powerful the concept of the *equation* of god and image was: the god was present and approachable in the image. Even though this does not exclude simultaneous contrary concepts such as withdrawal or other embodiments of the god, the cultic image was crucial for a salvific contact with the divine that stabilized the cosmic order.

In the Mesopotamian rituals for the production and consecration of images that Angelika Berlejung has discussed in her important monograph, *Die Theologie der Bilder*,[39] it is obvious that there was a sharp awareness that it was only at the moment when *the mouth was opened* during the concluding ritual of washing the mouth, signifying the definitive insertion in the communicative context of the temple, that the image *ceased to be an artifact* and became a more-than-human form of the god's appearing.[40] Previously the image was gradually separated from the context of the human world by the wise craftspeople, who were likewise specialists in ritual, and transferred to the context of action within the world of the gods; this latter accompanied all stages of the work from the beginning. (For Isa 40:18–20, where this was addressed polemically, see §2.4a below.)[41] One prayer with uplifted hands for the opening of the mouth of the cultic image reads, "When the god was created, when the pure statue was completed. Pure statue, completed in awe-inspiring glory. At your coming forth. Statue, born in a pure place. Statue, born in heaven."[42]

While the image is "created" and "completed," yet "born in heaven," it is, as the ritual says, "creation of the god, a human work."[43] It shares in both realms of being. In it the horizontal and vertical axes of the symbolic system are focused. It stands at the center of all religious actions, and the materials used in its production reflect its ties to all the regions of the cosmos (heaven, earth, subterranean freshwater ocean/Apsû; for the rejection of this idea in Deut 4 and in the expansion of the Decalogue's prohibition of images, see below, §2.3a). Like the temple, it is a cosmic point of intersection and, like it, it shares in stabilizing the world order. (Jan Assmann, in speaking of the Solar Phases Hymn that supported the sun's course in Egypt's temples, refers accurately to "keeping the world in motion.")[44] What was demonstrated especially in the cuneiform cultures of Mesopotamia is equally true, with variations, for Egypt, Syria/the Levant, and to some extent also for Greece.[45]

What is critical for our further reflections is a more or less conscious awareness of their "double nature" both in our dealing with the images and in reflection on their production/origin. Taking them as media of the presence of a deity, one may interact with them directly, thus following the social rules of contact with a superior; in that case the question of the "nature" of the images normally does not arise. But at the same time the presence given in and with the image resists any final definition, not only because one is dealing with a deity but also because the medium of a *visual* object (in its context) also involves a special set of *complex perceptions of otherness*. The classical philologist Fritz Graf summarizes the issue as follows in an important essay devoted to "The Obstinacy of the Divine Images in Ancient Religious Discourses" and thus to the *ambivalence* expressed in them:

The ambivalence rests ultimately in the divine image. Human and divine are fundamentally incompatible: their ways parted in Mekone, when Prometheus set up the sacrifices; so said Hesiod, and since then, for humans, the paths of communication with the divine have been difficult. Ordinarily it is the temples in which this communication takes place, in prayer and sacrifice; these activities repeatedly focus on the cultic image. In a certain sense the image is the connection (the interface, so to speak) between the two ultimately incompatible worlds. As such it is *a place of tensions and irresolvable contradictions*—the images represent gods who, however, are ultimately beyond representation if only because they are imperishable and timeless.[46]

Precisely at this point—the *indispensability* combined with a simultaneous *insufficiency* of the cultic images as media of contact with the divine—we can focus the problem of the "image" more precisely, as it was expressed in ancient philosophical critique of images and in the Old Testament-Jewish prohibition of images. (Cf. further the religious-philosophical considerations below in §III.4.3.) But first, as we approach the complex problematic, we must once again deepen our perception of the ancient Near East since, besides the anthropomorphic cultic images, there were *complementary visual representations*, symbolic and "aniconic" representations differing in time and region, that were of vast importance.

c. Symbols of gods: Equivalent or competing media?

Ancient Near Eastern temples and sanctuaries sheltered not only the central cultic images of the deities to whom they were dedicated; they also housed places for the worship of other gods and their images. Here we see an essential characteristic of polytheistic symbol systems whereby gods are always embedded in connections of relationship and hierarchy. We know that it was this multiplicity, together with the defined functional spheres of great deities, that made it possible for gods to be mutually identified and for the pantheons of cities and kingdoms to be open to one another.[47] A similar multiplicity (cf. Henri Frankfort's famous dictum about the "multiplicity of approaches")[48] was true also of the cults of the gods in a *single* temple, which were able to unite various forms of representation of the same god, his/her close circle of gods, and other deities as well. A further precondition for the placement of various forms of representation alongside one another was the *expansion of divinity* to things that, in the modern Western mentality, were "inanimate." Thus, for example, weapons or musical instruments such as kettledrums (^dLILISSU) or a stringed instrument (^dBALAG) could be written with the divine determinative (the cuneiform ^d = DINGIR for "god/divine").[49] These sacred objects were addressed by name, and sacrifices were offered to them. In altogether analogous fashion *metonymic* (*pars pro toto*) or *abstract symbols* (as sculptures/artifacts; often these were designated by Akkadian *šurinnu*, "divine emblems") could take on a cultic function in temple rituals. In this regard they had equal weight with cultic images, as is shown by the fact that the same rituals of mouth-washing and mouth-opening were performed on a divine symbol, such as a crescent moon, as on anthropomorphic images (see above): "Unless its mouth is opened this crescent moon cannot smell any incense, cannot eat any bread, [and cannot drink any water]."[50] The process for production of the crescent moon, a very common symbol associated primarily with the great moon god of the West, *Sîn of Ḥarran*, was also perceived simultaneously in connection with divine and human actions ("The crescent moon, creation of god, made by men").[51] Sometimes, probably because of some cultural idiosyncrasy, a preference for anthropomorphic or symbolic representations of deities in Mesopotamia shifted. Beginning with the rule of the Cassites in Babylonia (midsecond millennium BCE) it was very common practice to represent deities with symbols, for example, on boundary stones and contracts (*kudurru*).[52] Corresponding iconographies were stable and drew on an inventory of images that in many cases complemented the human figures of the temple-cult images. It is difficult to say whether theological intent played a role in this. There is scarcely any textual evidence from which to judge.[53] If the locus of the divine presence in ritual was determined by the cult as a whole, the symbolic context of interaction, and its architectonic frame, then the difference in forms of representation was probably not fundamental. That seems even more probable when we consider two perspectives that will be important for the development of our argument:

(a) Because the objects of the divine presence were media for actions/communication and were not constituted definitively by a relationship of *similarity, a nonanthropomorphic symbol could fully represent the god*, at any rate if it was made in such a way as to function correctly in the ritual.

(b) Together with the further visible components of a cult-like architecture or gesture, a common *imaginary world of imagery* played a decisive role that accompanied and structured the rituals and feasts. This was shaped above all *by speech and texts* whose (metaphorical) imagery was just as crucial for their being experienced and understood as were externally visible phenomena. Here we can speak with Tryggve N. D. Mettinger of a "mental iconography,"[54] a conventional world of imagination in which the primary form of the gods was physical and human. The phenomenon of *personal names* also contributed to this.[55] Having a name made a god an individual who could be addressed. Calling on the name automatically resulted in "locating." To that extent the (notion of a) form and the name were related: together, like the cultic image of the deity, they made communication possible.

A well-known example from the Middle Assyrian period (13th c. BCE, now in Berlin) furnishes a fine example (figure 4): the cultic pedestal of King

Figure 4: Symbol-ornamented pedestal of Tukulti-Ninurta I.
The relief on one side of the pedestal of a cultic symbol from the Middle Assyrian period shows the divine symbol that was once attached to it, together with two phases of the postures with which the ruler Tukulti-Ninurta I (1244–1208 BCE) venerated the symbol (standing and kneeling).
Source: Friedhelm Hartenstein, *Das Angesicht JHWHs. Studien zu seinem höfischen und kultischen Bedeutungshintergrund in den Psalmen und in Exodus 32–34*, FAT 75 (Tübingen: Mohr Siebeck, 2008), 299, plate 5.1 (= Black, Green, and Rickards, *Gods, Demons and Symbols*, 29, fig. 20. Drawing by Tessa Rickards).

Tukulti-Ninurta I shows two phases of the *proskynesis* of the ruler before a divine symbol that must at one time have really occupied the pedestal.[56]

On the relief both the pedestal itself and the divine symbol once located there are illustrated: it appears to be a stylus in front of a rectangular (writing) tablet. Both are attributes of the god Nabû, but they also serve for the vizier god Nusku, named in the pedestal's inscription, "who stands before (the face of) Assur and Enlil" and "who daily repeats the prayers of Tukulti-Ninurta [I], the king he loves, before Assur and Enlil."[57] Here Nusku was certainly not imagined "in the form" of the symbol, but was represented by it and thus thought of as standing in human form before the high rulers of the gods, a form of representation familiar to us from audience scenes and images on seals.

Things are still more complicated in a second example of divine symbolism, the tablet of the Babylonian ruler Nabû-apla-iddina from the year 853 BCE (figure 3),[58] already discussed. It has attracted much attention because here we have both a pictorial relief and an inscription referring to the same event. It is about the loss of the central cultic image from the temple of the sun at Sippar, destroyed by the Suteans. In its place, in the eleventh century BCE, a (sun)disk was installed as cultic symbol. The interim situation lasted until the middle of the ninth century BCE when, under Nabû-apla-iddina, a model of the lost anthropomorphic cultic image, enabling its restoration, was found, and the king ordered the cultic restoration to take place. The two-hundred-year absence of the cultic image is described in the inscription in terms of historical theology as "raging against Akkad" and as Šamaš "turning his face [lit.: neck] away." The god's turning back is indicated by the divine gift of the correct model for renewal of the cultic image. The evaluation implied is that the symbol is only an incomplete substitute for the anthropomorphic cultic image. The image relief on the tablet, however, does not make this clear; instead, the two appear here as complementary. Still, what the inscription clearly presumes is *the anthropomorphic presentation of the god as such* (turning of the face away and toward), which locates the sun god in the background, in his cosmic sphere, while the cultic image appears as a gift for the sake of human beings.

d. "Aniconic" cult symbols: Complementary or contrary to images?

Finally, as with symbols, which apparently were functionally of equal value with anthropomorphic temple cultic images, the same is true of so-called aniconic, that is, "pictureless" sacred objects. These have received increased attention in recent years in the context of inquiry about the origins of the prohibition of images or setting of a boundary against pictorial representations of gods in Judaism and Islam.[59] They are attested primarily in northern Mesopotamia (Assyria) and in Syria/the Levant, including Palestine, and as far as Arabia as well as in Asia Minor and Greece. For the most part these are *worked stones set up vertically*, in size ranging from less than a meter to taller than a human being.[60]

The forms vary from a simple pillar or rectangular form to the more common stele (tablet form with rounded upper corners or a semicircular top), but also include obelisks (Byblos). Common to these "standing stones" (Akkadian *sikkānum*, Hebrew *maṣṣēbâ*, Arabic *nuṣb*)[61] is their specific *materiality* (enduring stone) and *vertical* orientation. Philo of Byblos (2nd c. CE) referred to them with a much older Greek designation: *baitylos*,[62] a foreign word derived from the Semitic *bêt 'ēl/bīt ili*, "house of God" (see 1.1a above). These were regarded—as inscriptions testify—as the *dwelling of a god* or a (divinized) ancestor; accordingly, they are found in both sacral and sepulchral contexts. Their functions, otherwise attested, as memorial steles or documents for contracts are also clarified by their "animated" character, being, as they were, "ensouled" by a divine presence. They coexisted with anthropomorphic cultic images prominent from the Early Bronze Age (3rd c. BCE) until the Roman period, inclusive. Individually or in groups (often in rows of steles, e.g., in Gezer in Palestine) they were features both of open-air sanctuaries and of temples. In the latter they were mostly found, on the one hand, in courtyards, and on the other hand, rarely in clear relationship to or altogether within the *temple cella*. In some cases they occupied the *position of the central cultic symbol* (e.g., in the Bronze Age obelisk temple at Byblos or in the Iron Age Judaic fortress temple at Arad; see figure 5).

As a rule the stones are associated with cultic installations (often basins for water, sacrificial benches, altars, etc.) that make clear the fact that sacred pillars are to be treated like cultic images and embody the divine presence in the context of ritual: "In the temple, then, they are a sign of the divine presence. Outside the temple they also signify the presence of the god, which in addition can be coupled with guaranteeing a contract, certifying a boundary, or associated with a memorial, for example in the cult of the dead."[63]

In individual cases the idea of a heavenly origin may also have contributed to their supramundane quality (meteorites: cf. the legend in

Figure 5: Cultic niche in the fortress temple at Arad

In the elevated cultic niche in the small Iron Age Judaic temple built into the northwest corner of a quadratic fortress stood a smooth, red-painted aniconic stele/massebah as symbol of YHWH. Two small altars flanked the entrance to the niche, at the head of two stairs.

Source: Othmar Keel, *The Symbolism of the Biblical World: Ancient Near Eastern Iconography and the Book of Psalms,* trans. Timothy J. Hallett (Winona Lake, IN: Eisenbrauns, 1997), 148 and fig. 248 (p. 184; drawing by Hildi Keel-Leu).

Philo of Byblos according to which Astarte devoted "a star fallen from heaven" to a temple at Tyre;[64] see also, possibly, the famous black stone of the Ka'abah at Mecca).[65] In Aramaic-speaking regions, steles were often found also in exalted public cultic spaces on the outside or inside of the *city gates* (cf. Bethsaida and Dan in Palestine), where sacrifices were also presented to them.[66] It is striking that they were not always "aniconic," as shown by a whole series of examples from various times and regions (cf., e.g., the Iron Age relief stele at Bethsaida with a bull-symbolism that is difficult to interpret,[67] or the hands lifted to the moon on the front side of a central stele from the Late Bronze Age sanctuary at Hazor C [figure 6], which was built into the wall of the lower city).[68]

Figure 6: Sanctuary of steles in the western wall of the lower city of Hazor

In an enclosure/cultic niche open to the city side (6 x 4.5 m.) stood ten steles (up to 65 cm tall) set in a half-circle. The central stele is adorned with pictorial elements: two hands lifted to the crescent moon. On the left stood the statue of a man with a half-moon emblem. (It is unclear whether this stele sanctuary was devoted to the gods or was for veneration of ancestors.)

Source: Helga Weippert, *Palästina in vorhellenistischer Zeit*, Handbuch der Archäologie Vorderasien II/1 (Munich: Beck, 1988), 283, figs. 3–45 (= *Biblisches Reallexikon* 2 [Tübingen: Mohr, 1977], fig. 49.4).

In such cases it is better to speak of *"iconic"* *cult symbols*, which, for example, combine a stele with iconographic depictions. According to Jens Kamlah's definition, "iconic cult symbols" were "objects which represented a deity without depicting the deity's image. Though they avoided depicting the (anthropomorphic, theriomorphic or hybrid) figure of the deity, they were decorated with figures or figurative elements."[69]

Cultic symbolism in Palestine participated, from the earliest period, in this Syrian-Levantine tradition of "aniconic" and "iconic" symbols. But there is little to be said in favor of the idea that before the Old Testament's prohibition of images this was felt to be a deliberate contrast to the cult of images; instead, it was simply *a complementary variant of it.*[70] In the later distinctive practices of the monotheistic religions of Judaism and Islam, a new understanding of this unique religious-cultural feature of West Semitic and Arabian regions is *one* possible basis for dissociation from cult images (see below). The thesis of an age-old *specific difference* in the sense of an aniconism connected to a nomadic way of life, ethnic identity (Semitic iconophobia), or a more primitive stage of religion can no longer be maintained in the same form today.[71] Still, we have to deal with the question how deported Judeans at Babylon during their exile did, after all, obviously note a major cultural difference at this point, one that would become an effective mark of identity in the context of the now explicitly formulated monotheism (see below at 2.4a).

e. What do we know about Jerusalem's cultic symbolism?

The question, hotly discussed among Old Testament scholars, about the *cultic symbolism of the preexilic Jerusalem temple* also plays an important role as regards the traditio-historical preconditions for the prohibition of images. Othmar Keel, Tryggve N. D. Mettinger, and Jens

Figure 7: Relief of a god on the sphinx throne

The limestone stele (5th c. BCE) from Punic Hadrumetum (Sousse, Tunisia) shows a bearded god seated on a sphinx throne (possibly Melkart, the city god of Tyre), receiving an adorer in a *naos* surmounted by a winged sun (cultic encounter modeled as an audience). The god's right hand is raised in greeting/blessing (cf. also the gesture of the statue from Hazor, fig. 2). He holds a lance as scepter.

Source: Friedhelm Hartenstein, *Das Angesicht JHWHs. Studien zu seinem höfischen und kultischen Bedeutungshintergrund in den Psalmen und in Exodus 32–34*, FAT 75 (Tübingen: Mohr Siebeck, 2008), 302, plate 8.2 (= Sabatino Moscati, *Die Phöniker. Von 1200 vor Christus bis zum Untergang Karthagos*, Kindlers Kulturgeschichte [Zürich: Kindler, 1966], 487, fig. XXXV).

Kamlah have answered it by positing for the YHWH cult one or more *aniconic "visible token(s)" or "iconic cult symbol(s)."*[72]

A series of biblical texts report that the inner sanctuary of the pre-exilic temple consisted of a cubical wooden structure called the *debir* (a *naos* on the Egyptian model). In this "house in the house" stood two *cherubim* whose outstretched inner wings provided a throne for YHWH (cherubim = sphinxes: winged lions with a human face). YHWH's royal person was to be envisioned as seated on the "empty" throne, invisible but nevertheless concrete (cf. Isa 6:1–11). This constellation reflects the *sphinx thrones*, archaeologically attested especially in iconography of the second half of the first millennium BCE in Phoenicia, devoted to various gods (e.g., Astarte or Melkart; see figure 7).[73]

This type of throne is attested for human kings in Palestine (Megiddo) since the Bronze Age. It is not improbable that YHWH of Jerusalem possessed such a royal throne as symbol of his kingship. However, it is a matter of dispute whether in this case we should speak of an "empty space aniconism" as distinct from "material aniconism," as Tryggve N. D. Mettinger has suggested. The ostensible "emptiness" as represented by a throne occupied by a royal figure should probably be regarded instead as a mixed form *between* "aniconism" and a cult of images, what Kamlah calls an "iconic symbol." In any case it is *not known to have been contrasted with an anthropomorphic cult image*; rather, it participates in that concept in that the throne evokes a corresponding "idea of a figure." An archaeological witness discovered in 2006 in the excavations of David's city in Jerusalem may help us to further clarify the matter (figure 8).

This seal impression from Iron Age II A (ninth century BCE?) displays a throne with a winged sun on/over it.[74] The sun symbol, originating in Egypt and widely used in the Levant in the first millennium BCE, has a number of meanings: it possesses royal (cf. the official *lmlk*-king's seals on Judaic storage jars)[75] and cosmic (solar/celestial) connotations. From a social point of view, both in the ancient Near East and in Israel it was likewise associated with divine "justice" or "righteousness" (cf. Mal 3:20 [MT]). That the seal impression refers to YHWH of Jerusalem is quite possible: in that case the god would be represented—as in the biblical texts—not by a cult image but by the symbol of the empty throne with a winged sun, open to a royal YHWH evoking associations of light and splendour.

In this context we should point, on the one hand, to the debate about a "solarization" of YHWH in preexilic Judah,[76] and on the other hand to

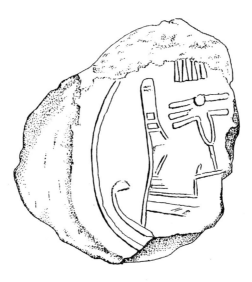

Figure 8: Seal impression from Jerusalem: Throne with sun symbol

Clay impression of a stamp seal found in the excavations by Ronny Reich and Eli Shukron (2006) in the area near the first Temple (Gihon Spring) and dating probably from the ninth century BCE. It shows an Egyptian-style, "empty" throne with a high back. Above/on the seat is a winged sun disk or sun symbol.

Source: Othmar Keel, *Die Geschichte Jerusalems und die Entstehung des Monotheismus*, 2 vols., OLG IV/1–2 (Göttingen: Vandenhoeck & Ruprecht, 2007), I: 304, fig. 191 (drawing by Ulrike Zurkinden-Kolberg).

the possible link with the biblical concept of divine glory (*kābôd*),[77] a "mental" symbol of Yhwh's presence from official Jerusalemite theology of the temple. As we will show more clearly below (§2.4a), from the time of the exile—in contrast to Babylonian imagery—Deutero-Isaiah, "P," and Ezekiel have recourse to this concept of presence. In the cultural contact with the Babylonian image cults, it is probable that Jerusalem's former material cult symbolism of Yhwh without an anthropomorphic image (and the associated "mental" concept of *kābôd*) was recognized as a mark of difference. In fact, an emerging awareness of difference in this regard may already have had its predecessor in the time of Josiah (cf. the destruction of the Asherah in 2 Kgs 23:6; see below at §2.4b.2).

On the other hand, there are thus far scarcely any credible grounds for the hypothesis presented, for example, by Herbert Niehr, Christoph Uehlinger, and Matthias Köckert, derived by analogy from "ancient Near Eastern normality," that until 587/586 BCE a cultic statue of Yhwh in human form stood in the temple at Jerusalem.[78] Probably what stood in Jerusalem in the cella (*dəbîr*), besides the empty throne, was the *chest-shaped sanctuary of the ark* with a stone/stones inside it, meant to be understood in the context of the tradition of the massebot (standing stones)[79] (cf. Gen 28:18, 22). In the biblical witness the two (throne and ark) were mutually related, but explicitly attested is this only in the Priestly writing (see Exod 25:10–22) after the destruction of the temple. Highly interesting, possibly also in regard to a comparable mixed form of "aniconic" and "iconic" cultic symbolism, is a Phoenician sphinx throne from the Lebanon (7th c. BCE, figure 9).

Here again the throne is "empty," but it may be that we should interpret the pillar-like structure on the back as a betyl (house of god) or massebah (standing stone); in that case we would have, in addition, an aniconic "visible token" as embodiment of the deity. In both types of

Figure 9: "Empty" sphinx throne from the southern Lebanese coast

The Phoenician limestone throne (7th c. BCE) flanked by two sphinxes is either "empty" or else the prominent central console of the throne's back is to be addressed as a betyl/massebah, so that the deity would be symbolized twice (invisibly seated on the throne and simultaneously manifest through the betyl).

Source: Martin Metzger, "Jahwe, der Kerubenthroner, die von Keruben flankierte Palmette und Sphingenthrone aus dem Libanon," in *Vorderorientalische Ikonographie und Altes Testament. Gesammelte Aufsätze*, Jerusalemer Theologisches Forum 6 (Münster: Aschendorff, 2004), 210, fig. 157.

interpretation its proper shape remains "invisible." In any case the object, coming from a preexilic period and a neighboring religion, attests to the close relationship to a throne symbolism like what we should presume existed in Jerusalem—without a temple cult image of human or animal shape. We may conclude our overview of ancient Near Eastern image cults and "aniconism," which ultimately brought us to Palestine/Israel, with the view of Othmar Keel, which in my opinion is the best-founded statement regarding the debate in question:

> The Jerusalem cult was not the only one in the ancient Near East to do without an anthropomorphic cult image. Niehr also speaks cautiously of "a symbol of a deity" as the possible focus of an ancient Near Eastern cult. For example, we may point to the famous cultic pedestal of the Assyrian King Tukulti-Ninurta I (ca. 1240 BCE) in Berlin. [See figure 4 above.] More pertinent is the small temple of YHWH in Arad in the northern Negeb, where, in the 8th–6th centuries BCE the deity, most probably YHWH, was represented by an aniconic pillar (massebah) to which, as the archaeological findings show, people also offered incense and brought sacrifices. [See figure 5 above.] The deity worshiped there was neither in the form of a chest (in the case of the Ark) nor of a stone figure (as in the case of a massebah).[80]

Instead, in the Old Testament texts we always find the idea of YHWH *in the form of a human being or, more precisely, as a royal persona* in the sense of the common ancient Near Eastern concept of gods.[81] The associated problem, already mentioned above, of the multiple "embodiments" of a god must now be addressed briefly in more detail. It is about a basic conceptual framework with the aid of which one could, on the one hand, "read" the ritual but could, on the other hand, relativize and transcend it.

1.2 The Cult's Frame of Reference: "Mental Iconography"

a. The bodies of the gods

Historical anthropology of ancient cultures also addressed the question of the *(imagined) bodies of the deities.* Jean-Pierre Vernant in particular has pointed out how much, on the one hand, the concept of divine bodies makes communication with humanity possible, and in that way is an indispensable precondition for the cult: gods, as bearers of names and so available to be addressed, are bound up in a network of social relationships (see above).[82] This is true of relationships among the gods themselves (kinship/rule) and in relation to humans (ritual/cult). On the other hand, the corporeality of the gods is of a sort that *far surpasses human limitations*:

> Visible and invisible, revealed and hidden, present and absent, here and elsewhere, everywhere and nowhere—in short, in the world beyond: the body of the god presents the problem of relationships between the divine, the form or forms, and individuality. The body is a form; it occupies a particular space and at the same time has its place in a particular location. These limitations through and in the body appear to be the necessary condition for an individual, in its uniqueness, to take on a form. The gods do seem to have individuality, but the superfluity of being and the life-force that characterize them cannot be confined within the narrow limits of a particular form.[83]

Hence Vernant speaks, from the perspective of comparative religions, of "polysomy," the multiple embodiments of the gods.[84] Biblical monotheism, which shapes the final version of the Old Testament, still employs *a number of older anthropomorphic symbols* for the personal god Yнwн; these indicate his "embodiedness" simultaneously with a transcendence and relativization of it.[85] This is clear from the literary and poetic images of the figure of God—body parts, clothing, and their functions—painted by Old Testament texts. These represent a *necessary precondition* for speaking of the God of Israel and make that God accessible to human beings.[86] These are anthropomorphisms that are not governed by the rejection of images (see §3.1 below). Thus the "voice," the "(right) arm," the "hand," the "feet," or the "face," shining or turned away in wrath, are *social metaphors* for God, statements related to action intended to evoke particular reactions from people. Behind the linguistic images lie *precise imaginative contexts*, such as the model of a *royal audience* (for the "face" of Yнwн) or a warrior king.[87] But these ideas, which can be described more precisely in light of ancient Near Eastern iconographic conventions, were, in Vernant's sense, constantly being surpassed and relativized. In that light all visual representations are subject to the tension, previously described, between what is visibly present and the impenetrable "other."

b. Transcendence of the divine beings

Ancient Near Eastern deities were not restricted to one form of presence (in either polytheistic or monotheistic systems). They were as multiple and many-shaped as their local and national cults, some of them with the most ancient of traditions. So, for example, Greek or Roman authors marveled at the manifold figures of gods in Egypt, so hazy and ambiguous to viewers from outside; they were especially fascinated by the numerous embodiments in animals or composite creatures. In Egyptian "theology" there was certainly an internal mythical logic at work according to which, behind the innumerable visages of gods, there stood a knowledge of the limitations of every form of appearance.[88] The greatest god, Amun-Re (Amun of Thebes, combined with the sun god Re, considered all-encompassing in the New Kingdom) incorporated in his very name, Amun, "the hidden one," the primeval space-time depths as the ineluctable horizon of being. Erik Hornung accurately characterizes the corresponding uniqueness of Egyptian "ideas of God":

> Terms like these [i.e., sun god, sky goddess, etc.] describe only parts of the divine reality which we should not consider to be the sole significant ones. Even new, improved terms will probably never encompass the entire richness of a god's nature. Nonetheless we are not freed from the obligation to try to comprehend a larger part of that nature and to achieve a closer approximation to it. Here the Egyptians themselves set an example for us: for them the nature of a god becomes accessible through a "multiplicity of approaches"; only when these are taken together can the whole be comprehended.[89]

Mesopotamia does not yield such a great multiplicity of forms as Egypt, but there are comparable phenomena to be found. We may refer, for example, to the *multiple names* for the same deities, especially Marduk, whose fifty names/epithets are listed in the doxological final section of the *Enuma Elish* (the Babylonian Epic of Creation; tablets VI–VII).[90] In their abundance they praise the greatness of the god, beyond all measure, whose rise was depicted in the preceding myth. We should also recall the special character of the astral trio of Šamaš (sun), Sîn (moon), and Ištar (Venus). Their primary way of appearing in the heavens is *cosmically given*, beyond all artifacts and symbolic forms, and—in the case of the sun—impossible to look at directly. But the heavenly bodies are not the gods themselves; they are *ma(n)zzāzu*, their "location," or *tamšīlu*, "images" of them.[91]

At least in the case of the astral trio, then, there appear cheek by jowl the idea of a human form, anthropomorphic cult images, symbols representing their astral appearance (like the sun disk shown above from the temple of Šamaš in Sippar), and the heavenly phenomena themselves: an example of polysomy (Vernant) and multiplicity of appearances (Frankfort, Hornung). Our question about the "nature" of a god in relation to the god's forms of appearance can, in light of the ancient Near Eastern "cultural semantics" (Benno Landsberger's *Eigenbegrifflichkeit*)[92] only be formulated in such a way that we take multiplicity *and* its internal tension as our starting point and inquire into its logic.

According to what has been said already, this logic lies in the *ambivalence of presence and withdrawal, what is given and what remains unknown/invisible*. In regard to a hermeneutic of the Old Testament-Jewish prohibition of images, we ought to sharpen the question whether the nature of the transcendence is not fundamentally altered when *the distinction between (creator)-god and world* is made in a deliberate way (Fritz Stolz).[93] Then the view on visual representations also changes, especially when these are regarded as "artifacts": now they are understood to be a part of what is made and belonging within this world. The later biblical polemic against images can most easily be understood in light of this distinction; thus it is also related to the pre-Socratic philosophical critique of images. For that reason also the following overview of the unique character and origins of the prohibition of images should begin with a broad view that includes ancient philosophical critique of images and the views of Greco-Roman antiquity regarding the image-free character of Jewish religion.

2. The Ban on Images: Character and Origin

2.1 The Pre-Socratics' Critique of Images

The pre-Socratics subjected cultic and religious practices to a critique beginning especially with the visual representations of the divine in the narrower sense in order to arrive at a more abstract and indefinite idea of god (cf. also §III.4.4 below). The corresponding arguments of Xenophanes of Colophon (ca. 570–475 BCE), a contemporary of Deutero-Isaiah (see below at §2.4a) and the Priestly writing (see below at §3.2c) are well known. His remarks on the nature of the gods, fragmentarily contained in the *Stromateis* (ca. 200 CE) of Clement of Alexandria, Origen's teacher, speak of the incomparability of the gods as regards "body" and "mind," which are altogether distinct from those of mortals.[94] At the same time, people of all cultures succumb to *anthropomorphism and anthropopathism*:

> But men have the idea that gods are born,
> And wear their clothes, and have both voice and shape.[95]

> But had the oxen or the lions hands,
> Or could with hands depict a work like men,
> Were beasts to draw the semblance of the gods,
> The horses would them like to horses sketch,
> To oxen, oxen, and their bodies make
> Of such a shape as to themselves belongs.[96]

> The Ethiopians [depict their gods] black with turned up nose,
> the Thracians with red hair and blue eyes."[97]

37

Xenophanes's contemporary, Heraclitus of Ephesus (end of the 6th c. BCE) criticized the worship of images of the gods even more clearly: "They pray to images, much as if they should talk to houses; for they do not know the nature of gods and heroes."[98]

Such an enlightened critique of religion, perhaps inspired in part by cultural contacts with the religion of the Persians (Achaemenids), which was nearly devoid of (cultic) images,[99] by no means succeeded in the broad scope of Greco-Roman culture, so that the absence of images and the polemic against them in *Judaism* was viewed by ancient observers for the most part as both conspicuous and irritating.

2.2 Ancient Jewish Critique of Images

a. Hellenistic-Roman authors on monotheism and prohibition of images: The view from outside

Given the central role of images for the cultic worship of deities, as well as for the ideas people formed of them, which prevailed almost without question in the ancient Near East and in antiquity in general, the *absence of images* in Jewish religion appears as highly unusual. This is true not only in light of the modern study of religion; it was remarked on frequently from the Hellenistic period onward. Beginning in about 300 BCE, the absence of images was a central element of the "classic" constellation of motifs used to describe the religion of Judea and the Jews.[100] The religious-cultural and philosophical view from outside regarded that religion as marked by worship of the "most high" god, one whose name remained as unknown as his form. There is a direct Hebrew and Aramaic equivalent for the term "most high god" (*summus deus*) in the late period of composition of the Old Testament and in early Jewish writings: *'ēl 'elyôn* or *'ĕlāhā 'illāyā*.[101]

Cosmologically, the Jewish God was almost exclusively associated with *heaven* in the eyes of ancient authors (perhaps first by Theophrastus, the pupil of Aristotle [372–288/287 BCE],[102] certainly by the historian Hecataeus of Abdera [*Aegyptiaca*, ca. 300 BCE][103]). Also, the god of the Jews was frequently *identified directly with heaven(s)* (or among the Stoics, with the whole world: Strabo of Amaseia [64 BCE–23 CE][104]). This association with heaven is directly attested by the very frequent linking of Yнwн with heaven in the Old Testament from the Persian period onward. Particularly relevant here is the significant title "God of heaven," used in the Old Testament primarily in situations of contact with non-Jews (so Ezra–Nehemiah, Chronicles, Jonah, Daniel).[105] In terms of the history of religion, YHWH's increasing relationship to heaven can also be associated with the greater and greater prominence in the second half of the first millennium BCE of the universal "Lord of the heavens," *Ba'al šāmēm*, in Syria and the Levant.[106] It was natural for Greeks and Romans to identify deities of this type with Zeus and Jupiter.

The *exclusivity* of worship of the one (heaven-)god by the Jews corresponded, in the eyes of ancient observers, with the most remarkable characteristic of that worship: its *lack of images*. Ancient voices clearly attest that this was solely a matter of *images for cultic worship* (ancient synagogues in Palestine/Syria were indeed decorated with pictures).[107] Besides the programmatic avoidance of images, other customs and rituals that separated Jews from non-Jews were constantly mentioned (such as certain animal sacrifices and male circumcision). Still, in the judgment of Greek and Roman authors (e.g., Livy [59 BCE–17 CE] or Lucan [39–65 CE]), which was often motivated by hostility to the Jews, these were seen as less odd than the absence of images, especially in combination with the "namelessness" of this god, or that the god's name remained hidden from outsiders.[108] The god of the Jews appeared in a sense to be "placeless" (not a member of the society of gods) and oddly opaque. For some authors the Jews were simply "godless" because no one could or wanted to imagine a god without an image and a name (thus the Egyptian priest Manetho [*Aegyptiaca*, 3rd c. BCE]).[109] Scholars like Terentius Varro (referring to the ancient Roman religion in his *Antiquitates*, between 63 and 47 BCE) or the historian Tacitus (referring to the Germans in his *Historiae* V.5,4, between 105 and 110 CE) gave religious-historical analogies for aniconism of deities and to that extent tried to relate Judaism to what was otherwise known (cf. also the Middle Platonist Celsus [*Alēthēs Logos*, between 177 and 180 CE] with an analogy to the aniconism of the Persians, referring to Herodotus).[110] However, as Peter Schäfer has demonstrated, the ancient judgments are almost all marked more by lack of understanding than by empathy:

> What clearly most strikes the Greek and Roman authors is the aniconism of the Jewish God, the evident fact, contrary to all the customs of the Greco-Roman world, that he is invisible and wants to remain invisible, that is, that he does not allow any image to be made of him. One possible and common response to this, which

can take a positive as well as a negative connotation, is to identify him with heaven, more specifically with the remote and invisible "heights of heaven" (together with this [identification] sometimes goes the notion that he is incorporeal). Related to the "heights of heaven" is the epithet "highest god" (*summus deus*), or "most high," which acknowledges the Jewish God as the highest of many other gods and therefore identifies him with Jupiter or Zeus. Another, and clearly negative, conclusion to be drawn is that he does not exist at all, that the Jews do not recognize any God and therefore are to be regarded as godless or atheists.

Between these two extremes we find the idea that the Jews do worship a God who, or whose name, is unknown (*ignotus* or, according to the later Neoplatonic terminology, *agnōstos*) to the Gentiles.[111]

As we have said, the expressions of "all-surpassingness" employed by the ancient authors to interpret the Jewish religion ("highest" of the gods, to be equated with heaven) in turn have a basis in Old Testament texts (cf. the late-deuteronomistic prayer of Solomon at the dedication of the temple in 1 Kgs 8:27: "Even heaven and the highest heaven cannot contain you, much less this house that I have built!" and compare Isa 66:1).[112] Worth noting are the well-known remarks of Tacitus in his ethnographic excursus in the *Histories*. These interpret Jewish aniconism in the sense of an ancient philosophical theology like that in Cicero's *De natura deorum*,[113] but the context of critique of Judaism makes them appear ambivalent:

> The Egyptians worship many animals and images of monstrous form (*animalia effigiesque compositas*); the Jews have purely mental conceptions of Deity, as one in essence (*mente sola unumque numen intellegunt*). They call those profane who make representations of God in human shape out of perishable materials. They believe that Being to be supreme and eternal (*summum illud et aeternum*), neither capable of representation, nor of decay (*neque imitabile neque interiturum*). They therefore do not allow any images to stand in their cities, much less in their temples. This flattery is not paid to their kings nor this honour to our emperors.[114]

This passage reveals knowledge of Jewish traditions, including the Old Testament, such as the argument about the materiality of images that draw the eternal God into the transitory realm (see §§2.2b and III.3 below). It is striking that the idea of God is interpreted as *mente sola*, an experience in thought of the most high and eternal one. In this view the Jews could not tolerate either anthropomorphic depictions of God nor a worship of earthly rulers (their own or the Roman emperor) as like God. The passage and its larger context illustrate the ancient struggle with the special character of Jewish religion; at its core lay the question of images. (In *Historiae* 5.3, Tacitus, like some of his predecessors, speaks at length of the exodus and its profound significance for the origins of Judaism).[115]

In inquiring about the tradition history of aniconism and the origins of the prohibition of images, we should note that as early as 300 BCE the following basic elements of Jewish religion were frequently mentioned by Greek and Roman outsiders:

1. The reference to Moses as lawgiver and the strong sense of identity, over against other peoples, deriving from his rules.
2. A special self-awareness on the part of the inhabitants of Judea/the Jews, grounded in the "exodus" from Egypt (usually interpreted not, as in the biblical tradition, as liberation, but instead as expulsion).
3. The worship of a (single) god as "most high," and his cosmic location in or identification with heaven/the heights of heaven.
4. The aniconism of the belief in this god, both with reference to the Jerusalem temple and also in principle—with the focus placed not on the prohibition of images as such but on the existing practice: for example, that Moses made no images of God "since he believed that God has no human form."[116] In this way the prohibition of images appears as a powerful distinguishing mark separating Judaism from the world around it, including a critique of images in the practice of other nations (as attested, e.g., by Tacitus; see above).

We should not underestimate the fact that the writings of ancient authors, who likewise built on the work of their literary predecessors, assumed a significance of the Torah that we find attested externally from the third century BCE onward. That significance lay for them *in the Jews' special concept of God*, characterized, in modern terms, especially by the elements of *monotheism*, *transcendence* (of a creator god associated with the heavens), and *aniconism*. As we have said, it appears that this last was not regarded by the ancient authors as imposed by any *prohibition* of images, which they do not mention as such. Instead, the avoidance of an image of God was regarded as a striking *religio-cultural peculiarity* that seemed to follow seamlessly from their special *idea* of God. To that extent it was, according to the Greek and Roman descriptions, adduced by the Jews themselves and was also used as a criterion for judging other religions. To put it again in modern terms: *aniconism and the prohibition/critique of images are a consequence of specifically Jewish monotheism.*

We need now to pursue this line of interpretation further, using it as a guiding concept, for in today's religious-historical perspective on the Old Testament and early Judaism it still retains the greatest probability. (The so-called Second Commandment appears to be a concretion and consequence of the First.)[117] In what follows we will begin with the relatively secure postexilic evidence of the writings later included in the Tanakh and further Jewish literature of the Greco-Roman period. From there the presentation will move back to the highly controversial problems surrounding the origins of the prohibition of images.[118]

b. Critique of images in ancient Jewish witnesses and texts of the postexilic period (5th–3rd c. BCE): The view from within

B.1) ANCIENT JEWISH TEXTS

The latest example, to be examined first, is the so-called *Apocalypse of Abraham*, an ancient Jewish tractate from the period after the destruction of the Second Temple by Romans in 70 CE (and to be dated possibly as late as the 2nd century CE).[119] It only survives in a translation (in Old Church Slavonic), presumably based on an original in a Semitic language. The first eight chapters tell the story of the patriarch Abraham's youth; here, as previously in the book of *Jubilees* (first half of the 2nd c. BCE), relevant gaps in the biblical story of Abraham (Gen 11:27–30 with Josh 24:2) are filled. In a fictive personal testimony Abraham describes how, in Mesopotamia in surroundings in which worship of images was a matter of course, he came to know the *one* Creator God. The stages of his process of emancipation in this regard are associated with various aspects of the critique of images of god/polemics against idols. Abraham came to know the images of god directly because his father Terah had a workshop that made them and he assisted in the family business:

> On the day when I was [planing] the gods of my father Terah and the gods of my brother Nahor, when I was testing which one was the truly strong god, at the time when my lot came up, when I had finished the services of my father Terah's sacrifice to his gods of wood, stone, gold, silver, brass and iron....[120]

Several situations illustrate his increasing insight into the evanescent materiality of the "gods" and their complete inability to act. First, the head of an idol called Marumath falls to the floor of the temple, and its body has to be repaired by Terah and Abraham so that the head will be secure (*Apoc. Ab.* 1:4–12). Then Abraham sets up five statues from his father's workshop for sale in the streets, but three of them fall from his donkey and break, so he throws them into the river, where they simply sink (*Apoc. Ab.* 2—3). Abraham recognizes that they were incapable of doing anything, even for their own protection. Finally, Abraham finds "a little god" engraved with the name Barisat among the wood shavings in the workshop and tries an experiment: he entrusts Barisat with caring for the fire in the stove, but the god simply falls down and is burned (*Apoc. Ab.* 5). Abraham reports this to his father, but he only praises what his son ironically calls Barisat's "love" as the basis of his self-sacrifice. From then on Abraham turns away from his father and the images and inquires into the powers of creation, the elements of fire, water, and earth, and the heavenly bodies—sun, moon, and stars. They all have power over one another but are also limited by their opposites (thus water extinguishes fire and the sun is darkened by night). In a leap of thought, therefore, Abraham seeks the originator of all the works of creation and finds it through a deep study of the *heavens*:

> Listen, Terah, my father, I shall seek in your presence the God who created all the gods which we consider! For who is it, or which one is it who colored heaven and made the sun golden, who has given light to the moon and the stars with it, who has dried the earth in the midst of many waters, who set you yourself among the elements, and who now has chosen me in the distraction of my mind? (*Apoc. Ab.* 7:11–12)

Thus the text presents a series of arguments that were also advanced by the great Jewish philosopher Philo of Alexandria (d. 40 CE in Rome) and the historian Flavius Josephus (ca. 37/38–100 CE), adopting Stoic ideas to give rational proof of the Jewish idea of God as found in the Bible.[121] Tacitus also, in his excursus in the *Histories* cited above (contemporary with the *Apocalypse of Abraham*), apparently applauded comparable attempts. The *basic presupposition of the critique of images*, which the *Apocalypse of Abraham*, as a very late testimony to the Jewish ridicule of idols shares with its predecessors, is the *identification of the images with the gods in the eyes of their worshipers*, as indicated in the Old Testament. Jewish criticism of images is above all a criticism of foreign gods. If we recall the differentiated ancient Near Eastern "theology of images" sketched above (see §1.1b above), we can clearly see the radical foreshortening that has taken place: it applies the monotheistic insight that nothing this-worldly, no element of the works of creation, nor even the universe as a whole is able to represent or reflect the creator god who is radically different from the world. Other early Jewish texts from the Hellenistic-Roman period (*Bel and the Dragon*, an addition to Daniel probably from the 2nd century BCE; the *Epistle of Jeremiah*, 4th–2nd century BCE; Wisdom of Solomon 13—15, between the 2nd century BCE and the 1st century CE) argue similarly. They all have in common a critique of images (= idols) that in turn rests on the corresponding anti-image polemic in the Old Testament, attested from the time of Deutero-Isaiah (6th–5th c. BCE).[122]

B.2) OLD TESTAMENT CRITIQUE OF IMAGES FROM THE POSTEXILIC PERIOD

A condemnation of the nations' worship of images as a false trust in empty things and self-deception characterizes the critique of religion in many Old Testament texts from the postexilic period (Deutero-Isaiah, Jeremiah, Ezekiel, the Psalter, etc.). Even if at first glance the arguments applied against the "idols" and "nothings" seem stereotypical, it is worthwhile to pay attention to their different aims. The very fact that broad sections of the Old Testament literature reveal such polemics against gods (i.e., their cult statues) may possibly be regarded as a sign of *unclarity in the question of images and conflict situations within their own religious community*. After all, the texts are not directed primarily at external addressees; their primary purpose is to be taken seriously within Judaism, then in the process of constituting itself. (Differently from Christianity and Islam, ancient Judaism hardly ever engaged in active proselytizing.)

First let us consider the Hebrew Psalter, which, despite the complex evidence from the Qumranic texts, probably acquired its final form in the late Persian and early Hellenistic periods. An important compositional and redaction-critical "cross brace" in its architecture is the connection of the fourth and fifth books of Psalms by means of Psalm 135, which I see as stemming, at the earliest, from the late Persian era. In verses 15–18, that psalm reprises the criticism of images in Psalm 115 (vv. 4–8).[123] Psalm 135 was deliberately placed before Psalm 136 and thereby adopts some of its wording. I will concentrate here on the model, Psalm 115, which can scarcely be dated much earlier (probably also in the 4th century BCE). This psalm's whole subject is "apologetics": it begins with the *non-Jews' question about "where" God is*, and so—in modern terms—enters from the outset into an interreligious debate. The nations appear to distrust the imageless god:

2   Why should the nations say,
        "Where is their God?"

3   Our God is in the heavens;
        he does whatever he pleases.[124]

Very much in the sense of the ancient witnesses to Judaism we have named, the answer to the peoples' question about the "location" of the god worshiped by those who pray the psalm is that God is in *the heavens*, and consequently his power is not bound by *any earthly limitations* (in dogmatic-theological terms one would speak of God's "omnipotence" or sovereignty). The continuation shows clearly that this is a dialogue about the *question of images*:

4   Their idols are silver and gold,
        the work of human hands.
5   They have mouths, but do not speak;
        eyes, but do not see.
6   They have ears, but do not hear;
        noses, but do not smell.

7   They have hands, but do not feel;
        feet, but do not walk;
        they make no sound in their throats.
8   Those who make them are like them;
        so are all who trust in them.

In a fashion very similar to the much later *Apocalypse of Abraham*, here the *bodies* of the gods, thought of as identical with their images, are dissected as altogether "dead" and mortal; the valuable materials, silver and gold (possibly an ancient starting point for Old Testament critique of images; see §2.4b.1), do not alter that fact. Instead, it is precisely the artifact-character of the "gods" that makes visible the illusion associated with them—assuming that one has knowledge of the one, universal creator god. (The text appears, moreover, to know exactly how a cult image was imagined in the ancient Near East as integrated within a context of actions and communication; see 1.1b.) The quotation from Psalm 115:7 is expanded still further in Psalm 135:17b: "there is no breath [*rûaḥ*] in their mouths."[125]

Finally, a nuance in Psalm 115:8 is revealing: it is not only the "makers" of the (images) of god(s) who will share their mortal fate but likewise "all who trust in them." This postscript does not exclude members of one's own community of faith. It may be, in fact, that the impulse to the psalm's argumentation lies here—in addition to the quarrel with the "nations." Verses 9–11 appeal to Israel's *trust in God*, to the Aaronide priesthood, and to "those who fear YHWH" (thus also proselytes or those among the nations who understand). According to verse 12, they may all expect "blessing" (the verb is *brk*) from YHWH:

12   YHWH has been mindful of us; he will bless us;
        he will bless the house of Israel;
        he will bless the house of Aaron;
13   he will bless those who fear YHWH,
        both small and great.

14   May YHWH give you [ever more blessings],
        both you and your children.
15   May you be blessed by YHWH,
        who made heaven and earth.
16   The heavens are YHWH's heavens [= belong to YHWH],
        but the earth he has given to human beings.

The monotheistic God of the heavens does not abide in transcendence; rather, this God's lifegiving power is continually manifest in *blessing*, which gives fertility and posterity (vv. 14–15; cf. also Ps 67, where the blessing is universalized to encompass the world of the nations).[126] This, too, can be read in such a way that it is not merely about setting boundaries (and a gesture of superiority) toward those outside but also concerns an internal struggle in view of a "plausibility gap" in one's own religion caused *by the aniconism and absence of anything tangible.* For Psalm 115, blessing is the solution: a mediation between transcendence and immanence. Other texts in the Psalter, and also in Deutero-Isaiah, activate more ancient elements of Jerusalem's cultic traditions with similar functions, such as the personified divine active powers *ḥesed* and *ʾemet*, "kindness" and "faithfulness," or "righteousness" and "justice" (cf., e.g., Ps 85:10–14; Isa 45:7–8).[127]

In Deutero-Isaiah, which we will have to consider in more detail, we find a whole series of polemics against idols; for a long time these were regarded as one redactional unit (especially Isa 40:[18], 19–20; 41:[5], 6–7; 44:9–20; 46:[5], 6–7). But it seems likely that these texts are distributed across a variety of stages in the development of Isaiah 40—55.[128] Among the later (Hellenistic?) examples is the *ridicule of idols in Isaiah 44:9–20,*[129] inserted immediately before the central saying about Cyrus in 44:24—45:8, the core of the basic literary layer of Deutero-Isaiah (ca. 539 BCE). The ridiculing of idols in Isaiah 44 served as a model for many successors, clearly including the author of the *Apocalypse of Abraham* (see above). The text describes how the carvers (*yōṣrê pesel*, "cultic-image-makers," v. 9) are incapable of insight and knowledge: they are only human beings, and yet they think they can confect gods. They are deaf to their bodily needs (weariness, hunger), which must remind them of the fleetingness of their existence and of their products. Their blindness is demonstrated especially in the famous block of wood from part of which a god is made while the rest is thrown into the fire to create warmth and make it possible to bake something:

> [15] Then it [the wood] can be used as fuel. Part of it he [the carver] takes and warms himself; he kindles a fire and bakes bread. Then he makes a god [*ʾēl*] and worships it [bows down to it in *proskynesis*], makes it a carved image [*pesel*] and bows down before it. [16] Half of it he burns in the fire; over this half he roasts meat, eats it and is satisfied. He also warms himself and says, "Ah, I am warm, I

can feel the fire!" [17] The rest of it he makes into a god [*'ēl*], his idol [*pesel*], bows down to it and worships it; he prays to it and says, "Save me [*nṣl* {Hiph.}], for you are my god [*'ēlî*]!"

The text clearly presumes the explicit prohibition of images in the Decalogue ("You shall not make for yourself [*ləkā*] an idol [*pesel*]" (Exod 20:4//Deut 5:8 [see below]), and develops its argument from there: that a lack of insight into one's own status as mortal human being leads to blindness in regard to self-made "gods." Here the critique of images comes very close to that of Xenophanes (see above at §2.1; below at §III.4.4). However, one significant difference is the *definition of a god* formulated in the prayer to the image, which Deutero-Isaiah (basic layer) is the first to advance (repeatedly) against the Babylonian conception of a god: "*Save me*, for you are my god!" From this point of view it is characteristic of the God Yнwн that he alone is able to save, and so to demonstrate divine power in history (of the world, of the nation, of individuals).[130] The prayer, correct in itself, is accordingly directed to the wrong addressee; it lacks insight into the "nature" of the creating and saving God of Israel. It is revealing that this text also *remains vague as to the identity of the "makers" of the idols.*

This is about the ways of humans in general (vv. 11, 13, 15: keyword *'ādām*, "human being"). In the context of Deutero-Isaiah one is inclined to think primarily of the Babylonians, but it is true here also that the intended readers are members of one's own community who felt insecure in their identity in face of the wealth of images in Babylon. (This must be considered in more detail because here we can most clearly locate the context in which the explicit prohibition of images originated; see below at §2.4a). As in Psalm 115, then, the critique of/polemic against images in Isaiah 44 is directed *both outwardly and inwardly*. Likewise, as with the "blessing" in Psalm 115, so also in Isaiah 44:17 it is the experience of "rescue" (*nṣl* Hiph. means literally "snatch out" [of the hands of enemies/of danger]), which is able to reveal God's presence without the medium of an image.

Jeremiah 10:1–16 speaks directly against the attractions of the cult of images for the members of the "house of Israel" (the postexilic addressees of the Book of Jeremiah) who are "vulnerable" in this respect. This is the third example we will give here; it is also a late insertion in its context and one that clearly presupposes Deutero-Isaiah:[131]

2 Thus says YHWH:
Do not learn the way of the nations,
    or be dismayed at the signs of the heavens;
    for the nations are dismayed at them.
3 For the customs [or: statutes] of the peoples are false:
a tree from the forest is cut down,
    and worked with an ax by the hands of an artisan;
4 people deck it with silver and gold;
    they fasten it with hammer and nails
    so that it cannot move.
5 Their idols are like scarecrows in a cucumber field,
    and they cannot speak;
they have to be carried,
    for they cannot walk.
Do not be afraid of them,
    for they cannot do evil,
    nor is it in them to do good.

In what follows (Jer 10:6–16), the prophetic voice never tires in emphasizing for the addressees, in light of this critique, the incomparability and greatness of the world king, YHWH (v. 7: "King of the nations"); though nothing is said directly about YHWH's uniqueness, it is profiled in terms of God's mighty deeds in creation and history in contrast to the nations and their gods/idols. Those who worship images are "stupid and foolish" (v. 8), while YHWH "made the earth by his power...established the world by his wisdom, and by his understanding stretched out the heavens" (v. 12). Here again the argument of creation, of the world but especially of the heavens, marks the specific difference.[132] This is made particularly clear in the still-later (Hellenistic) Aramaic insertion at verse 11, which sought actively to make the idols vanish:[133] "Thus shall you say to them [the nations]: The gods who did not make [Aramaic *ăbad*] the heavens and the earth shall perish from the earth and from under the heavens."

Conclusion: The intensity of the confrontation within postexilic polemic over idols is not always at the same level, but it is clear that precisely monotheistic, aniconic Judaism in its formative phase, living according to the demands of its guiding texts, over a long period *had to contend with the power of the images.* Discoveries of interest to religious

historians, including terracotta figurines and Zeus iconography of YHWH
on coins from the Persian province of Yehud (as well as Samaria)[134]—
even though not related to sanctuaries—also point to a *greater pluralism
of forms of religion* (between "official" and "private," "urban" and "rural")
than had long been supposed. (Even so, it is true that anthropomorphic
figurines are less frequently to be found in Yehud than, for example, in
the neighboring coastal regions of the Levant [Phoenicia]):

> In any case we *cannot* derive from the material findings dating to
> the Persian period the actions of an orthodoxy that was, on the
> whole, intolerant, working from the center toward the periphery.
> What is crucial is that the overall picture of the formative phase of
> early Judaism cannot be equated with the biblical scenario of an
> early post-exilic Judaism dominated by a hierocratic elite in Jeru-
> salem (as in the biblical texts); rather, the reconstruction must *also*
> include Elephantine (the Jewish colony on the like-named island
> in the Nile, in Egypt) and Egyptian diaspora Judaism, southern
> Judea or Idumea (i.e., Edom/the Nabateans), and the western
> Shephelah (the coastal hinterlands influenced by the Phoeni-
> cians). A consideration of Samaria and the developments associ-
> ated with Yehud further widens the view. The scholarly evaluation
> of this greater pluralism as heterodoxy, in contrast, arises from a
> picture of a Yahwism that is fundamentally unified, but this is not
> equally reflected in the findings.[135]

The early Jewish monotheistic theologies of a unique God who chose
to remain invisible were the great exception in the ancient world; in a
context in which worship of images and their cult were the norm, they
had to demonstrate *and* maintain themselves both toward the outside
and within.

In this light, what was the meaning of the Old Testament prohibition
of images? How and when was it formulated? What religious-historical
contexts and tradition-historical preconditions for it can we name?
These questions have been matters of dispute in Old Testament research
for a long time.[136] The next section will attempt in the briefest possible
compass to give a possible, if not probable answer: *There are no adequate indications pointing to a great antiquity of the prohibition of images
or to its formulation altogether independently of the First Commandment*

(prohibition of foreign gods). In this connection it is important to distinguish two phases of origin and development:

(a) The easily identifiable phase after the *explicitly formulated prohibition of cultic images in the Decalogue* and similar prohibitions of images in other legal contexts in the Old Testament (none of them prior to the 6th c. BCE). These formulated prohibitions constitute the reference point for what is portrayed in the next sections (§§2.3, 2.4). The explicit prohibition of images is constantly presupposed in the just-discussed late texts critical of images (§2.2b.2), but not yet in the basic layers of Deutero-Isaiah and Ezekiel (see below at §2.4a).

(b) Two strands of a longer *prehistory* in the form of a *critique of images* in the preexilic state period may be isolated in the eighth through seventh centuries BCE (cf. §2.4b):

- the critique of the bull images in the Northern Kingdom of Israel in the Book of Hosea and in Exodus 32
- the Jerusalem temple in the Southern Kingdom of Judah, very probably conceived without a cult image of Yhwh, whose uniqueness served as a criterion of distinction (at first within the religion itself) in the so-called cultic reform under Josiah (and in the measures undertaken by his predecessor, Hezekiah).

The starting point for our overview is, first, the prohibition of images in the Decalogue (§2.3a) and, following that, its parallel formulations (§2.3b).

2.3 The Ban on Images: Origin, Variants, Rationale

a. The Decalogue's prohibition of images

When we speak of the prohibition of images in the Old Testament we think first of the Decalogue, the "Ten Words" (Deut 4:13) of Sinai/Horeb. As we know, in the Hebrew Bible the Decalogue is given twice, in Exodus 20 (vv. 2–17) and in Deuteronomy 5 (vv. 6–21).[137] The ban on images appears in Exodus 20:4–6 and Deuteronomy 5:8–10. In the

Christian tradition of numbering, the Orthodox, Reformed, and Anglican churches count the ban on images as a separate commandment (the second). In older Jewish tradition and in the Roman Catholic and Lutheran way of counting, the prohibition of foreign gods and the ban on images are joined (for Jews it is the second commandment, with God's introductory self-description as the first; for Roman Catholics and Lutherans it is the first).[138] Structurally, the prohibition of images appears in the Decalogue as a *concretization of the prohibition against foreign gods.*[139] The two are surrounded by a deuteronomistically influenced frame (cf. the reference to Exod 34:7 in Exod 20:5b // Deut 5:9b). The *inclusio* is also nicely indicated by the twofold formula of self-presentation, "I am YHWH, your God" (Exod 20:2, 6b // Deut 5:6, 9b) (A // A'). The following translation schematizes Exodus 20:2–6:

> A: 2 "*I am YHWH, your God*, who brought you out of the land of Egypt, out of the house of slavery.
> B: 3 You shall have <u>no other gods</u> before me!
> > C: 4 You shall not make for yourself an idol,
> > *[that is]*[140] *in the form of anything that is in heaven above, or that is on the earth beneath, or that is in the waters under the earth.*
> B': 5a You shall not bow down <u>to them</u> or worship <u>them</u>!
> A': 5b For *I YHWH your God* am a jealous God, punishing children for the iniquity of parents, to the third and the fourth generation of those who reject me, ⁶ but showing steadfast love to the thousandth generation of those who love me and keep my commandments. (Exod 20:2–6 // Deut 5:6–10)

In this sentence structure the ban on foreign gods is continued through and beyond the ban on images (note the underlined portions). Verse 3 (B) forbids the presence of "other gods" (pl.) in YHWH's presence; according to verse 5a (B') "they" (pl.) are not to be offered worship or service. Between these verses stands the prohibition stated in the singular: "You shall not make for yourself an idol" (v. 4 [C]). If we read the whole—which was deliberately constructed as a *concentric* figure, as indicated by the A-C-A' structure—together, the plural "them" in v. 5 must include the idol(s). The rejection of the worship of foreign gods also forbids their antecedent cultic representation in images. The close relationship of the two commandments that begin the Decalogue is obvious and is supported also by the frequent *identification of images and gods* elsewhere in the OT. (On this see also the examples of postexilic polemic against the idols given in the previous section.)

On the other hand, besides the incongruent number (gods [pl.]—image [sg.]) the *relative independence of the formula forbidding images* in verse 4 is striking: "You shall not make for yourself an idol!" Read in isolation, the command is not clear: *is it primarily the images of foreign gods that are here banned, or are images of YHWH also included?* This ambiguity is supported by the definition of *pesel* (sculpture/cult image) in the second half of verse 4, according to which nothing is to be made "in the form [*təmûnâ*] of anything that is in heaven above, or that is on the earth beneath, or that is in the waters under the earth." The only direct terminological and material parallel to this is found in the single extended explanation of the ban on images, Deuteronomy 4 (see §3.2 below). This postexilic text (one of the latest in Deuteronomy) already presumes Deutero-Isaiah and the Priestly writing.[141] In compositional terms, it was deliberately placed ahead of and in the external deuteronomistic frame of the Decalogue in Deuteronomy 5, so that the latter would be read in light of it. Deuteronomy 4 adjures the reader also to rightly understand the theophany on Sinai (Horeb in Deuteronomy):

> [15] Since you saw no form [*təmûnâ*] when the LORD spoke to you at Horeb out of the fire, take care and watch yourselves closely, [16] so that you do not act corruptly by making an idol [*pesel*] for yourselves, in the form of any figure—the likeness of male or female, [17] the likeness of any animal that is *on the earth*, the likeness of any winged bird *that flies in the air*, [18] the likeness of anything that creeps on the ground, the likeness of any fish that *is in the water under the earth*. (Deut 4:15–18)

This implies two things:[142]

(a) The argument from *creation theology*, already familiar to us from the later witnesses, according to which nothing this-worldly is able to represent the (heavenly) transcendent God (cf. Deut 4:11, 36: YHWH is concealed within the heavens; Deut 4:32: God's universal creation of humanity under the whole heavens; Deut 4:39: Israel is to know "that YHWH is God in heaven above and on the earth beneath; there is no other.")

(b) A probable reference to the cosmological implications of the *manufacture of idols in Mesopotamia* (see §1.1b above). There the image/the god was located, ritually and by means of the materials used, in the center of the "coordinate axes" of the three-story world: heaven, earth, and the freshwater ocean beneath the earth (cf. Deut 4:18 for the "water under the earth," as also in Exod 20:4 // Deut 5:8, a statement otherwise scarcely to be found in the OT).

Thus the argumentation in Deuteronomy 4 is primarily concentrated *on the command not to make images of YHWH*, because no "form" (*təmûnâ*, as also in the explanation of the Decalogue in Exod 20:4 // Deut 5:6) was seen at Horeb/Sinai.[143]

In this way the text states the grounds for the ban on images (still lacking in the Decalogue) by looking at its narrative context: the *ban on images* of the one God follows from the aniconism anchored, for Deuteronomy 4, in *Israel's founding event at Sinai*. The text goes on to make a striking link between *foreign gods* and images. Those who had been at Sinai, after all, had to be immune to the fascination the foreign gods exercised—and yet Deuteronomy 4 announces that in exile Israel will "serve" them. In this way the god images are described, using the familiar critique of the material (cf. §2.2b: Ps 115, etc.), as incapable of communication or action:

> [28] There [i.e., in exile] you will serve other gods made by human hands, objects of wood and stone that neither see, nor hear, nor eat, nor smell. [29] From there you will seek the LORD your God, and you will find him if you search after him with all your heart and soul. (Deut 4:28–29)

Hence on the one hand Deuteronomy 4 grounds the aniconism of Israel's worship of God in the theophany at Sinai. (For the relevance, in terms of a hermeneutics of images, of the altogether visual "surrogate" appearances there, see below at §§3.2a–b; §III.7.) On the other hand it points in anticipation (in fact, of course, retrospectively) at the fascination the images of gods would exercise over Israel in the alienation of exile (the thought is certainly of Babylon; cf. v. 19 on the worship of celestial bodies/beings [see below] and in v. 16 the mention of the three-story picture of the world in relation to the visualization of YHWH).[144]

Recent scholarship assumes that the Decalogue's ban on images was redacted again at a later time in light of Deuteronomy 4, by a cosmological annotation on heaven, earth, and the waters under the earth in Exodus 20:4 // Deuteronomy 5:8.[145] If we remove this quotation from Exodus 20:4aβ.b // Deuteronomy 5:8aβ.b, the basic form of the ban on images in the Decalogue remains: *lō' ta 'ăśeh ləkā pesel*, "You shall not make for yourself an idol!" (Exod 20:4 // Deut 5:6). The following points concerning this sentence should be emphasized:

(a) With the concept of *pesel*[146] a three-dimensional (sculptured) object is forbidden (cf. the verb *psl* Qal for the working of stone in Exod 34:1, 4; Deut 10:1, 3; 1 Kgs 5:32; Hab 2:18). However, the word is open to a variety of materials (and metal is not excluded). From the etymology, the focus is primarily on the *working of the material to shape an image* and is not per se about worship. On the other hand, the concept of *pesel* otherwise appears almost always in polemical contexts (cf. §2.2b.2), where it has the connotation of "image venerated in a cult," which is why it can also be translated "idol" in Exodus 20:4 // Deuteronomy 5:6.

(b) Similarly, the very common verb for manufacturing/producing/making (*'śh*) is not focused on particular methods of manufacture; it points primarily to the intention to denounce the *action of crafting/creating* the idol. The emphasis on "making" suggests associations with (in modern terms) *autonomy and self-deception* about the status of the "thing made" (on this see expressions such as "[inferior] work [*ma 'ăśeh*] of human hands,"[147]).

(c) Finally, because it receives too little attention among scholars, we should emphasize the preposition *lamed* with the suffix of the second person (*ləkā*, "for yourself"). This dative/reflexive indicates the self-referential character of an action, including *taking possession* of what is made.[148] It underscores clearly again what was noted in (a) and (b): no "image" is to be "made" *on one's own initiative and to satisfy one's own needs* ("for yourself"). This *dativus commodi* has a probable precursor in the critique of images in Hosea (Hos 8:4; probably postexilic is Hos 13:2 [see below, §2.4b]).

As we can see, all the components of the formula for the ban on images in the Decalogue (Exod 20:4 // Deut 5:6) accord very well *with the reflections on the ontological status of the images that mark the late Old Testament and ancient Jewish polemic against images against the background of monotheistic aniconism* (see above at §2.2b.1–2). Nothing can be found in the commandment that speaks in favor of an early (pre-exilic) origin. With its "anthropological" orientation (and the absence of any reason given in the basic form) it is most likely an expression of the creation-theological argumentation clearly emerging after the exilic period, with its view of Yhwh's transcendence and incomparability, which disallows any *self-referential making of images*. This is not about a prohibition on "artistic creativity" as such; it is about the problem of a production of images that is exposed to the danger of self-deception. The common verb for "making" or "producing" used here, *ʿāśâ*, is also often found, as a *terminus technicus*, in creation-theological contexts. This terminology, in turn, is not a pointer to a particular dating. Recent research on the Decalogue, which agrees in positing *at the earliest an exilic origin* for Exodus 20 and Deuteronomy (with varying prioritizations in time), and likewise posits postexilic expansions (especially in the reasons given for the Sabbath commandment) suggests a narrow window in time for the formulation of the (unexpanded) ban on images in the Decalogue.[149] Within the Decalogue it is clearly to be read as an *enhancement of the prohibition of foreign gods*, which thereby becomes altogether unambiguous:

> The "gods" of the ban on foreign deities, likewise with the formula "not for yourself" (Exod 20:3 // Deut 5:7; cf. *ləkā* in Exod 20:4 // Deut 5:8) in fact appear *only in light of the ban on images* as lifeless illusions. Without the explicit prohibition of images the ban on foreign gods is less clear regarding the status of the "gods": after all, according to Exod 20:3 // Deut 5:7 the gods are primarily to be excluded *locally* (*ʿal pānāy*, "before me/my face," that is, mainly, so it seems, in the sanctuary). With that, on the one hand, their existence is not completely denied; Yhwh is simply separated from them (a hint at the history of the first commandment; see below at §2.4b.2). On the other hand, the problem of *images* is already implicit here, because the form of presence of gods "before Yhwh" would probably be that of cultic "visible tokens" (cf. Exod 20:5: "you shall not bow down before them or worship them"). The constellation of the ban on foreign gods, which in my opinion points back to the preexilic temple cult in

Jerusalem (excluding a coexistence of Yhwh with other gods; cf. Josiah's reform [see below, §2.4b.2]) is stripped of all ambiguity in the composition of the Decalogue by the explicit prohibition of images in the sense of a fully developed monotheism.

In Deuteronomy 4 (still Persian period) *the ban on images then moves altogether into the foreground* (here the so-called second commandment dominates the first). The situation moves in precisely the same direction also in the later polemic against images in the Old Testament that we have already considered (see above, §2.2b.2): the multiplicity of apparent gods is contrasted with the one God of heaven; the former are merely "artifacts," "the work of human hands," and to that extent represent a problem not so much for theology as for anthropology (the human longing for images [cf. §III.3]).

Does this entirely exclude the possibility that the ban on images in Israel is older? In principle, no, but the indicators for it are weak. The Decalogue, a "burning glass"[150] of Old Testament legal history according to Eckart Otto,[151] does bundle together various precepts of older cultic, legal, and tribal or family law, most of them going back to the royal period. Likewise, a correspondingly early and even undetectably ancient beginning of the ban on images has regularly been postulated by scholars (including, still, W. H. Schmidt; in his case not recently in that formulation but "in substance").[152] With that focus, however, we would be dealing only with a question of the tradition history of something no longer explicitly evident. There have been attempts to contrive arguments for this through comparisons with other Old Testament formulations of a ban on images, and in the next section we will examine those formulations in more detail.

b. Further explicit prohibitions of images in the Old Testament and their relationship to the Decalogue

Besides the Decalogue, all the important collections of laws in the Old Testament contain further bans on images (Exod 20:23; 34:17; Lev 19:4; 26:1; Deut 27:15). It is striking in these cases that they appear as "solitary" and scarcely, if at all, part of a series of commandments: that is, they are more loosely anchored in their context. We will consider them in the literary-historical sequence of the law collections to which they belong and compare them with the Decalogue's ban on images. The bodies of laws in the OT arose in this order:[153]

Book of the Covenant (BC): Exodus 20:22–23:33: from eighth/seventh centuries BCE

Deuteronomy (Deut): from seventh/sixth centuries BCE

Holiness Code (H): Leviticus 17—26: in the sixth/fifth centuries BCE

Additional note: The so-called privilege law of Yhwh in Exodus 34:10–26 (also called the "cultic decalogue") was long regarded as a relatively old, pre-Deuteronomic tradition.[154] Today its core is fairly often treated as still late preexilic (and pre-Decalogue), but with a deuteronomistic (postexilic) redaction. In all, a relatively great age of individual commandments (especially the calendar of festivals in vv. 18–26*) is still not to be excluded.[155] But late datings are also advocated on good grounds.[156]

(1) *Exodus 20:23*: The later framing around the royal-period Book of the Covenant contains, successively, as a "preamble," a ban on images (20:22–23) and then a (probably older) law regarding the altar (20:24–26); to these two, in the end frame, correspond a ban on foreign gods (23:13b) and (again older) a festal calendar (23:14–19). The "secular" Book of the Covenant is secondarily theologized by a twofold frame and simultaneously anchored in the Sinai narrative of the Book of Exodus, in the course of which it appears as an unfolding of the Decalogue in Exodus 20. The fact that it opens programmatically with the ban on images could, on the one hand, already be a reaction to the Decalogue, but on the other hand it may be shaped by its context within the narrative (Deuteronomy 4 interprets the ban on images as a consequence of the theophany in Exodus 19).[157] The wording strongly suggests this, if we take Exodus 20:22–23 as a literary unity:

[22] The LORD said to Moses: Thus you shall say to the Israelites: "You have seen for yourselves that I spoke with you from heaven. [23] You shall not make [*śh*] gods of silver [*ʾĕlōhê kesep*] alongside me [*ʾittî*], nor shall you make for yourselves [*lākem*] gods of gold [*ʾĕlōhê zāhāb*]."

The Ban on Images: Character and Origin

The fact that Yʜᴡʜ's transcendence in verse 22 is marked by hiddenness in the heavens during the Sinai theophany (already against the background of Deut 4? In the context of Exod 19 that link is only indirectly maintained) adds inherent weight to the ban on images in verse 23. Two points favor the idea that this is a reaction to the preceding Decalogue:

(a) The difficult *'ittî*, "alongside/beside me," should most likely be understood in the sense of the *'al pānāy*, "before me," in Exodus 20:3; this would link to the ban on foreign gods and images as expressed also in the identification of "gods" and images.

(b) "Making [*'śh*] for yourselves [*lākem*]" directly echoes the formulation in the Decalogue.

The *emphasis on precious metals* strikes an accent different from that in the Decalogue. (In context, of course, it may also point toward the golden calf in Exod 32 [see below at §2.4b]. Favoring this is also the fact that the "gods *of gold*" are directly tied to "mak[ing] for yourselves.") On the whole it is highly improbable that we have a pre-Decalogue formulation of a ban on images in Exodus 20:23.[158]

(2) *Exodus 34:17*: After the introductory, deuteronomistically formulated bans on foreign gods and making covenants with foreign peoples in the so-called cultic decalogue in Exodus 34:10–26, there stands in verse 17, unrelated to anything else, a brief prohibition of images (cf. before this in v. 13 the deuteronomistic demand for destruction of the cultic symbols of the inhabitants of the land, as in Deut 7:5). There is also no direct connection with the older festal calendar that follows in Exodus 34:18–26*:

'ĕlohê massēka lō' ta 'ăśeh-lāk, "You shall not make cast idols for yourself." (Exod 34:17, trans. by author)

Here the Decalogue's formulation, "you shall not make for yourselves," is adopted word for word, except that the object is replaced with " *'ĕlohê massēkâ* [cast god/gods]." The reference to the image of the calf in Exodus 32:4 (*'ēgel massēkâ*) and its identification with "your god/gods" (*'ĕlohêka*) in the same verse is clear (for Exod 32 see below, §2.4b.1). Given the renewed making of the covenant (with Moses alone) that follows in Exodus 34, following the breaking of the covenant through worship of the golden calf (Exod 32), Exodus 34:17 is above all to be read within its context and belongs to the (deuteronomistic) redaction.[159] Here also we are not dealing with a pre-Decalogue tradition.

(3) *Leviticus 19:4 and 26:1*: In the late Priestly (obviously postexilic) Holiness Code we find a first ban on images in Leviticus 19:4. Chapter 19 appears to have been written in light of the Decalogue[160] (the preceding v. 3 is about the commandments regarding parents and the Sabbath). Verse 4 then offers a combination of the bans on foreign gods and images:

> Do not turn to idols/nothings [*'ĕlîlîm*] or make [*lōʾ taʿăśû lākem*] cast images [*'elōhê massēkâ*] for yourselves: I am Yʜwʜ, your God. (Lev 19:4)

Probably not only the Decalogue but also Exodus 34:17 ("cast idols") are received here. Again, it is not a matter of an ancient prohibition of images. The same is true for the ban on images in Leviticus 26:1, placed prominently at the beginning of the passage that introduces the major chapter on blessings and curses that concludes the Holiness Code:

> You shall make for yourselves [*lōʾ taʿăśû lākem*] no idols/nothings [*'ĕlîlîm*] and erect no carved images [*pesel*] or pillars [*maṣṣēbâ*], and you shall not place figured stones [*'eben maśkît*] in your land, to worship at them [bow down before them]; for I am Yʜwʜ, your God. (Lev 26:1)

This variant not only looks back to the Decalogue but expands its generalized formulation to cover the long period of unproblematic massebah/stone monuments in the cult of Yʜwʜ (cf. Jacob at Bethel in Gen 28:10–22, with the Priestly reference to it in Gen 35:14), as well as stone reliefs and steles (on which cf. Ezek 8:12; Num 33:52). Late deuteronomistic iconoclastic statements like those in Deuteronomy 7:5 are also adopted and the previous ban on cult images is extended in the direction of a universal ban on cultic symbols. This ban on images, unique in breadth, is late (probably it is the latest of the variants here presented: 5th/4th c. BCE?).[161]

Another striking feature in the late introduction to Leviticus 26 of verses 1–2 is also that there for the first time the ban on images is directly *connected with the Sabbath commandment* (v. 2: "You shall keep my sabbaths and reverence my sanctuary: I am Yʜwʜ"). It is clear that the ban on images expanded to include the day of rest serves the proper veneration of the "sanctuary" (though probably the second temple in Jerusalem).[162] To that extent this confirms the supposition that, besides male circumcision and the Sabbath, the aniconic nature of the cult (and the ban on images) was becoming ever more important as the third crucial criterion that distinguished early Judaism from the "nations" (see below at §2.4a).

(4) *Deuteronomy 27:15*: Chapter 27 is, in whole or in part, a later insertion into Deuteronomy (compositionally it comes after the conclusion of the law corpus in Deut 12—26 and begins the closing frame of the book, whereby chap. 27 corresponds to Deut 5 in the opening frame; what we have here is a secondary introduction to chap. 28 on blessings and curses; cf. Lev 26). In Deuteronomy 27, Moses acts together with the Levitical priests in a ritual involving both the building of an altar and the erection of an inscribed memorial stone (27:1–8). Then follows a *blessing*, and in Deuteronomy 27:14–26, a cursing ritual for serious secret offenses. This so-called Sichemite Dodecalogue in verses 15–26 "presents an archaizing list of serious offenses. It was composed as a programmatic counter-code to the Decalogue in 5:6–21 to conclude the deuteronomic law and in a sense ratifies it in an oath-ceremony."[163] The series of offenses begins again (in a renewed first positioning; cf. the Book of the Covenant, the Decalogue, and Lev 26) with a ban on images:

> "Cursed be anyone who makes an idol or casts an image [*ya ʿăśeh pesel ûmassêkâ*], anything abhorrent to the Lᴏʀᴅ, the work of an artisan, and sets it up in secret." All the people shall respond, saying, "Amen!"

Even though here it seems to be less a matter of defending against images in "official" worship and more, perhaps, about household cults (cf. what was said above about the Persian period and in addition the narrative in Judg 17—18, which in its final form should probably be located there),[164] the location in parallel to the Decalogue of Deuteronomy 5 as well as the formulations ("make an idol" as in Exod 20:4 // Deut 5:7, and "work of an artisan") show that this is a post-Decalogue formulation.[165]

Result: None of the five bans on images beyond the Decalogue can be located literarily before it. Rather, they all appear to refer back, in different ways, to the basic formulation in the Decalogue: "You shall not make for yourself an idol," and to repeat and sharpen it for their particular contexts.[166] With Exodus 20:22–23; 34:17; Leviticus 19:4; 26:1; Deuteronomy 27:15 we find ourselves in a realm of tradition in which the so-called second commandment has acquired a dominant significance: in the *postexilic period (as regards the finalizing of the Torah, probably Persian to early Hellenistic Period, 6th–4th centuries BCE)*. The Decalogue in Deuteronomy 5 (and Exod 20) precedes all of them.

Thus the question arises: *Why was the apparently oldest ban on images, that in the Decalogue, created in the first place?* We have seen that it appears to be relatively independent of the ban on foreign gods (see above at §2.3a). At the same time, however, nothing seems to indicate that it had a completely independent prehistory *in (cultic) law*, but it did have a *prophetic-theological background in the critique of images in the Book of Hosea* (see below, §2.4b). As in the comparable case of the explicit Sabbath commandment, it could have been formulated shortly before, or even precisely for the context of the Decalogue (within the framework of the basic form of the Decalogue, which we regard with Hossfeld[167] as early deuteronomic, probably in the last third of the 6th century BCE; the ban on images and the Sabbath commandment also share the later expansion [see above], which increases the weight of both of them). Why was it necessary? Such a comprehensive rule was not simply created for no reason. A (late-) exilic or early postexilic origin must be made plausible in terms of religious and theological history. Decisive here is the question whether the ban on images has a *specific problem as its background*, beyond the first commandment, that was especially virulent at the time the commandments were formulated.

Therefore we need to continue, step by step, to probe the question, moving backward from later to earlier, and in a brief sketch of the exilic/early postexilic period (second half of the 6th, first half of the 5th centuries BCE), expand the textual basis beyond the ban on images itself in order to get a more precise view of the conditions under which it arose. This shall be done—for reasons to be explained immediately—with reference to Deutero-Isaiah. What can we learn from Isaiah 40—55 about the *image problem*, and which older presuppositions are being relied upon in dealing with the problematic?

2.4 Preconditions for the Beginnings of a Prohibition of Images

a. Judaic-Babylonian cultural contacts and the origins of the ban on images

Most studies are still agreed that the basic layer of so-called Deutero-Isaiah was created in the heart of the Babylonian empire (before and after 539 BCE, extending into the Persian period).[168] It would have been this one situation of confrontation between two traditions with which the deported representatives of a marginal culture (on the periphery of small conquered states in the Levant) had to contend, in the face of an empire that was in every sense "wealthier" and superior, and against its representatives (see below at §III.4). For the literary productions of the deported upper class of Jerusalem (to whom, in my opinion, not only the authors of Deutero-Isaiah and Ezekiel but also the earliest composers of the Priestly writing belonged) this meant the challenge *to redefine their identity at a distance from their homeland and to formulate it in terms of the traditions they had brought with them.* In this way the differences from Babylonian culture and religion could be transformed from a feeling of inferiority to an attitude of superiority. Thus the Priestly writing depicts keeping the weekly Sabbath (simultaneous with the Decalogue?) and the circumcision of males as criteria of differentiation and marks of identity.[169] Even before this, Deutero-Isaiah emphasized especially the *universal power of the one God (Israel's own)*, in contrast to and competition with the claims of the principal Babylonian god, Marduk, whose significance for state polity revolved around the cult of images in the principal temples of Babylon (see above, §1.1a). In view of the impressive staging of the cosmic-theological central symbolism of Babylon (above all in the festal cult; see §1.1b above) it seemed to many exiles that their own God was disempowered and irrelevant (Isa 40:27: "Why do you say, O Jacob, and speak, O Israel: 'My way is hidden from the LORD, and my right is disregarded by my God?"). The starting point from which explicit monotheism arose and, combined with it, the critique of images (in view of YHWH's incomparability) was, in the first place, the experience of the *absence and hiddenness* of God in history.

As Christina Ehring has shown, it is for that reason that YHWH's return is a major theme in Deutero-Isaiah, very probably developed against the

background of a long-established historical-theological model of interpretation in Babylon.[170] From the Babylonians' point of view the high
god Marduk had in the past surrendered his city to enemies a number
of times because of the sins of its inhabitants, and was himself imprisoned (in the form of his cult image; see §1.1b above). He returned each
time, after the end of the time of punishment, in triumph: on the political level this was evident in the actual bringing back of the cult image.
Evidently the prologue to Deutero-Isaiah adopts this pattern and in Isaiah 40:3–5 has Yhwh emerge from concealment in a royal triumphal
procession and return to his people (and his dwelling place) before the
people leave Babylon in a "new exodus" and return to their homeland.
What is important for the image question here is that the new presence
of the god is marked by a *mental image* (using the concept of *kābôd*,
"glory," from temple theology: Isa 40:5), but *not by a cult image*.[171] In all
likelihood it is precisely this that constitutes an *expression of the awareness of a specific religious-cultural difference with regard to images*.

A very comparable concept of this sort is represented also by the
texts of Ezekiel and the Priestly writing when they describe Yhwh's
presence (in the sanctuary and in motion outside it) as *kābôd*.[172]
The latter is both locally fixed (at the location of the divine throne)
and also dynamic and mobile (cf. Ezek 1:28, 8–11; 43:4–5; Exod
40:34–35). As a result these texts make reference—despite all differences—to an apparently *existing concept of presence with visual
and luminous aspects* stemming from the preexilic Jerusalem temple (cf. *kābôd* in the Jerusalem Psalms: Ps 24:7–10 [mobility as
aspect of Yhwh who comes from without: "king of *kābôd*"]; Ps
29:3 [title: "God of *kābôd*"]; Ps 29:9: reciprocity of *kābôd* in Yhwh's
palace; all these are acknowledged to be ancient; similar also is Isa
6:1–5 [v. 3b: "the whole earth is full of his *kābôd*," corresponding to the divine garment of light that, according to v. 1b, fills the
temple.])[173] The *kābôd* here refers above all to an appearance of
Yhwh in brilliant light, which must also go back to ancient elements of Syrian and Mesopotamian concepts of divinity ("terrifying brilliance"); this may be indicated by a "solarization" of Yhwh
beginning with the royal period.[174] In terms of iconography we can
probably point to the winged sun disk of Judah's official *lmlk* seal
and the depiction of an empty throne with a winged sun from the
earlier royal period in Jerusalem (see figure 8 and §1.1e above). It

was not without reason that the Septuagint mainly translated the corresponding passages with *doxa*, "steely brightness"/"glory."

As we have said, the prologue to Deutero-Isaiah, in Isaiah 40:1–5, uses the brilliant phenomenon of *kābôd* exactly in the position of the cult image of Marduk when, in Babylonian interpretations of history, it returns from banishment after being exiled. In place of a material "visible token," the *interpretatio israelitica* imagines a mental image of the return of the altogether real and vital royal brilliance of God. That only seems plausible if it was not an ad hoc invention but something drawn from memory of the temple theology proper to Jerusalem. As with Sabbath and male circumcision in the Priestly writing, Deutero-Isaiah (as well as Ezekiel and "P") refers back to something familiar that one may hold up to foreigners as superior: this is about a visual conception of the divine presence that presents no "form" to "be known" apart from light and power, and that is also able to withdraw again in two ways: in *history* (Ezek 8—11; 43: departure from and return to the temple; Isa 40:3–5: return from concealment) and in the ideally conceived *sanctuary* (a concept of the Priestly writing with the prior dwelling of Yʜwʜ in the "tent of meeting" in his *kābôd* in Exod 40 in the dialectic with the "cloud"; cf. Lev 9. Previously, in Exod 24:17, "P" interprets the visual phenomena accompanying the Sinai theophany, especially fire, as *kābôd*; for Sinai, see further below at 3.2a). What does the picture of Babylon's images look like in light of this newly imagined "imageless" (for this, cf. what was said above in §1.1e regarding the preexilic Jerusalem cultic symbolism) but now consciously "image-critical" imagery of Yʜwʜ? In this regard we should look first at the basic layer of Deutero-Isaiah in *Isaiah 46:1–4*:[175]

1 Bēl [= Marduk] falls on his knees, Nabû stoops,
    their idols [*ăṣabbêhem*] are on beasts and cattle;
  these things you carry are loaded
    as burdens on the weary [animals].
2 They stoop, they kneel down together;
    they could not save [*mlṭ* Piel] the burden,
    and/but they themselves [*napšām*] have gone into captivity.[176]

The text envisions images of god being carried away, as we know such events from Neo-Assyrian depictions or the Babylonian historical texts already mentioned: after a city has been conquered, the deities of the conquered are carried off as booty. In dating the text, scholars have pointed out that nothing similar is attested for the Persian seizure of Babylon in 539 BCE; instead, the cult of Marduk appears to have continued and become even stronger. Consequently Isaiah 46:1–2 must either be dated before 539 BCE or much later under Darius I, or possibly even Xerxes.[177] But all of this remains uncertain. Instead it is more promising to read the text, with Ehring, primarily as a *symbolic* (though historically significant) scene intended to bring the addressees to a fundamental insight:

(a) Verse 1a *first, by naming the deities as such, calls to mind* that their being moved involuntarily means that they are imagined in bodily form—and yet they reveal weakness and immobility.

(b) In the further course of verse 1, *the view shifts to the (cultic) images*, which are heavy objects ("burdens") borne by humans and animals. Here the "your" in the second person plural suffixes ("things you carry") is open to a variety of meanings: is it Babylonians or, in light of verses 3–4, Judeans who are being addressed? Both are possible here, even if they are not depicted with the same clarity as in many postexilic polemics against images (see §2.2b.2 above).

(c) The beginning of verse 2 takes up the verbs of motion "stoop" and "kneel" (also: "submit oneself") from verse 1a and emphasizes *the ineffectiveness of the gods*, who are unable to rescue human beings or even themselves (*napšām*, "their life"); instead, they are going into imprisonment (active formulation!).

We should note that for this text there is *no separation between the gods and their images; they are regarded as practically identical.* The text draws its argument from that identification, which marks most of the texts against images: Marduk and Nabû cannot even help themselves because they are described as *burdens to be borne*. In direct contrast, Yhwh's "I" in the following verses, Isaiah 46:3–4, reminds Israel that it has been *carried by Yhwh* throughout life. Verse 4 deliberately repeats the verb *mlṭ* (Piel), "save" from verse 2:

> even to your old age I am he
> even when you turn gray I will carry you.

I have made, and I will bear;
I will carry and will free/save [*mlṭ* {Piel}]. (Isa 46:4)

The result is a contrast between the gods and YHWH:

Marduk and Nabû	YHWH
Personal name(s)	"I" (implicitly: personal name)
Physicality/inactivity: kneeling, stooped	Physicality/activity: bearing, carrying
Cult image/immobility: borne	No cult image/mobility: working, doing
Unable to save (*mlṭ*)	Able to save (*mlṭ*)
No communication: (mute)	Communication: address

A comprehensive ability to act ("bearing, saving") and independence of an immobilizing tie to a place or object (*ăṣabîm*, "cult images"; cf. as early as Hos 8:4; see §2.4b.1 for more detail) distinguish YHWH from Marduk and Nabû. The gods are not denied their "existence," but their *ability to act*. The scenery from political propaganda, depicting the gods (or their images) as impotent, extends over a span of text, creating a *deliberate contrast to YHWH's return without a cult image* (but in his *kabôd*) in the prologue to the basic text in Isaiah 40:3–5.[178] Jerusalem's earlier (an-)iconic cultic symbolism (without an anthropomorphic cult image; see §1.1e) and theology (which included the concept of *kabôd*) was thus perceived in cultural contacts with Babylonian religion as a distinguishing mark of identity. That has consequences for our judgment of the other "idol" texts in Deutero-Isaiah (see §2b.2 above on Isa 44:9–20); many of these, like the verses in Isaiah 46:1–2 just discussed, may well lie at the level of the basic document.[179] The corresponding passages are found primarily and secondarily almost always *in connection with the idol polemic in the narrower sense* and, like those, are limited to chapters 40—48 of Isaiah. The conflict with the gods in Deutero-Isaiah seems to have been bound up from the beginning with the question of images; it may even have been kindled by it.[180]

Interim conclusion: It has become obvious that the ban on images in the Decalogue (like the other such prohibitions) is so closely bound up with the ban on foreign gods that the two can be distinguished but not completely separated. Evidently it was precisely *the identification of the great gods of Babylon with their (primarily anthropomorphic) cult images* (see §1.1b above) that became the point of attack for the Deutero-Isaianic critique of images (though in Isa 46:1–2 it lacks the characteristic terminology of the ban on images). Thus it seems probable that this is the point at which we should locate the *different experience* that at the same time, or a little later, led to the explicit prohibition of images: since the tradition of the Jerusalem temple most probably had, initially, no image in human form at its center, but perhaps an empty throne (with sun connotations? See §1.1e above), something that in the ancient Near Eastern context was nothing unusual, could become, in the eyes of Judeans struggling to secure their identity, *a fundamental criterion of distinction—though only in an interplay with the emergence of a differentiation of God and world.* After all, it was the same Deutero-Isaiah who, in the contest over the authority to interpret the historical events to which Israel had been subjected, *was the first to locate the long historical action of God in the context of God's role as Creator* (again in contention with the Marduk theology that attributed that role to the principal god of Babylon).[181] Here again the critique of images played a role from the outset, because it was about YHWH's incomparability.

This can first be demonstrated in the programmatic disputation in Isaiah 40:12–31, which, recent research agrees, belongs to the basic layer (at the earliest probably ca. 539 BCE). Here we find the creation-theological foundation for the message of salvation in the texts of Deutero-Isaiah, which responds to the lament of the addressees about God's hiddenness in verse 27 (see above). The very first verse subtly introduces the clash with the Babylonian gods:

> Who has measured the waters in the hollow of his hand
> and marked off the heavens with [his: cf. Q[a]] span? (Isa 40:12)

To the first question one might respond, for example, with an eye to the *Enuma Elish*, Tablet V, with the name of Marduk, who seizes control of the waters after slaying Tiamat. But the second question about the *origin of the heavens* is not so easily answered. Marduk completes the heavens and furnishes them, but their beginning is associated with his grandfather, Anu. YHWH precedes them both in time and space as the primal architect of the heavens.[182] The text then twice emphasizes YHWH's *incomparability* ("to whom then will you liken/compare [God]?" vv. 18, 25). The language pattern derives from the polytheistic context. It is no accident that it reflects *two prominent forms of visible appearance* by Mesopotamian deities:

(a) In *verses 19–20* the text refers to the *cult images* (which are here called *pesel*, as in the ban on images, but without otherwise referring to it). Differently from Isaiah 46:1–2, they are now viewed in the context of creation, *as regards their manufacture* (cf. the "not toppling" of the base in v. 20):

> ¹⁸ To whom then will you liken God [*'ēl*],
>   or what likeness [*dəmût*] compare with him?
> ¹⁹ An idol [*pesel*]?—A workman casts it,
>   and a goldsmith overlays it with gold,
>   and casts for it silver chains.
> ²⁰ As a base one chooses mulberry wood
>   —wood that will not rot—
> then seeks out a skilled artisan
>   to set up an image that will not topple. (Isa 40:18–20)

The images are to be seen as clearly contrasting with the creative artisan YHWH from verses 12ff., who has made every part of the world; that is why no image is appropriate for *him* (i.e., this statement is not primarily against the idols; it is about YHWH's uniqueness). We should pay particular attention to the fact that in Isaiah 40:19–20 (and in this it is comparable to Isa 46:1–2)—there is *no openly derisive polemic* like what we find in later texts against the gods and their images (cf. Isa 44:9–20, on which see above at §2.2b.2), which focuses especially on the transitory materiality of the images. Instead, attention is diverted more subtly to what the Babylonians understood to be their *supernaturally rooted production* (see §1.1b above), which is confronted with YHWH's superior creative abilities.[183]

(b) In *verse 26 it is the stars*, in a sense natural "images" in the firmament, that the addressees are called upon to consider:

> ²⁵ To whom then will you compare me,
>   or who is my equal? says the Holy One.
> ²⁶ Lift up your eyes on high and see:
>   Who created these?
> He who brings out their host and numbers them,
>   calling them all by name;

because he is great [firstborn] among the strong,
 mighty in power,
 not one is missing. (Isa 40:25–26)[184]

The luminaries were created (nondescriptive verb *bārā'*) by YHWH, master of the heavens, but they have names and are called "strong, mighty." Thus they are certainly granted *a (derived) might* (cf. the quite analogous warning in Deut 4:19, according to which YHWH has given the stars to be worshiped by the nations but not by Israel; see §2.3a above). Here again we may say, with Matthias Albani, that the immediate fascination with the worship of the stars in the context of late Babylonian religion probably plays a role.[185] As Deuteronomy 4:19 also shows, there the great lights of heaven were taken to be *ma(n)zzāzu*, "positions," or *tamšīlu*, "likenesses" and at the same time forms in which the astral triad (Šamaš, Sîn, and Ištar) appeared (see above at §1.2b). In both cases, however, Isaiah 40:12–31 is interested in reshaping older, preexilic Jerusalem's ideas:

(a) Regarding an *idol*, which did not represent anything comparable to YHWH against the background of the "empty" throne (see §1.1e above): the older, still implicit creation theology of Jerusalem, according to Psalm 93*, had as its primary goal the securing of the world's stability, and that depended on the divine throne and the temple.[186] Isaiah 40:22 then takes up that idea in contrast to the *idol* in 40:19–20 and expands it: *the whole world now becomes the divine throne room*, beneath the baldachino of heaven ("who sits above the circle of the earth...who stretches out the heavens like a curtain").[187] The inhabitants of the earth seem "like grasshoppers" (v. 22). In this way the "not toppling" of the idol as the intention of the Babylonian artisan (Isa 40:19–20) fits organically within the picture (cf. the "not moving" of the earth [*tēbēl*] in dependence on God's throne in Ps 93:1–2, as also elsewhere).

(b) Regarding the *lights of heaven*, which have no independent power alongside YHWH: the stars, as superhuman phenomena in the firmament, are interpreted *against the background of the ancient royal metaphor of YHWH's court* (cf. "their host," Isa 40:26), something retained also in the older Jerusalem cultic name YHWH Sabaoth, "lord of hosts."[188]

Thus Isaiah 40:12–31 disempowers the gods in their most important manifestations, against the background of the idea of the creation of the world, but here—differently from the later texts—we still find ourselves in a contest over the interpretation of being. *It seems to me that the Decalogue's ban on images lies within the framework of this situation; it means to focus or clarify the concept*: different from the ban on foreign gods but at the same time indissolubly related to it.

Conclusion: In the ban on images—as in the cases of Sabbath and male circumcision—we see an emerging awareness of something that had long been laid down in Israel's traditions. In the process of religious history, innovations are usually transformations of what is already present. What is implicit becomes explicit. It seems to me very probable that this is true also of the ban on images. Here earlier Jerusalem cultic traditions and the older theology of the temple are being reevaluated and placed within a comprehensive frame of reference (that of monotheism with its distinction between God and the world).[189]

Now, in a last step in the historical investigation of the origins of the ban on images, we need to take a closer look at some important older presuppositions that led to the prohibition of images: *critique of images*, but not yet forbidding them, had existed long before the contacts between Judah and Babylon. These concerned the bull images in the Northern Kingdom of Israel, and also reform measures undertaken in Jerusalem. Without those longstanding situations the ban on images would not have arisen in the way described.

b. Two older preconditions for the ban of images in Israel and Judah: Critique of certain visual representations

B.1). THE BULL IMAGERY AT BETHEL IN THE NORTHERN KINGDOM OF ISRAEL: HOSEA AND EXODUS 32 (8TH/7TH C. BCE)

Prophetic criticism in view of the threat of Assyrian expansion westward after the middle of the eighth century BCE focused especially on the images of bulls or "calves" at Bethel in the Northern Kingdom of Israel.[190] We find its first clear expression in the Book of Hosea (8:4–6; 10:5–6; 13:1–2). The age of these texts is, we must add, hotly disputed in current discussions about the character of preexilic written prophecy.[191]

If—contrary to the opinion that the oldest kernel of the prophetic books did not yet contain any warnings of calamity for their own land and that it was a feature that only emerged in the wake of deuteronomism—we continue to reckon with prophecies of *judgment* as the beginning of the prophetic books, then there is no reason to dispute that such is possible in the Book of Hosea. Its oldest texts are to be located within chapters 4—11.[192] In fact, we can read in the two passages critical of images in Hosea 8:4–6; 10:5–6 an older stratum from the eighth century BCE, if we remove later overpaintings that appear most clearly in the style of the postexilic polemic against images (in Hos 13:2 the mention of the calf image may be altogether postexilic).[193] In the passages cited below, the first redaction in each case (but not necessarily the identical redaction) will be *italicized*, while the postexilic polemic overpainting will be signaled by <u>underlining</u>. The basic layer will be given in plain type. In the fundamental text going back to the prophet Hosea, the primary interest at first was neither in criticizing the image *as such* nor only in the danger of *worshiping foreign gods*, no matter how much the calf symbolized both YHWH and an attribute of the (Syrian) weather god Ba'al (see below). Hosea uses it as a vehicle for a prophetic criticism, on the one hand, of a specific *ambivalence in the worship of God*, something he also attacks elsewhere. On the other hand, the prophet rebukes above all the *self-representation of the state* in the "calf of Samaria," and the making of images without YHWH's instruction:[194]

4   They made kings, but not through me;
        they set up princes, but without my [ac]knowledge[ment].
        *[From] their silver and gold they made idols [*ăṣabîm*]*[195]
        for their [or: its] own destruction.
5   Your calf is rejected, O Samaria.
        My anger burns against them.
        How long will they be incapable of innocence?
6   <u>For [what has Israel to do with it?]</u>
    <u>An artisan made it;</u>
        <u>[thus] it is not God.</u>
    The calf of Samaria
        shall be broken to pieces. (Hos 8:4–6)[196]

5   The inhabitants of Samaria [seek shelter
        with] the calf of Beth-aven.

Its people shall mourn for it [i.e., the calf],
    and its idolatrous priests [kōmer]…over it,
    [they rejoice] over its glory [kābôd]. It [the people?/the glory?]
       has departed [into banishment].
6 The thing itself [the calf] shall be carried to Assyria
    as tribute to the great king.
Ephraim shall be put to shame,
    and Israel shall be ashamed of [its plan]. (Hos 10:5–6a)[197]

1 When Ephraim spoke, there was trembling;
    he was "exalted" in Israel;
    but he incurred guilt through Ba'al and died.
2 *And [that was not enough;] now they keep on sinning*
    and make a cast image [massēkâ] for themselves
of silver made according to their skill/understanding *[təbûnâ],*
idols [āṣabîm]
    all of them the work of artisans.
"Sacrifice to these," they say.
    People are kissing calves! (Hos 13:1–2)[198]

A still-open question regarding these texts is whether the polemic against the *material* of the images, so typical later, has some basis we cannot discern. It is striking that the Hosea passages are not, for the most part, based (as are the postexilic idol polemics) on the "inanimate" materials incapable of action, but first and foremost are guided by a vehement *rejection especially of the precious metals, silver and gold* (Hos 8:4; 13:2); in Hosea 8:6, and less clearly in 13:2, we can point to the familiar criticism of "artisan work" typical of later polemic against images (see above at §2.2b.2). The rejection especially of precious metals in the redactional layers may be explained not simply by rational hostility to the materials. Instead, silver and gold appear in the first place to represent power and status. For that reason they were treated in the prophetic tradition as objectionable.

Is there a powerful strand of tradition, especially in the north—certainly evident to literary-historical criticism for the first time in Hosea 8:4—in which negative emotions were loudly expressed because of the poverty of images and/or materials in the tradents' culture? Othmar Keel saw it that way when he spoke of "a particular abhorrence of idols forged from expensive metals"[199] as a specific feature in the run up to the explicit ban on images whose origins are lost to us:

> It is one of the distinctive features of Israel and Judah that, well into the period of state-construction, peripheral traditions and voices remained loud and living (Elijah from Gilead, Amos from Tekoah, Micah from Moresheth Gath). That is one of the characteristics of Israelite-Judahite culture that cannot be demonstrated in the same way in other cultures of Syria-Palestine. Hostility to anthropomorphic cult images, especially those made of precious metals, may well be traced to this feature.[200]

Particularly in the Northern Kingdom of Israel there is also the problem—again not plausible as a later invention—of a *theriomorphic* (= animal-like) *image of YHWH, namely, the calf, at the center of cultic worship.* As is already attested from the Bronze Age in Syria-Palestine, statues of bulls or calves were primarily symbols of the weather god (the Early Iron Age image of a bull/calf from the neighborhood of Dothan in Samaria may represent Baʿal or Hadad, or possibly YHWH; see figure 10).[201]

As the literature (Elijah and Elisha cycle: 2 Kgs 9—10; Hosea) whose core stems from central Palestine shows, in the ninth/eighth centuries BCE, Baʿal was YHWH's strongest opponent in the north.[202] The two deities were scarcely distinguishable in their symbolism or in their functions. Hence in the Hosean critique of the manufacture and worship of the "calves of Samaria," the issue is not yet—as it is in the later polemic against images, for example in Deuteronomy 4—rejection of a representation of God by something created; it is concretely about the calf. The theme of foreign gods was associated with it from the beginning because in the Northern Kingdom YHWH and Baʿal were evidently similar enough to be confused (cf. the Elijah cycle, and again the Book of Hosea). Even when the texts were expanded and revised by continuation and integration in larger works (such as the Deuteronomistic History), the *religious-historical state of conflict* preserved in them appears authentic: the Northern Kingdom was associated both with a dissociation from calves as images of YHWH and possibly also with the rejection of precious metals as their material. According to Hosea 8:4–6*; 10:5–6a, positive emotions of the city inhabitants and servants of the cult were bound up with the calf image. From the prophet's point of view, it stood *at the center of their religious attention.* The self-deception

Figure 10: Bronze statues of calves/bulls from the neighborhood of Dothan

This bronze figure from Iron Age I (12th/11th c. BCE), found in an open sanctuary on a height in the Samaritan hill country, may, in the context of Bronze-Age Syrio-Palestinian bull symbolism, represent the figure of a weather god (Ba'al, Hadad, YHWH?).

Source: Othmar Keel and Christoph Uehlinger, *Göttinnen, Götter und Gottessymbole. Neue Erkenntnisse zur Religionsgeschichte Kanaans und Israels aufgrund bisher unerschlossener ikonographischer Quellen*, QD 134, 5th ed. (Freiburg et al.: Herder, 2002), 135, Plate 142 (= Amihai Mazar, "The 'Bull Site'—An Iron Age I Open Cult Place," *BASOR* 247 [1982]: 27–42, at 30, figures 2 A–B).

that saw protection and praiseworthy beauty in the images was to be brought to light in that the image was carried away by the Assyrians as booty (Hos 10:6a): as an eloquent, staged motif for the end of Samaria, which fit well with the corresponding Assyrian propaganda (see above at §§1.1b and 2.4a).

A hundred years later, in the late preexilic period (end of the 7th c. BCE?), this figure recalling the fall of the Northern Kingdom was reworked in the story of the golden calf at Sinai (Exod 32); thereafter it went through a number of stages of redaction.[203] Here it is revealing that in Judah, in the brief interval after the end of Assyrian domination and before the increasing pressure from the Babylonians, efforts toward an integration of the traditions of North and South chose precisely the problem of the calf image as a paradigm for the "primal sin" of *all Israel* at Sinai/Horeb. It would have been easy enough to seize on their own native Manasseh, the arch-villain of the later deuteronomists, for that purpose (cf. 2 Kgs 21). The fact that they did not do so probably points to the already-existing stability of the older remembered figure of the "golden calf" as the foundation point from which to initiate a critique of images inspired by YHWH himself. In the basic narrative of Exodus 32, which probably goes back to the late part of King Josiah's reign, we find a significant *narrative reflection on images as ambivalent—in modern terms hermeneutical—phenomena*:

> [1] When the people saw that Moses delayed to come down from the mountain, the people gathered before/around Aaron, and said to him, "Come, make gods [or: a god] for us, who shall go before us [or: our face]; as for this Moses, the man who brought us up out of the land of Egypt, we do not know what has become of him." (Exod 32:1)

The initiative toward making 'elohim (god/gods) comes from the people and is motivated by fear of being abandoned by God now that Moses has spent forty days on the mountain, wrapped in clouds that appear impenetrable from below (Exod 32:1 links to Exod 24:18, according to which Moses has gone up/in to YHWH). Moses, who had led the flight out of Egypt, has vanished, and the uncertainty caused by God's silence leads to the solution of creating the presence of God for themselves in the form of 'elohim fashioned by the priest Aaron. The grammatical form of 'elohim is deliberately left indeterminate, shifting between God and gods; the image represents a potential multiplication of YHWH, who would thereby become unrecognizable. But the still greater danger associated with this can be perceived when we consider the *material* for the future image:

> [2] Aaron said to them, "Take off the gold rings that [are] on the ears of your wives, your sons, and your daughters, and bring them to me." [3] So all the people took off the gold rings from their ears, and brought them to Aaron. [4] He took [the gold] from them, formed it [with his hands] [in a mold?], and cast an image of a calf; and they said, "These are your god/s, O Israel, who brought you up out of the land of Egypt!" (Exod 32:2–4)[204]

The golden amulets worn in the ears are associated elsewhere in the Old Testament with connotations of foreign gods, and here—in canonical sequence—are perhaps to be identified with the gold and silver ornaments brought out of Egypt (cf. Exod 3:22; 12:35). To that extent the molded image in Exodus 32:2–4 is seen as having something foreign about it because of its material (cf. what was said above about the calf images of the weather gods and the polemic in Hosea). Also important is the interaction of Aaron and the people in the making and consecration of the image. It is the people who solemnly declare the "image of a calf" to be the god who has rescued them from Egypt. Thus there can be no doubt that this is about an image of Yhwh, as becomes altogether clear in the subsequent *cultic staging of its ability to communicate*:

> ⁵ When Aaron saw [this], he built an altar before it [or: before its face]; and Aaron made proclamation and said, "Tomorrow shall be a festival to Yhwh." ⁶ They rose early the next day, and offered burnt offerings and brought sacrifices of well-being [shelamim]; and the people sat down to eat and drink, and rose up to revel. (Exod 32:5–6)

Since Yhwh, together with Moses, has withdrawn from sight into the vertical axis of the mountain of God and so is unapproachable, Aaron stages a direct contact with God on the horizontal plane by building an altar. It is (as in the Jerusalem temple) placed *in the visual field of the image* ("before it") and is used for purposes of the sacrificial cult, that is, the regulated encounter with the deity. The new cult is inaugurated the next day with a festival during which the smoke of burnt offerings rises and a common banquet is celebrated before the face of the idol: eating, drinking, and ecstatic movement (with excessive aspects? cf. the corresponding connotations of the verb ṣāḥaq Piel, "play/make sport of") indicate the intense communion between the people and the idol.²⁰⁵ Clearly, then, the image is only able to function when it is placed within a *sacred space* (a sanctuary) in relation to other symbols (altar as point of contact) and so is known to be able to be called upon and ready to communicate (ready, that is, to accept the burnt offering). In the course of the "festival to Yhwh" the image the people themselves have made will fully become the presence of God; for them, "worship of images/idols" is worship of God.

Here, differently from the later polemic against idols and ban on images, the accent lies on the "original sin" of Israel, which is not yet characterized as confusing Creator with creature but rather as *celebrating what is visible*: to use the philosopher Jean-Luc Marion's terminology,[206] it is about the *lust of the eyes*, satisfied by viewing the visible thing and attempting to hold fast to the self-withdrawing dynamism of God; that is the central point of the depiction in Exodus 32.[207] The danger of a manufactured image (that YHWH has not commanded) is the "fusion of intentionality,"[208] which from the outset prevents the image from being anything other than an idol. It reflects the desire for immediacy and so makes the image itself into a mirror.

If we are inspired by the astonishing multilayeredness of the biblical text, enabling it to enter completely into a level of reflection devoted to image theory and phenomenology (cf. §III.5), we should note that it is in the nature of a pictorial artifact *to evoke two ways of seeing*:

(a) An image can become the *medium of a transcendent excess of meaning* and thus a "window" through which a "more" than what is visible is indicated without appearing fully. Then the image belongs to an "appeal structure" that shows the visible precisely *as limited* and thus deepens and broadens the perception of it in light of the still greater invisibility.

(b) But an image may also—as in the story of the golden calf—*capture and fully focus the view*, so that it gets lost in the infinite multiplication of the visible: the image becomes opaque. As Marion has shown, this twofold seeing of the image is not inherent in the image itself. Rather, it is the *intentionality of the looking* that makes the image reflective or transparent. Phenomenological analysis can explain both the power and the illusion of images that oscillate between visibility and invisibility when the eye of the viewer is directed at them. Cult images in the ancient Near East, and as late as medieval art, present an especially welcome object for investigation by such a hermeneutic of the image, for, as we have seen, the cult image requires a cultic space and sacred time and action; it requires a *context of interaction* in order to become a making-present of the invisible.

In fact, the narrative in Exodus 32 seems much more subtle in its perception of phenomena and its ability to link to current (religious-) philosophical debates over the "power of images" (cf. §III.6) than does

later monotheistic creation-theological critique of images with its reduc-
tionist and rationalistic orientation (see §III.4.3 below). But it must be
maintained that the explicit prohibition of images in the Old Testament
(in all its variants), against the background of the traditions of the calf
image, is by no means only a part of the later, theologically grounded
rejection of cult images; rather, it targets an anthropological fact (see
§2.3a above): *the fundamental human desire for images, which the Old
Testament by no means denigrates* (in this context cf. again the danger
of self-referentiality so emphatically addressed in prayer formulae and
other texts: "for you" [singular and plural]; see above at §2.3a).

Old Testament texts take account in a variety of ways of the desire for
images as a basic need of the human, something we describe nowadays,
for example, in the tension of *Homo pictor* (Hans Jonas) and *Homo sym-
bolicus* (Mircea Eliade) (see part III of this book). In the closing hermeneutical reflections we will take up this thread from an exegetical point
of view. But first we need to follow a second strand in the prehistory
of the explicit ban on images: this leads again (as does Exod 32) to the
Southern Kingdom of Judah and the period after the end of Assyrian
domination. It has to do with the so-called cultic reform of Josiah and
the restoration of the YHWH symbolism of the Jerusalem temple around
622 BCE, supposedly connected with that restoration. Associated with
it were also measures that, despite the difficulty of reconstructing them,
allow us to draw conclusions about the iconographical traditions of
YHWH in the Southern Kingdom, or rather about their characteristic
absence.

B.2) JOSIAH OF JUDAH'S REFORM MEASURES (END OF THE 7TH C. BCE)

Since the nineteenth century (de Wette, 1806)[209] the account of King
Josiah's efforts to restore the worship of the Jerusalem temple in 2 Kings
22—23 has been regarded as the "central axis" of Old Testament literary history.[210] This important part of the deuteronomistic depiction of
history at the end of the Books of Kings bundles together crucial nodal
points in Judah's cultic policy at the end of the seventh century BCE
whose closest parallels have been seen, since de Wette, in deuteronomic
law and especially in the law of centralization in Deuteronomy 12: above
all it concerns, on the one hand, the *purification* of the Jerusalem temple
of abuses after the end of Assyrian domination, and on the other hand,

the *concentration of the cult* at the sanctuary in the capital city of Judah. In the narrative context King Josiah acquires the criteria for his program of cultic purification through the discovery of a written document in the temple. In light of its contents—unfortunately not specifically stated—it appears that the way worship was then being conducted and a whole series of its installations were illegitimate and perverse. Since de Wette's proposal (see above), scholarship has been inclined to identify the writing with the oldest core of Deuteronomy, even though that can, at best, only be deduced indirectly. The received text of 2 Kings 22—23 is clearly marked by the shaping hands of deuteronomistic redactors. But it contains, in 2 Kings 23:4–20, the so-called *account of the reform* in the narrower sense, and the special features of its language and content make it at least possible that it may, perhaps in part, be a document from the time of Josiah (though it may also have been written at a time not too far distant from it). For our question about the *image-critical predecessors to the origins of the ban on images* it is again unnecessary to enter more closely into the controversial state of debate over the text. As regards the literary-historical alternatives that have been discussed,[211] we can only indicate that, rather than there being two extreme positions—complete authenticity of the account or a pure postexilic fiction[212]—a middle course seems most advisable: even if we can scarcely reconstruct an ancient wording that will hold water,[213] we do find in 2 Kings 23:4–20 a series of inexplicable details that may indicate proximity to the Jerusalem cult at the end of the preexilic period. Also notable is the agreement of many of the religious practices/installations described with archaeological and iconographic finds from Iron Age IIC.[214] What follows here is oriented primarily to the comprehensive monograph by Michael Pietsch on the reform account, a work that should point the way for further research.[215] His most important conclusions are as follows:

> With some caution we may regard 2 Kings 23:4–20* as a (religious-) historical source for the late preexilic period (the last third of the 7th c. BCE). It is true that we find redactional elements from a later period within it (vv. 4b, 9, 13–14, 15*). But these are fewer than is often supposed. The basic document can be dated to the last part of the royal period. It is clearly evident from it that Josiah's measures applied both to the *ordering of worship* and to *centralization of worship*: the goals are purity and unity of worship, but *not yet in the sense of later deuteronomistic thought and the explicit*

prohibition of foreign gods and images. Instead, it appears that the measures associated with Josiah applied to "official religion" but were motivated more by pragmatism than by plan. In terms of the history of religions we are somewhere between "already" (in the sense of an "inclusive" mono-Yahwism) and "not yet" (in the sense of the programmatic and exclusive monotheism of the later period).

These measures are marked by a tendency to an *inner-religious standardization of an existing pluralism of YHWH-religion in Judah.* Besides that, emphasis should be placed on the factually strengthened *special position of Jerusalem* (after Sennacherib's besieging of the city but failure to conquer it).[216] What we have are *processes of self-differentiation* in the internal reflections of a religion that are interpreted as drawing boundaries against what is outside.[217] In that context it seems that almost none of the cultic installations that Josiah removed, according to 2 Kings 23:4–20, were simply remnants of "polytheism." Instead, Pietsch offers the illuminating possibility that, for example, the "Asherah" removed according to 2 Kings 23:6 (see below) was a cultic symbol whose appearance and function cannot be any better described but may have been phytomorphic (i.e., in the form of a plant) that stood beside the altar for burnt offerings in the court (with Deut 16:21: "You shall not plant any Asherah [tree as a sacred pole] beside the altar that you make for YHWH your God").[218] Be it noted that this refers to a symbol of YHWH's blessing that had been rejected because, given the dipolar structure of the sanctuary with *cella* and court, it was too much in the foreground (also as regards the "visible" elements).[219]

In regard also to the further reform measures, Pietsch presents a series of cautious reevaluations:[220]

There remains uncertainty about the meaning of *bāmâ* (usually given as "high place"; 2 Kgs 23:5), and the "passing through fire" of children as offerings to Molech in the Valley of Hinnom (2 Kgs 23:10). The latter appear, in light of newer studies, to have more likely been funerary rites (of the YHWH religion?) at the burial of children who died young. The thesis established by Hermann Spieckermann[221] regarding the oracular function of the horses of the sun/sun god (2 Kgs 23:11) against an Assyrian background has been rendered improbable in light of an unbroken reconstruction of the corresponding Akkadian ritual texts that has since been made possible.

In general, Pietsch (following the Assyriologist Steven W. Holloway)[222] offers an important correction to common assumptions when he points out that the Assyrians exercised no religious pressure on their vassals, and in that sense Assyrian influence was rather minimal. Likewise, his review of the iconographic materials from the glyptic art of Iron Age IIC allows him to challenge the supposition, widespread since the work of Keel and Uehlinger,[223] that the astralization of the idea of god gave special importance to lunar aspects.

On the whole, we get the impression that the measures decreed in the account of the reform represent not so much an event that occurred at a particular point in time as what was possibly a series of changes in the liturgical practice of Jerusalem extending over a longer period. In this way the *concentration on a single place for worship* would have been a logical consequence of the growth in importance of Zion theology after 701 BCE. The *restoration of temple worship* seems to be connected to a tendency to worship YHWH of Jerusalem alone ("mono-Yahwism" within and "monolatry" without). In this same context we may point to the two possible readings of the *Shema Israel*, "Hear, O Israel!" in Deuteronomy 6:4, emphasized in recent religious-historical research ("YHWH our God, YHWH is *one* [= one YHWH]" or "YHWH our God, YHWH is *unique* [the only God]"),[224] which stems from the same phase of the late preexilic period. Likewise, in the first commandment of the Decalogue, the ban on worship of foreign gods is formulated in such a way that there are to be "no other gods before me" (*'al pānāy*) (Exod 20:3 // Deut 5:7)—that is, the exclusion is first related to place;[225] it is not a matter of principle as in later exclusive monotheism (cf. §2.3a above). Apparently Josiah's measures in 2 Kings 23:4–20 were undertaken in the sense of the local meaning of the later first commandment: removal of elements of Aramaic/Assyrian-influenced religious practices and symbols from YHWH's temple on the one hand and—something that cannot really be separated from this—removal of some elements of the cultic-religious practice of the YHWH cult such as the Asherah on the other hand.

YHWH's Asherah (with possessive suffix in most inscriptions), as worked out by religious-historical research since the text discoveries in Kuntillet 'Ajrud and Khirbet el-Qôm, was a blessing entity associated with YHWH that oscillated uniquely between goddess and personified symbol, always with a clear ordering to and under YHWH (much like YHWH's "court" made up of nameless sons of God, or the personified forces such as *hesed* and *'emet*).[226]

The deuteronomists (in 2 Kgs 21:7) associated the Asherah that was removed from the temple and destroyed (2 Kgs 23:6) with a cult image (*pesel*) whose manufacture was attributed to Manasseh. Canonically read, then, the Asherah removed by Josiah in 2 Kings 23 seems (against the background of the Decalogue) to have been an anthropomorphic statue.[227] The account of the reform in 2 Kings does not require that interpretation (unless one wants to interpret the cloth mentioned in 2 Kgs 23:7, woven by the women "for Asherah," as clothing for a statue).[228] In any case, however, "Asherah" denotes a "visible token" that, against the background of Deuteronomy 16:21, would more likely have stood next to the altar of sacrifice in the court of the temple than in its interior:

> The account of the reform, however, in agreement with the polemical notice in Deut 16:21, attests *that* in the late pre-exilic period there was a symbol of Asherah in the Jerusalem temple that Josiah removed. The believability of this information should not be doubted: it is neither suspect of being the product of a cultic historical account nor does it contradict the other religious-historical findings in the late period of the Judahite kingship. On the other hand, no cult of Asherah is attested among the official acts of worship in the Jerusalem Temple during the post-exilic period.[229]

Was there, then, together with the tendency to mono-Yahwism/ monolatry, also a special *peculiarity of the visual representation of YHWH in Jerusalem that acted as a critique of images*? Why was it distinguished especially from the images/symbols of other numinous entities/deities by the exclusion of the latter from the sanctuary? Let me recall again the *close association of the bans on foreign gods and images* (see §2.3 above). In answering the question, we may consider, on the one hand, that despite the great number of iconographic finds, the *absence of a recognizable YHWH iconography* is well attested—no small argument in light of the transregionally and regionally rooted iconographies of deities in Palestine during the Bronze and Iron Ages. On the other hand, we should point again to the *aniconism*, mentioned above, of the god in the *cella* of the Jerusalem temple (cf. §§1.1d and 1.1e; §2.4a), at least as regards an anthropomorphic statue. The central cultic symbol of YHWH was first, in all likelihood an "empty" throne (with sun connotations), and second, the ark, a chest containing, perhaps, one (or two) *maṣṣēbâ/ maṣṣēbôt* (stones).[230] The specific feature of an *(an-)iconic (nonanthropomorphic) YHWH symbolism,* at first associated only with the history of this cult but later of essential importance as a reference point both for the treatment of the question of images in the monotheistic texts beginning with the late exilic period (Deutero-Isaiah, "P," and Ezekiel; see §2.4a above) and for the explicit ban on images, may have influenced Josiah's orders:

> In the process of self-reflection on the faith in YHWH that underlay Josiah's cultic reform the fending off of such tendencies [i.e., the possibility of a much-increased valorization of visual and more accessible YHWH symbols such as the Asherah] led to an exclusion of Asherah symbolism (and other symbolization of YHWH?) from the worship of YHWH; this in turn recalled the first commandment, in which there is an echo of the spatial conception of the Jerusalem temple area when it says, "You shall have no other gods *before me* (עַל־פָּנַי)" (Exod 20:3 // Deut 5:7). YHWH is enthroned and invisible in the Holy of Holies; all other pictorial representations of his presence are excluded from cultic worship as not being identical with him.[231]

In conclusion we should recall that the deuteronomistic historical work also reports, in 2 Kings 18, an earlier "cultic reform" by Hezekiah of Judah (end of the 8th c. BCE).[232] At least the removal of a *single image of a serpent* made of metal (attested for Bronze Era sanctuaries in Palestine[233] and also for the Samaritan temple on Mount Gerizim[234]) appears historically possible (cf. 2 Kgs 18:4 with Num 21:9 and the seraphim surrounding YHWH's throne in Isa 6:1–11). Unfortunately, apart from the deuteronomists' stereotypical evaluation of royal behavior ("he did what was right in the sight of YHWH," 2 Kgs 18:3), it is not clear what motivated Hezekiah to remove the serpent symbol called Nehushtan. (The name contains the Hebrew word for the metals copper or bronze, *nəḥōšet.*) We would not go wrong in supposing a situation of competition within the YHWH symbolism in the Jerusalem temple in regard to this serpent idol similar to the one that provoked Josiah's later measures. What is decisive in all this is the apparent *high degree of stability* *of the "(an-)iconic" throne symbolism of Y*HWH *in the cella* and the associated absence of an anthropomorphic cultic statue. This is indirectly confirmed also by the little fortress temple at Arad, mentioned above (§1.1e), in which only a standing stone represented the state god of Jerusalem.[235]

Conclusion: Once again a specific "poverty of images" at the center of the cult appears at first to be an insignificant fact but then proves to have major historical consequences. As soon as what was self-evident became no longer so in new historical contexts, this situation was recognized as a *distinguishing identifying mark*, both inside and outside, of Judaism as it was coming into being.

This brings us to the end of the sketchlike religious-historical segment. We have sought, by means of an examination leading from certainly decipherable later features to less-and-less-clear earlier ones, to find the vertices of the origins of the Old Testament and Jewish ban on images, but above all to make clear the uncertainty of it all. In what follows we will formulate, with necessary brevity, the *hermeneutical consequences* for the interchange with the philosophy of religions and appropriately interested cultural studies, as well as with other theological disciplines, systematic theology in particular.

3. Consequences for a Hermeneutics of the Ban on Images from an Exegetical Perspective

What hermeneutical conclusions can we draw from the preceding sketch regarding the ban on images, the context in which it originated, and its prehistory? Important, to begin with, is the observation that critique of and the ban on images in the Old Testament is completely focused on the *problem of images that are worshiped*; the Hebrew Bible is not interested either in an overall ban on images or in forbidding art. (This must be maintained in light also of a number of excesses in the course of the long history of the Bible's influence.) The biblical ban on images addresses an anthropological constant (among other things; cf. also §III, esp. §III.3): the *desire for images and the latent danger of the visible* that is omnipresent alongside it. The push toward *making* images—from the perspective of the ban on images—involves both *arbitrary* action and the invasion of something *foreign* because of the fascination exercised by the image. *Worship* of the thing made seems to follow, because such worship is experienced as a locus of epiphanies and a powerful presence. Hence the bans on images and foreign gods are coupled from the beginning, not only historically but also functionally. Both the critique of images in the Northern Kingdom of Israel (calf at Bethel, self-representation of the state and symbol wavering between YHWH and Ba'al) and the exclusion of mono-Yahwist problematic "visible tokens" in the Judahite south (Asherah as symbol of YHWH's blessing) point to the *interaction of the worship of one god and defense against images* that is given in the Decalogue's later ban on images. Central Old Testament texts on the topic then ultimately revolve around the impossibility of making an "image" of the special, later the only, God YHWH. The *boundaries of the visible* are here measured with astonishing subtlety (if we meld hermeneutically what has been worked out above):

1. Regarding YHWH images or symbols surrounding him there is an effective *distinction* made between the God experienced *in action* (above all God's saving deeds) and the possible *freezing of his dynamic presence (and withdrawal) in the image.* The image can lead to a fixing and narrowing of the idea of God that affects the relationship to God in an elemental fashion as soon as it becomes entirely absorbed into the presence of the visible thing. Particularly relevant to a description of this problem is, above all, the narrative of the "golden calf" (Exod 32).

2. The problem of *decoupling* continues to plague both YHWH images and those of other ("foreign/strange") deities, that is, the issue of reduced *attention* to the one God who, in appearing, immediately conceals himself again (cf., e.g., Exod 3; 19; 33:18– 23).[236] The *poverty of visual artifacts/material representations* that is central to the Old Testament conceptions of God appears on the one hand as a strength (marker of the difference of Old Testament–Jewish identity beginning with the exile, especially in cultural contacts with the Babylonians). On the other hand, the intensity of the treatment of the problem of images in late Old Testament texts (and the writings of early Judaism) also reveals a subliminal awareness of what is perceived as a real *weakness* in Israel's religion: the rejection of the images seems by no means directed entirely outward but *also always inward—* because of the anthropological dimension of the desire for images reflected in the texts. It is probable that behind this latter rejection lurk practices involving images in Yehud/Judea (and/ or Samaria) during the Persian and Hellenistic periods that the texts' authors regarded as heterodox.[237] It was precisely in the face of the claims of a ban on images that the *experienced lack of the visible* was felt to be both a source of *attitudes of superiority* as well as (indirect) *self-criticism* on the part of the Jewish religion that was coming into existence. It could be that it was from this point that the religious-historical processes of

self-identification—already manifest in the prophetic critique of images and Josiah's reform—may have continued after the formulation of the explicit ban on images.

3. *An explicit ban on images* and *a monotheistic concept of God* are elementarily connected (cf. §III, esp. §III.4). The points of view named in 1 and 2 above received further monotheistic development in the late, clarified theology of the later prophetic books, the Psalms, and the critical Wisdom writings. The altogether *rational theology of a Creator separate from but attentive to the world* who is simultaneously present in it and capable of working everywhere within it plays out the problem of the divine presence especially in terms of a *critique of images*: nothing created (= mortal) can adequately represent the invisible, transcendent, and eternal God YHWH (Deut 4, et al.). According to the normative texts, especially those of the Persian period, it is this God alone who decides *how* he is to be imagined and addressed (in the Torah these are the Sinai texts and the cultic ordinances). God's holy *name* and literarily given (auditory and visual) *signs of divine presence* (fire, cloud, thunder, etc.), all of them simultaneously opaque and transparent as well as time-limited, respond to the enduring desire for imagery (see §3.2a below). The *written* will of God (the Torah of Sinai, e.g., also in the form of the motifs of the two stone tablets [Exod 24; 32—34]) can thus appear as a *sculpted word*. Another manifestation is the experience of the power of *blessing* for Israel and the world, which bridges the gap between the distant God, God's own people, and the nations (cf. Ps 67, et al.).[238] Finally, we should point to the idea of the human as *imago Dei*, "image of God" (Gen 1:26–28) (see below at §§3.2c, III.5.3). But *poetic imagery* and the collective and individual imaginings about YHWH should also be mentioned. A *poetics of transcendence*, ultimately bound up with narrative, that is, founded on narrated history (above all the accounts of the rescue of the people and individuals) was not restricted either in the Old Testament or in early Jewish writings by the ban on images.

3.1 The Ban on Images and the Image of God Conveyed in Words

a. Biblical metaphorics as limit conceptuality

It is precisely the *metaphorical language* of the Bible that, in its ineluctable character, not only drives forward processes of reflection but creates a *specific imagery* for the question of and the imagining of God (cf. also §III.7). The Old Testament, from this perspective, is a *book of images*, although certainly within the dialectic of a visually liminal symbolism of God between presence and withdrawal. The "iconic" character of biblical texts (above all the Psalms; see §3.1b below), fruitful also for a literary and philosophical aesthetics, is rooted in an enduring conventional world of symbols from which emerge ever-new variations on tradition-bound linguistic images produced by creative language. The adequate concept for describing biblical metaphor is thus not solely what is called in broad sections of modern (literary-critical and theological) discussion of metaphors the "living metaphor,"[239] but rather a continuing *symbolic variation*. With Paul Ricoeur, I understand *symbols* as bound metaphors, that is, signs with multiple meanings, anchored cosmically and socially in something beyond language.[240] They shape the Old Testament texts. The Hebrew Bible, as a universe of religious expression, is impregnated with an inventory of signs from the cultures (and cultural contacts) from which its texts are derived.[241] In the course of the *use* of linguistic symbols and their consequent continual *transformation* arises the new thing we call meaning, as revealed in metaphorical understanding.[242] This is a dynamic of irresolvable but not arbitrary ambiguity.[243] Images expressed in biblical language open and shift horizons of perception of a God who is experienced as dynamic. They are metaphorically realistic *limit-concepts* in the interpretation of religious experiences.

Here we may refer, by way of example, to the concrete *horizon* character of the cosmic metaphor of *heaven/the heavens*, which plays a major role in biblical monotheism. The view of the all-enveloping "tent" by day and the myriads of stars by night ("the hosts of heaven") became in the Old Testament a point of reference for a metaphorical "measuring" of the human (cf., e.g., the statements about the anthropology of the heavenly horizon in Pss 8:4–5; 139:8–10;[244] 147:2–5;

cf. Gen 15:1–6). How is this *movement on the borders of the visible* associated with *imaging*? Was the cosmo-theological experience of horizon in the image thematic in itself, or did every limited experience of image appear in light of it as an inadmissible "freezing," a stopping? Both these possibilities are realized in the biblical texts. Their authors themselves—together with those who testify to nearly all religions—were unable to stop "finding meanings in the sky"[245] when they tried to make the distant-and-near YHWH available to the imagination. YHWH was manifest above all on the margins of experience, both spatial and temporal,[246] in paradigmatic narratives and poetic compositions.

b. Iconicity of the Psalms

Once we have grasped the warnings of the biblical critique of images and the appeal of the ban on them, and if we regard both as setting limits to the anthropological desire for images, what appears in the Old Testament is precisely the "seeing" and "beholding" God as the primary focus of religious experience, which must therefore be defined as aesthetic experience.[247] Above all in the Psalms the speaker desires to see (*rā'â*) or behold (*ḥāzâ*) God, God's face, God's form (cf. Pss 16:11; 17:15; 27:4, 13; 42:3; 63:3–4, and frequently). This is bound up with a synesthetic abundance of sense experiences: light, fullness, movement, security with/before God as king.[248] On the other hand, *not seeing God's countenance* means, in this system of reference, being delivered up to darkness, hunger, bodily failing, and the dissolution of all social ties (cf., e.g., Pss 13; 88).[249] It is the *pictorial* character of believers' imagination drawn by the Psalms that is precisely the strength of these sensible—and for that very reason sense-*filled*—texts. They are media of a shared world of the imagination in which interaction with the personal God is, above all, dominated by the visual. In the pictorial language of the Psalms the imaginary/internal and real/external, as well as the cosmic and social, overlap and blend ("mutual modelling").[250] The temple appears, within the framework of its symbolic world, as the epitome of life (cf. only Pss 36; 63). The veracity of the experience of intensified life, or of threats to it or loss of it, is irrevocably concrete for the ancient communities living with the Psalms.

A religious community of interpretation today that uses biblical texts is therefore already impregnated, on a precritical level, with this concreteness and thus through poetic experience shares—though with alterations determined by individual perspectives—elements of ancient ways of perceiving. Such participation partly determines the perceptions of believers even today and calls them both to be attuned to and to maintain a critical distance.[251] The fact that a theologically responsible reception of the Bible requires approaching it by means of a historical-critical hermeneutics need not diminish the appeal of various approaches to understanding the Bible. Rather, a historical awareness makes it possible to open up the text anew, as a demonstration of the strangeness of the familiar or the familiarity of the foreign. Looking into the distant mirror of the Psalms shows us (with Martin Luther; cf. his preface to the Psalter, 1528)[252] *ourselves* in our fears, desires, and need for consolation, as well as the places to which we flee in our homelessness (for Luther's understanding of imagery, see below at III.5.2). The Old Testament does not construct a *concept* of metaphor, as Greek philosophy did (cf. Aristotle's *Poetics*). Hence in Old Testament texts reflection takes place *in* images, narratives, and confessions. Precisely because these are so varied ("multiplicity of approaches")[253] they contain an awareness of the notion of *boundaries* that at times is even their guide.

3.2 Models of a Critical Hermeneutics of Imagery in the Old Testament

The uninhibited and intensive way in which the Psalms give expression to the desire to see God (cf. §3.1b) is relativized in Old Testament statements about the difficulty, danger, or even impossibility of seeing God. The best-known text is Exodus 33:18–23:

[18] Moses said [on Sinai, after the golden calf incident], "Show me your glory, I pray." [19] *And he said, "I will make all my goodness pass before you, and will proclaim before you the name Yhwh; and I will be gracious to whom I will be gracious, and will show mercy on whom I will show mercy.* [20] But," he said, "you cannot see my face; for no one shall see me and live." [21] And Yhwh continued, "See, there is a place by me where you shall stand on the rock; [22] and while my glory passes by I will put you in a cleft of the rock, and I will cover you with my hand until I have passed by; [23] then I will take away my hand, and you shall see my back; but my face shall not/cannot be seen."

This passage, too, is multilayered in its literary history and should be read in the probable sequence of its creation as continued reflection on epiphanies in the light of "critical imagery" (Exod 33:18–23 is already aware of the ban on images, though it does not speak of it explicitly).[254]

(1) Verses 18 and 21–23 (unmarked): The oldest version of the plea for a theophany asks for the "beholding" of the royal "glory" of God (*kābôd*; cf. Ps 63:3–4 and Isa 6:3) that is otherwise associated with the Jerusalem temple. It anticipates the theophany subsequently depicted in Exodus 34:5–6, in which YHWH does *not* come "face-to-face" with Moses but only "passes by" (*'ābar*). This deviation from the beholding of God that is asked and longed for in the Psalms constitutes the point of connection for the interpretations in Exodus 33:18–23. Elsewhere in the Old Testament YHWH's "passing by" has connotations both of mercy (cf. Amos 7:8; 8:2) and of destruction or rejection (cf. Exod 12:22–23; Job 9:11–12). Evidently Exodus 33:18, 21–23 has both of these in mind and deliberately has Moses protected by YHWH from his presence (which in the context has elements of wrath) by means of his "hand" and the cleft in the rock. *Even Moses may only see YHWH's back, not his face.* The text emphasizes a dialectic between near and far, revelation and concealment of YHWH: it is only *in the tension* between beholding God and protection that Moses can encounter YHWH in this situation. In this way the blessed nature of seeing the "face" of God, so clearly formulated in the Psalms, is placed under a restriction that cannot be removed by human beings.

(2) The two continuations in verses 19–20 each shed a different light on this tension:

(a) The latest part, in verse 20 (<u>underlined</u>) shifts the—situationally conditioned—problem of seeing God's "face" (probably under inspiration from v. 23b) to something fundamental (*whoever sees God must die*)—a pointed statement that, with hermeneutical precision, emphasizes the character of God's "face" as representing a *limit expression*.

(b) In contrast, verse 19 (*italicized*) replaces the "glory" and "face" prayed for with two different manifestations: YHWH's "kindness" (*tûb*) (a collective noun for YHWH's life-sustaining gifts), familiar, for example, from Psalm 27:13, and—as a further model of assurance of God's nearness that became more and more important after the exile—the divine name, the tetragrammaton Yʜᴡʜ, prominently interpreted in the succeeding text in Exodus 34:6–7 as a revelation of God's nature (in the so-called grace formula).

Texts like Exodus 33:18–23 that very deliberately portray God's visibility (of which there are very few in the Old Testament, although those few developed a great deal of influence; cf. §III below) must be understood against the background of the perception (illustrated in the example from Exod 32 [2.4b.1]) of the *latent danger of the visible*, applied to the (cultic) ban on images. Because in terms of religious history the God Yʜᴡʜ had no proper iconography and very probably was present in Jerusalem only through the royal symbol of an "empty" throne in the temple (see §1.1e above), the cultic absence of imagery from the exilic period onward, with its monotheism, appeared as a mark of distinction from the "world of the nations" (retrospectively also from Israel's own past: "Canaanites"). Various strands led to the development of an identity for Israel that could be maintained at a distance from Jerusalem and the temple. Together with male circumcision (cf. Gen 17, basic layer of the Priestly writing) and keeping the Sabbath (Gen 1—2:4a; Exod 16; 31 [secondary layer of the Priestly writing]) the *imagelessness* of the cult of Yʜᴡʜ appears as a criterion of difference, not previously applied in this way, marking its uniqueness (see §2.4a above). Hence it is no wonder that in the texts of the *Sinai pericope* (Exod 19—24 and 32—34 // Deut 9—10 and, in reaction thereto, Deut 4) that founded the identity of emerging Judaism and received their literary form especially after the exile, *nonpictorial symbols of Yʜᴡʜ's presence* move into the foreground, not only in the wake of the story of the "golden calf" but also in the "preceding Sinai pericope" with the theophany of Yʜᴡʜ on the mountain of God and the proclamation of the ordering of life for Israel. These *nonpictorial symbols* appear like a *linguistic imaging ("iconic") realization* of the presence of God for God's own people, made manifest in the *saving deed of the exodus event: transitory* and assigned to the collective imagination and memory (see §3.2a–b above).

a. The Sinai theophany: Transitory imagery and the image in words

In an explicit expansion of the ban on images, the major tractate in Deuteronomy 4 (considered above; see §2.3a) sheds light on the special, indirect image quality of the Sinai experience and its shift of media toward the "sculpted word" (see, for more fundamental detail, §§III.4.7; III.7). Deuteronomy 4 is a postexilic foundational text, inserted before the Decalogue in Deuteronomy 5:[255]

> [9] But take care and watch yourselves closely, *so as neither to forget the things that your eyes have seen* nor to let them slip from your mind all the days of your life; make them known to your children and your children's children—[10] how you once stood before YHWH your God at Horeb, when YHWH said to me, "Assemble the people for me, *and I will let them hear my words, so that they may learn to fear me as long as they live* on the earth, and may [also] teach their children so." (Deut 4:9–10)

The purpose of Moses's warning to the people is to ensure that they will not forget the encounter with God at Sinai/Horeb, because there YHWH not only showed himself in a unique way as he desires to be worshiped, but also made his will known in such a way that Israel's whole life is to be directed by it in the future. Emphasis is laid on the fact that it is precisely what was seen that is decisive. But at the mountain of God the vision of God is characteristically indirect:

> [11] You approached and stood at the foot of the mountain while the mountain was blazing up to the very heavens, shrouded in dark clouds. [12] Then YHWH spoke to you *out of the fire. You heard the sound of words but saw no form; there was only a voice, [a sound].* [13] He declared to you his covenant, which he charged you to observe, that is, the ten commandments; and he wrote them on two stone tablets. (Deut 4:11–13)

Well-established assessments positing that in the Old Testament hearing is elevated above seeing (see below, §III.7) appeal especially to Deuteronomy 4:11–12.[256] But the very emphasis in verse 9 (not to forget everything "that has been seen") shows that that interpretation was too hasty. The fact that a "figure" (*təmûnâ*) of YHWH was not visible, though YHWH's voice could be heard, does not mean, as one often reads, that therefore one had to imagine the God of Israel as formless (cf. the consequences, at §III.5). Instead—as the tradition-historical comparison shows—Deuteronomy 4 supposes, as a matter of course, a royal figure of God in the "innermost heaven."[257] That figure, however, remains veiled and hidden. Dialectically, the cosmic symbols *fire, cloud, darkness, and cloudy darkness* point to its transcendent existence in relation to the question of cultic figures.

These ideas link to the ancient tradition of the (concealed) way the weather gods, associated at an early period with YHWH, manifested themselves (cf. Ps 18; 1 Kgs 8:12–13 [MT], et al.).[258] The Sinai theophany is by no means stingy with its visible manifestations: they are the very things that are to be remembered. But it is shaped in such a way as to ward off the danger of freezing the view and so venerating the image: we have here a field of imagery that, contrary to the calf image in Exodus 32, *is only able to function iconically and is immune to being turned into an idol*: fire, darkness, clouds, and cloudy darkness are to be seen, but they indicate a spatially withdrawn presence, visible *and* impenetrable. They make the invisible present and thereby call attention to *seeing as such*: its irreducibility and its limits.[259] Then add the time dimension: fire, darkness, and clouds are by nature "passing." These make it clear that something is happening that requires the utmost attention because it will cease and afterward will remain present only in memory (the text). The Sinai narrative prevents the idolization of images of the divine by generating an illustrative process of perception of manifest withdrawnness characterized at depth by *passing away in time*. It allows powerful signs of presence to appear behind thick barriers—but ultimately they are visible as figures of devouring fire, sweeping smoke, flying clouds, and a sound that falls silent. From now on only their enduring "traces" (above all the Torah itself) are available to the understanding; these are to be read and interpreted as an orientation for life. This *imagery aware of its brokenness* in the Sinai narrative can, I believe, be fruitfully brought into conversation with modern theories and hermeneutics of the image, above all with those that are not tied to artistic works in the narrower sense but also advance the question of the *imagination* (e.g., when it arises out of narrative) and—connected to it—the experience ahead of the "image," the *passivity* of the encounter with the image.[260]

Comparable, finally, is the depiction of the Sinai theophany in Exodus 20:18. Here the perceptions of all the phenomena accompanying the divine presence are synesthetically combined in the concept of "seeing":[261]

When all the people *witnessed* [saw: rā ʾâ] *the thunder and light-ning, the sound of the trumpet, and the mountain smoking*, they were afraid [with LXX, Sam., et al.] and trembled and stood at a distance. (Exod 20:18)

"Seeing" or "witnessing" stands here collectively for the perception of the appearance of God. It is neither subsumed in the visual (thus the phenomena of sound and the impenetrability of the smoke are emphasized) nor is sight able to hold fast to it: what is seen is a *living dynamism of God* without any fixed form. The people react with fear, as previously in Exodus 19:16 (where their "trembling" before the theophany of Yhwh finds a striking terminological correspondence with the cosmic "shaking" of the mountain at the moment when Yhwh descends [Exod 19:18; each time the verb is *ḥārad*]).

> This is *the same fear* that distinguishes other instances in which a superfluity of divine nearness is described (Isa 6; Judg 6; 13; Gen 32:22–32; Exod 4:24–26, etc.). Add to this that in such cases the subject is generally an *unmediated* encounter with God, not one occurring according to (cultic) rules. This line of expression ("whoever sees God must—in principle—die/cease to exist") has its most famous presentation in the text mentioned above, Exodus 33:18–23: even Moses, the only one to whom Yhwh is present without obstruction (Exod 33:7–11; Num 12:1ff.; Deut 34:10, etc.) *is only able to see the back of God, who is manifest solely in "passing by."* Anything else would have to result in death, even for him—it would be an act of boundary violation, and the later verse, Exodus 33:20, very matter-of-factly draws the conclusion: "for no one shall see me and live" (see above).[262]

These (literarily late) texts reflect engagement with the problem of images: they secure the idea of Yhwh by using literary means to steer the readers away from idolization. They propose a metaphorical "mental" iconography of an idea of God in the form of its opposite: it is precisely the God who withdraws who is also present; the self-concealing God alone is able to save (cf. Gen 22).[263] But despite its importance—for Christian theology as well—this line of thought must not be made absolute. The seeing and beholding God in the Psalms, which does not display a relativized theology of images in exactly the same way, retains its own value. But the contrary statements about not being able to see or not being allowed to see Yhwh are instructions for conscious application.

b. The "enduring disappearance" of the theophany as "figure" of memory

At this point a link to the recent discussions of the *figura* in the field of the study of images seems opportune as a point of reference for the hermeneutics of imagery in seeking a more far-reaching religious-philosophical understanding. That discussion in turn points back to older theological-hermeneutical presuppositions.[264] Attention must be paid to the doubleness of the "figure" as visual and cognitive phenomenon of *memoria*: for cultural memory the figure must be anchored in a paradigmatic *narratio*, in this case the Moses-exodus narrative of the rescue from Egypt and guidance through the wilderness, if it is to develop its meaning. The narrative constitutes the necessary background for the "appearance of the figure" of Yhwh in the text.

"Form" and "figure" reveal themselves as pictorial/image phenomena by the fact that, on the one hand, they are perceived willy-nilly by the observer (cf. the well-known reversal in a flip-flop picture), and on the other hand they indicate in a pointed way the *inseparable tie between image and time*. As Gottfried Boehm in particular has repeatedly pointed out, material and concrete images follow the same *basic visual contrast* between the visible and the (still or enduringly) invisible, such as a linguistic image (e.g., a metaphor). Boehm speaks here of an *iconic difference*.[265] In focusing especially on the phenomenon of the figure, Boehm has investigated the fact that this is not about something static but concerns a *movement in time* that profoundly affects the reception of the image. Figures rise out of their background or substratum, whereby a spatial layering occurs in the image, something it does not "have" from the beginning but that arises again and again when the figure "appears."[266] Figure and figuration, as the perception of figure, are in the same relationship to one another as image and kinesthetics, as a particular way of imagining. And that relationship is fundamentally *temporal*. So Boehm concludes "that the iconic difference has a temporal sense.…Time is not one particular characteristic alongside others; it is the one that makes itself apparent, that opens the viewer's eyes."[267] If we start with this working hypothesis the questions of image, ban on images, and "mental images" in the Old Testament appear *elementarily related to one another.* Approaches that resolve only one aspect do not bring us to the goal. The origins of the critique of images in the Old Testament, which, together with that of the pre-Socratics, remain essential for our own culture, are in need of a consideration that will bring together the *viewpoints of the hermeneutics of images with those of a (production- and reception-aesthetic) poetics.* Such a consideration would enable the advance of a fruitful dialogue between exegesis and systematic theology.

If we draw this line out further we may suppose the following about God's *"achieving* form" and *"changing* form" in the Old Testament: in "passing by" (Exod 33:18–23), and that means primarily in "history," retrospectively and prospectively "read" and imagined, the *active* God is manifest. This is not a rejection in principle of anthropomorphic ideas of God and the acceptance of a divine "form." Rather, the pictorial phenomenon of the *figura* fruitfully shows how inaccessibility and withdrawal combine with *imprecise visibility.* The leitmotif is not the formless, invisible, bodiless God but the dialectics of God's presence and withdrawal in time (cf. also §III.6, esp. 6.5). The paradigmatic recollection of the rescue in the exodus is interwoven with the accompanying image-critical circumstances of the Sinai event: both point to something unique and never to be repeated. Above all the Torah, which gradually became a new "word" making present the word from Sinai, became the crucial organ of mediation of a memory, yet image and word did not become false alternatives (cf. again Deut 4). The appropriation of the Decalogue and the Torah remain bound back to the basic narrative of their communication on the mountain of God, which is in turn introduced and legitimated by the exodus event (cf. Exod 20:2). The "epiphanies" of exodus and Sinai are narrative symbols, "iconic" kernels of foundational "figures of memory" *that evoke and guide an imagination of the "enduring passing away" of the divine presence.* Alongside the visual aspects there always remains the unique *proper name* of God, the tetragrammaton Yнwн. Its increasing holiness and tabooing—certainly to be read as an image-critical dimension of the idea of God—cannot be pursued further here. Instead we will discuss, in conclusion, one last strand of an "image-critical system of imagery" in the Old Testament whose influence is especially important, namely, the *imago Dei* of the human in the Priestly writing.

c. Humans as image of God in the Priestly writing and relevance for a hermeneutics of imagery

A final point of divergence in the Old Testament texts regarding a critical system of imagery in light of the ban on images, one that is important for hermeneutics and extends into questions about the basis of human dignity, appears in the theme of *imago Dei*. It is probably just as relevant as the ban on images itself for the Jewish-Christian history of meaning and its secular reception history (see below at §§III.2.1; III.3.6; III.5.3).[268] Even though ancient traditions of interpretation have established the link between the prohibition of images of God and the human as image of God, the exegetical-linguistic findings warn us to begin cautiously. The concepts of image in Genesis 1:26–28, the Priestly writing's account of the creation of human beings from the Babylonian/early Persian period,[269] are indeed not those belonging to the tradition-complex of critique of images, polemic against images, and bans on images:

[26] Then God said, "Let us make humankind in our [representational] image [*bə* + *ṣelem*], according to our similitude/likeness [*kə* + *dəmût*]; and let them have dominion over the fish of the sea, and over the birds of the air, and over the cattle, and over all the wild animals of the earth, and over every creeping thing that creeps upon the earth."

[27] So God created humankind in his [representational] image [*bə* + *ṣelem*],
in the [representational] image [*bə* + *ṣelem*] of God he created them;
male and female he created them. (Gen 1:26–27)

There has been a lively discussion of these concepts of image in recent decades, resulting in an affirmation of their ancient Near Eastern background.[270] The Akkadian word *ṣalmu*, from a root also related to Hebrew *ṣelem*, is the most general and frequent term for an image in Babylonian and Assyrian texts, describing an image as a separate entity independent of a concrete visual medium or vehicle, but it can also include the vehicle (a cliffside relief, etc.) together with the image.[271] The thing represented or, better, embodied by the image is present in it, in all its power and validity. It does not matter whether it is an iconic (e.g., anthropomorphic) or symbolic representation:

> In the ancient Near East a ṣalmu was located both actively and passively within a framework of action. It possessed a lifelike quality, an essence capable of communication, which is why it was ensouled, cared for, and protected, but the reverse as well: it could also be mishandled and killed. Ṣalmu accordingly served as a designation for an object that was created in order to assume a representative function. In accordance with that function ṣalmu was, strictly speaking, not an appropriate term for an image; it was, rather, a representative; accordingly it was confronted not by a viewer but by a user for whom the denotative relation to the object represented was more important than the aspect of similarity.[272]

These semantic observations regarding the Akkadian equivalent to the main term for "being an image" in Genesis 1, though not explicitly directed at Genesis 1:26–27, contain a series of important points regarding an appropriate interpretation of the *imago Dei* statements in the Priestly writing: a living image, to be regarded as having the function of a representative, with no primary relation to similarity in appearance, but very probably a powerful correspondence in action and effect.[273] Old Testament scholarship has for a long time pointed, against the background of Mesopotamian and especially Egyptian sources, to the well-established concretion of such an understanding of images as regards the correspondence between the human being and deities, namely, the statements about rulers in the *ancient Near Eastern ideology of royalty*:

> Despite open questions about the path of tradition, the Old Testament *imago Dei* idea probably originated in the ancient Near Eastern ideology of kings. But it is scarcely the result of an inner-Israelite "democratization" of the royal image; rather—after the end of the Judahite kingship—it was the result of a *universalization of the idea of rulership* in which, through the Priestly writing, it appears that royal-ideological metaphors were deliberately inserted ("royalization" of the image of the human; cf. Ps 8:6–7).[274]

The human being created by God in Genesis 1 (using the nondescriptive verb *bārā'*, which allows no associations with concrete actions such as the shaping of a pot) is a *royal human* (as "man and woman," i.e., the emphasis lies beyond the difference of the sexes). The royal role of the two is also indicated in the so-called *dominium terrae* in Genesis 1:28, in the verbs of action *rādâ* and *kābaš*, "tread down," and "take possession of [land]."[275] For these also there are direct root equivalents in Mesopotamian royal statements, with comparable semantics. We cannot here pursue the ideology-critical question in view of the concept of rulership thus expressed; we may only point to the positive dimension of care and preservation of animals here contained, alongside the (legitimated) power aspects.[276] Above all the concept of the human (*all* humans for the Priestly writing) *is limited in relation to God, the human's vis-à-vis whom the human represents*[277]—in that it is an original property of human nature, independent of concrete action. In this regard we should also point to the preservation of the image-of-God character after the flood, which the Priestly writing explicitly affirms in Genesis 9:6: "Whoever sheds the blood of a human, by a human shall that person's blood be shed; for in his own image God made humankind." In the conception of the exilic/early postexilic Priestly writing, the human being as "living statue of God" assumes *the spatial position* of a cultic image at the center of the created world. According to the cosmological concept of "P" the world structure established in Genesis 1, with the human at its center from the beginning—following an ancient Near Eastern model in which temple and cosmos mirror one another—is shaped to correspond to the later sanctuary in the wilderness (the portable temple manufactured at Sinai). The terminological parallels between the conclusion of the work of the six days of creation in Genesis 1:1—2:4a and the conclusion of the building of the temple in Exodus 39—40 have often been noted.[278]

The "emptiness" of the Holy of Holies in the "P" concept of the temple, which by no means is conceived in relation to a cultic image in human shape (cf. Exod 25 with the "chest" of the ark and its lid as the place of God's epiphany), corresponds on the other hand to the "figure" at the center of the structured world: the *royalized human being*. Bernd Janowski describes the consequent relationship between God and human as follows, incorporating also the second image concept from Genesis 1:26 (*dəmût*), which indicates a relationship of similarity/correspondence:

> Whereas *ṣelem* emphasizes the functional aspect of imaging God in the sense of the *idea of representation*, the *dəmût* phrase,

expanded with *kə*—in order to avoid identifying the image (the human) with what it images (God)—makes this aspect more precise in the sense of a *correspondence* of the human to God, but not in the sense of a theomorphic quality of the human in the image of God. Both qualifications—*representation* and *correspondence*—express the exclusive relationship of the creature to its creator (connection with God), which is then made explicit and concrete by the twofold charge to govern (connection to the world).[279]

Finally, Rüdiger Lux, in an instructive essay,[280] has with good reason reminded us once again that there is at least *one* central text in the Old Testament for the ban on images, one that refers quite clearly to the *imago Dei* concept as a critical counterpart to the forbidden cultic images of YHWH. This is again, and not accidentally, the great text in Deuteronomy 4 forbidding images, which terminologically and in its substance is not only representative of late Deuteronomistic theology but explicitly plays on Deutero-Isaiah and the Priestly writing as well. In Deuteronomy 4:15–18 (already discussed above in relation to the Decalogue; cf. 2.3a), which also represents the matrix for the later expansion of the Decalogue (see above), it is said of the created world:

> [15] Since you saw no form [*təmûnâ*] when YHWH spoke to you at Horeb out of the fire, take care and watch yourselves closely, [16] so that you do not act corruptly by making an idol [*pesel*] for yourselves, in the form of any figure—the likeness of *male or female*, [17] the likeness of *any animal* that is on the earth, the likeness of *any winged bird that flies in the air*, [18] the likeness of *anything that creeps on the ground*, the likeness of *any fish that is in the water under the earth*. (Deut 4:15–18; emphasis supplied)

Lux writes regarding the obvious reference here in Deuteronomy 4 back to Genesis 1 as well as to the Decalogue's ban on images in Exodus 20 // Deuteronomy 5:

> This text is a genuine mixture of the bans on images in Exodus 20:4–5; Deuteronomy 5:8–9; and the creation of humans in Genesis 1:26–28. The depiction of the humans as "man or woman" along with the making of images of gods in the form of "animal[s] on the earth," "bird that flies in the air," "fish…in the water," and

even "anything that creeps on the ground," all of which are spoken of here, constitutes the last part of our chain of argumentation and makes clear that the thesis that the texts forbidding images have nothing to do with the *imago Dei* texts can scarcely be maintained. Instead, in the debate over image theology between the post-exilic Deuteronomists and the Priestly circles the living human being as image of God came into focus and in so doing replaced the forbidden images of deities.[281]

With this insight we conclude our reflections on the hermeneutics of the ban on images from an exegetical point of view. It again shows, with great clarity, the equally constructive and critical significance of the Old Testament's ban on images. The same is true for the ongoing ancient Jewish tradition[282] and also—under changed circumstances— christological transformations of the Old Testament theme of images in the New Testament writings. Thus, according to 2 Corinthians 3:18, all people exist in an eschatological relationship of representation to the *vera icon*, Jesus Christ: "And all of us, with unveiled faces, seeing the glory [*doxa*] of the Lord as though reflected in a mirror, are being transformed into the same image [*eikōn*] from one degree of glory to another; for this comes from the Lord, the Spirit" (2 Cor 3:18).

Likewise, in the perspective of a theology of the *one*, two-part Christian Bible in which Old and New Testaments stand in a correlative and contrastive relationship to one another,[283] attention must be paid to the complex relations among ban on images, aniconism, and being the image of God. Against this background, too, there appears a *critical theology of the (living) image*. It is enabled and accompanied by a *hermeneutics of the ban on images* (cf. §III, esp. §III.10). For without the tension between the desire for images and its fulfilled impossibility of fulfillment, we can say as little about human creativity as about the perception of images as islands of presence, withdrawn in the flow of time. Here let us listen once again to Gottfried Boehm:

> The imaging process that leads to presence has a paradoxical structure. For that reason it is impossible to point to a beginning and an end *in* time. A discipline that focuses on the internal linkage of representation, presentation, and presence is therefore necessarily a discipline of completion and experience. Its stimulus is the effort to translate back into the actuality of perception and reflection, as

a critical moment, everything that has solidified itself historically or analytically. Its discourse serves the insight that images are as much bodies subject to historical determinants as the effects and powers they generate and that have a claim to validity. When representation is primarily intended to establish presence, the meaning of images is fulfilled in the act of perception, at the moment when they make a co-presence available to the viewer, when what we look at also looks at us, and regard encounters regard.[284]

III

Systematic Perspectives

1. Contexts

Bans draw boundaries. They exclude some action and so interpret it in terms of a rule that limits the opportunities of the actors. For example, prohibiting people from boarding a train as it is entering the station is framed by the expectation that, normally, people standing on a train platform intend to do just that, and that they are allowed to do so. But it is now forbidden and out of the question. Certainly there are also bans that simply rule out some action; that is, they not only sort out some possibilities but reject a sphere of action as a whole, without regard to specific situations and circumstances. Besides unconditional forbidding of what is lawful, the taboo is a pregnant example of this. When, in archaic cultures, a place was declared unapproachable or an object untouchable, or when today a topic is made taboo in discussions, it is not simply about the exclusion of an action from the agenda; rather, it is about an ultimate boundary that defends not merely a different order of things[1] but the differentness of the order itself. At that point one can no longer decide what one wants to say about such a topic or choose how to deal with an object because the boundary no longer separates one possible attitude from another. Instead, it removes something altogether out of reach, withdraws it from communication and the grasp of the actor.

The ban on images is not a prohibition within the order that allows some things and excludes others; rather, it represents the basis on which order is introduced. It can therefore only be understood if one considers the specific limits it marks in each instance. But precisely for that reason it is remarkable, and truly fascinating, to observe the multiplicity and heterogeneity of interpretations of the ban on images in its long history of interpretation and reception, and this in relation to quite different oppositions to which the rule of exclusion, "not this but that," can be applied. Whether the biblical ban on images forbids only an image of *God* or all images whatsoever; whether it excludes only sculpture in its three-dimensional concreteness or paintings as well; whether it is only images on the altar that are forbidden, or paintings on the walls and floor mosaics are included; whether it is only adoration or also every kind of honor that is negated—each of these establishes categorically specific boundary lines for different cultural orders. These in turn are further differentiated, depending on whether it is the opposition of spirit and body, reason and sensibility, invisible and visible, or hearing and seeing that is formative. If the ban on images is solely the result of the categorical difference between the infinite and the finite or (to speak theologically) between Creator and creature, the cleft deepens. The excluded other side becomes the "wholly other" that can only be designated by the manner in which the boundary is drawn. The ban on images operates on the threshold between everyday affairs and the extraordinary.[2]

The task of a hermeneutics of the ban on images, including the historical understanding of the ways in which religious practice shaped various cultures and especially aesthetic traditions, arises against this background, calling us to orient ourselves to the boundaries that each interpretation of this ban involves.

This is to say that we need to keep in view that this is not about just any ban that the divine lawgiver has issued alongside other commandments and prohibitions. The theological potency of the ban on images, rather, lies in the fact that it is about the divinity of Godself, God's transcendence and freedom, about the exclusivity manifest in the first commandment as YHWH's self-presentation ("I am the LORD your God, who brought you out of the land of Egypt, out of the house of slavery; you shall have no other gods before me!" [Exod 20:2–3]) and that evidently finds its precise expression (cf. §II.2) in opposition to the image ("You shall not make for yourself an idol…in the form of anything…" [Exod 20:4]). The only possible God for those thus addressed demonstrates in the exclusion of images that he is absolutely transcendent. Certainly, though, this *theological* sense of the ban on images may be *anthropologically* motivated: the negative contrast between God and the image, however it may be clarified within the horizon of the differences mentioned above, need only be emphasized, and the distancing between God and the image need only be inculcated because the addressees of the divine self-presentation have an inclination to confuse the two. What is found *sub specie Dei* to be simply different can apparently, *sub specie hominis*, not be so self-evidently kept separate. Otherwise there would be no

108

need for a prohibition. Consequently we may suppose that the boundaries set by the ban are drawn precisely because the other side—so rich in variations—that is thus fenced off from the human being has something tempting, fascinating, or at any rate immediately plausible about it. Such attractiveness of the image must be explained, and the source of human desire to cross boundaries must be made understandable if the heft and rigor of the ban is to be understood. The degree to which the ban is emphasized shows how improbable it is that the human will remain within the boundaries of the established order. What is it that the image exposes, so that human beings are so inclined to mistake it for God? What does the image offer that makes it something to be banned?

A hermeneutics of the ban on images must therefore clarify the phenomenon of imagery in anthropological terms if it is not to make the unconditioned nature of the ban appear theologically as a kind of overreaction and idiosyncrasy on the part of God who dislikes competitors. Reflection on boundaries and what they respectively exclude, seen against the background of religious-historical studies and current exegetical research, thus links with the question of why dealing with images was made a paradigm for human boundary-crossing.

Or to put it another way: Why do humans (notorious border crossers that they are), make this move? Why does the being capable of transcendence grasp after images, or a single image? If the biblical ban on images is intended to preserve the difference between God and the human, that explains its relevance in light of a boundary crossing (i.e., transcending) that can mistake the transcendent itself or at least displace it. Consequently, interpretations of the ban on images may be distinguished from the point of view of what immediately appears as the danger of confusion in each case: if the confusion is grounded in the quality of the imagery itself, the ban on iconic representation of God casts a shadow on all other images as well. If, on the contrary, it rests exclusively on a human weakness and marks a wrong attitude toward images, then it is not primarily the image itself but the human imagination that is the source of the problem. But perhaps not even imagination as such. It is also possible that a specific way of image usage tempts and steers the human imaginative power in the wrong direction, so that it is neither the images nor the power of imagination but solely a misguided *use* of images that explains why the boundary is drawn precisely here.

Alongside the exegetical and historical questions treated in the previous main section and besides the anthropological questions implied in the iconic turn and raised in both main parts of this book, a hermeneutics of the prohibition of images also has systematic-theological dimensions. It is to the systematic-theological aspect we will turn in what follows. Of course, these sections are interrelated, just as they are also linked to broader perspectives, but they can and must be considered sequentially, each according to its particular focus. In the systematic-theological reflections that follow, it will appear that interpretations of the ban on images are connected to interpretations of the images, their forms of representation, and their limits, so that the hermeneutics of the ban on images will reveal itself as a special case of a hermeneutics of imagery.

2. Powerful Images

We would misunderstand the ban on images if we were to regard it as solely a concern of religion, the special world of its rituals, or the interior of temples and churches. Cultic questions are, in reality, questions of power. They reveal who is entitled to rule and to be free, before whom knees must be bent, who is to be acknowledged as possessing the highest power, and how the human person is able to respond to the one she or he trusts to have the last word. We are underestimating the phenomenon of liturgy and the acts of worship if we do not take into account their inner connection with the representation of rule and domination and thus the basic problems of political theology. Since a hermeneutics of the ban on images includes an understanding of the power of images, we concentrate first of all in terms of images of power through which political domination presents itself.

2.1 Representations of Dominance

Scarcely anything so clearly links the history of ancient Near Eastern religions in which the ban on images was articulated and the Roman cult of imperial ideology as does the presence of power as represented in pictures, sculptures, symbols, and other media. The early Christians rejected that cult, but it was later transformed in the image world of the Christian church with modern concepts of sovereignty. The statue of the emperor, the picture of the sovereign, or the photograph of the ruler manifest an order of power whose presence is linked to visibility, to the iconic representation of the one in power. This figure embodies the claim to ultimate sovereignty, no more so in ancient and medieval royal ideology than in the forms of presidential politics of imagery such as we can witness in exemplary form in portrayals of Vladimir Putin. Power depends on representation and finds its first image in the body of the one in power. The personality cult of dictators only serves to drive that to the extreme.

The biblical concept of *ṣelem*, which grounds the designation of the human as image of God in Genesis 1:26, in itself, because of its linguistic relationship to the Akkadian lexeme *ṣalmu*, leads us back to the function of such standing images representing dominance in the political realm (see §II.3.2c above).[3] The image serves as a medium of power, depicting it and making it present when the power holder is not personally present and above all when presence is not possible. There is an affinity between images and bodies (see §3 below) that makes it possible to illustrate the presence of the ruler and that ruler's power to create order, and also makes it believable. The sovereign is who possesses a comprehensive view and in the final instance sees everything and everyone. That very sovereignty ought to be visible everywhere ("Big Brother is watching you").[4] Power stabilizes itself through the images in which it manifests itself. Hence a change of rulers is signified by an exchange of images, and the victory of the opposing power is shown by its assault on the representational forms of the vanquished.

In the Mesopotamian, Egyptian, and Roman orders of power this expectation regarding images was based on the idea that the ruler was him- or herself a living image of the governing god-king whom he or she represented.[5] Hence the ruler's legitimacy was not the result of a secondary, external conferral of power—a "private person" exercising office, as we might say—but came from the presence of the deity who dwelt within the royal body or had taken possession of it. This was made clear above all in the making of laws: as the god establishes and creates the good order of the world, the *kosmos* by his rule, so he preserves it, makes it concrete, and establishes it as the order of things in the entitlement of his representative to command and claim power. The idea that the political ruler is the image of the royal god then sheds light on the images representing the ruler. Their production, or at least their positioning, is itself a sacred action.

When the Roman emperor (Gaius, Domitian, Aurelian) bore the title *dominus et deus* (Lord and God), it was intimately related to the cult of images through which the emperor was revered as *divinus* (divine). Imperial power was itself a cultic reality from whose public performance only a *religio licita* (permitted religion) like Judaism was exempt. In that case the state tolerated what otherwise would have been sanctioned by death penalty: that those subjected to the ruler did not accept the presence of divine ruling power by showing reverence to his image. Image worship is a recognition of the highest ruler. Because the holy is present in the ruler's own person, his image is set into the temples and on the altars in and on places where people serve their gods. Sacrifices were brought to the emperor (e.g., Augustus) as represented by his image, and *proskynesis* (bowing the knee in front of the statue) was performed. *Son of god* is the title of majesty due to the ruler; it signifies his legitimacy. That title was certainly not to be interpreted in a naturalistic sense so that it would imply physical descent; it was a religious-political symbol oriented to the living embodiment of the divine law and the power of the supreme will. Despite numerous differences between the Greek East and the Latin West, political theology in the form of a civil religion of imperial power received its significant cultic expression in the image of the ruler. In it is present the power to which the ruler himself is obligated.

When Christianity became a state religion under Constantine the multitude of polytheistic forms, statues, and images of gods lost their public meaning and significance. But, despite every accommodation of religious culture to the biblical God, one image remained so powerful that thereafter it shaped the depiction of Christ as Lord of the universe, while the Christian emperors were able to retain the title *divus* (divine) for themselves: the title of the emperor as world ruler in whom the highest power was embodied[6] or even incarnate (cf. plate 1, *Christus Pantokrator*, p. I.1).

2.2 Bodies and Images of Kings

The political theology of the Middle Ages was also shaped by this cluster of images. In the king—as Ernst Kantorowicz has shown[7]—was embodied the *dignitas* (dignity) that grounds all order, in such a way that its transcendent divine character could absorb even the mortality of the king. At his death an effigy of the king was set up, and it was regarded as the bearer of sovereignty and thus ensured the continuity of the kingship during the interregnum ("The king is dead. Long live the king!"). In death, body and image exchanged symbolic significance: while the body of the ruler decays, the image represents the living power of the kingship until a new sovereign is installed. (Significantly, the new ruler was not allowed to encounter the effigy, and in the course of his enthronement ceremony it was burned.)[8] Ritual honor was also paid to the ruler in his image (*in effigie*), so that the faithful depiction of the royal body, for example on the coffin of the dead person, concealed the mortality of the individual body. The image manifests the presence of true governance by shifting the view from the mortal fate of the bearer of divinity. At the same time it withdraws the eternal kingship from time, which rules inexorably over the king's physical being.[9] The image represents the incorruptible and immortal divine background of order that survives the fate of any particular ruler and is not affected by his death. So, the king's body is present in a twofold way: as effigy and as body. But precisely that doubling represents the divine majesty as one that dwells within the holder of power.[10] For the brief time of the change of rulers, what had come together in the life of the king—the union of divine power and human-earthly existence—separated. Power manifests and asserts itself in the visible, inasmuch as within the cult the image takes the place of the person, as it does in its normal reference, so also in death. For it is precisely in the image that it becomes evident that the king has acted not as an individual force, not as an arbitrary ruler moved by his private interests, but as the representative of divine dignity. Thus, the kingship, through the medium of the image, thwarts death, because the image prevents it from showing the body of the king to be powerless. The royal figure remains transparent for the governance it exercises. The king manifests the divine, which of its nature, that is, *per definitionem*, is immortal and, in the power of the image, escapes from death.[11]

Our modern minds, on which are inscribed the difference between image and reality, between the effigy and the real body of the king, need as much support to grasp the unique nature of the medieval kingship as to understand the relationship between the *figura*, the sign, and the true body of the Lord in the traditional interpretation of the sacramental reality of the Lord's Supper. Neither the royal ideology nor the eucharistic theology, neither the royal ritual of imagery nor the sacrament can be grasped in terms of a nominalistic interpretation of images and signs. The connection between the two thematic fields is anything but accidental. In the one case as in the other it is a question of a *reality* that consists entirely of representation. In both instances an idea of incarnation lies in the background—with different accents, but not without internal connection. Thus the "body of Christ" is just as much the bread of the altar as the unity of the church that receives this bread (*corpus mysticum*), and "the political body" is just as much the body of the king as the unity of the members subject to his rule (*corpus politicum*).[12]

Thus, the fact that the Roman emperor could regard himself as *deus in terris* (God on Earth) or *deus praesens*[13] (present God)—and, above all, wanted to be seen as such—is a matter of image theology. Thus, the investiture struggle was not only about issues of papal versus imperial primacy in the empire; at the same time, it was about competing theologies regarding the representation of God. Whether God is most fundamentally represented in the image of the ruler or in priestly-sacramental power was a crucial question in the struggle between spiritual and worldly orders. The internal connection of the two forms of representation is explicitly emphasized by Thomas Aquinas when he asserts, "*Et ideo quando ipse Christus in propria specie a discipulis discessurus erat, in sacramentali specie seipsum eis reliquit; sicut in absentia imperatoris exhibetur veneranda ejus imago.* [Consequently, when Christ was going to leave His disciples in His proper species, He left Himself with them under the sacramental species; as the Emperor's image is set up to be reverenced in his absence.]"[14] We will return later to this relationship between image and sacrament (see §6.7 below).

The image of the emperor makes the absent ruler present; it participates in that divine power that fills him. The power of the image that grounds *reverence*, worship, and the offering of sacrifices, is derived from ideas of embodiment and incarnation that are anchored in the king's body and encroach upon his image, thus linking together the representation and the one represented in the continuity of a single sphere of power (cf. the analogous relationship in the cultic images of the ancient Near East, at §II.1.1b above).

2.3 Prohibition of Images as Critique of Power

While medieval political theology dealt with the harmony between the political representation of the world ruler as creator and lawgiver and the sacramental representation of Christ (the son to whom all power is given), there was also competition between early Christianity and the imperial cult of Rome over the either/or of worship of the emperor or confession of Christ. When young Christianity lost the protection accorded a messianic movement within the Jewish *religio licita*, it found itself in a situation in which it was evident that—and why—the "ban on graven images…is political in nature."[15] In the context of representations of sovereignty, the ban on images opposes not the visible and perceptible but the power that makes itself present in the image and through it as an immortal entity, ultimate and supreme, and thus seeks to assert itself. It should therefore be thought of as a critical rejection of the (self-)staging of political power, as when the Mishnah arrives at the following explication of the ban on images: "All images (ṣəlāmîm) are forbidden…because they are worshiped one day a year [words of Rabbi Meir]. Other sages say: only those ṣəlāmîm holding a rod or a bird or a ball (are forbidden). R. Shimon b. Gamliel says: All (are forbidden) that are holding any thing."[16]

The nexus of the argumentation leads from images as such to the insignia of the Egyptian, Hellenistic, and Roman rulers (who, e.g., held a shepherd's staff) and then to a universal critique of all forms of grasping at power and the glorification of them. Thus the ban on images is read here also against the background of the ancient cult of rulers and the connection between power and representation. Wherever that connection's influence continues or extends even farther, the reception of the ban on images turns into an iconoclastic critique of power.

3. Image and Body

Those who give reasons for the ban on images often justify or explain it in terms of characteristic features of the images that are intended to make the normative drawing of boundaries seem comprehensible. Among those characteristics, bodiliness, that is, a particular affinity between image and body, plays a central role. Hostility to images and iconoclasm thus appear as expressions of a specific hostility to the body in certain religions, like what Nietzsche diagnosed in Judaism and Christianity. As "Platonism for the 'people,'"[17] Christianity established a metaphysical dualism between soul and body, the spiritual and the sensual (*mundus intelligibilis, mundus sensibilis*), and thus a two-worlds theory oriented to a devaluation and despising of the body. Such religion finds its positive expression, or systematic foundation, in thinking of its own highest object as imageless and worshiping it as such. In short: God must be worshiped aniconically because God is to be thought of as incorporeal. Accordingly Hans Belting, one of the most impressive students of imagery, writes, "When the Jews refused to look at their God in an image, it was because they did not wish to make a body for a god who had no body."[18]

The exegetical reflections and observations presented above have disputed the conclusion about Yhwh's having no body (see above, §II.3.2a), and now it is time to present some systematic reflections on the question.

3.1 God Has No Body?

Hans Belting's assertion just cited is, at any rate, accurate to the extent that Christian critique of images frequently makes use of that motif. Thus Andreas Bodenstein von Karlstadt (1486–1541) provoked and justified the iconoclasm in Wittenberg in 1522 in his *Von Abthuung der Bilder*

117

(On the removal of images) with the twofold reasoning that all images refer to the flesh, but in the Bible's judgment and in agreement with the Lord's saying, "the flesh is useless, it counts for nothing"[19] (referring to John 6:63, a text that also became central in the debate between Zwingli and Luther about the Lord's Supper). The critical saying against cult and temple in the same Gospel, that God is to be "worshiped in spirit and truth" (John 4:24) was explained by a deep gap between spirit and flesh, and this argument was used in the attack against superficiality and works righteousness in the contemporary papal church. The Reformation, which turned from doing to believing, from works—especially the Mass as sacrifice—to the word and the proclamation of the gospel, thus tended to the removal and banning of images from the place where true worship was performed and presented.[20] The "putting away" of the flesh, the "slaying" of the old Adam was accomplished by abolishing the worship of images and false gods and was understood as the fulfillment of the Old Testament ban on images by a church whose concern was to reestablish God's word in its purity.

John Calvin (1509–64), who, unlike Luther, saw the ban on images as a second commandment alongside the first, also interpreted it as the essential mark of a worship of God that properly corresponds to YHWH's self-identification: ("I am the LORD, your God…you shall have no other gods before me" [Exod 20:2–3]). The image is forbidden because God is spirit and therefore cannot and may not be worshiped by the flesh: God is the supreme majesty and as such God is "incorporeal."[21] In this line the Geneva Catechism declared it blasphemy to try to confine the eternal and spiritual in an image and thus within the sphere of the corporeal. As a result of these statements, the removal of images from churches became a hallmark of Reformed churches.[22]

We can find elements of this line of argumentation even in late ancient Christianity when Eusebius of Caesarea (†339), at the beginning of the conflict over the legitimacy of a pictorial representation of Jesus, argues with the second commandment against images and by referring to the Son's participation in God's essential nature: since Jesus is God's Son he cannot be represented by an image (picture). Eusebius also justifies the ban saying that since Easter morning the risen Christ has overcome all mortality and shed everything bodily. Hence there is nothing left to paint.[23] This position shows that corporeality was thought of as an immanent feature of the image, and not only as regards the material of the painting or sculpture, which consists of colors and shapes, but also regarding the objects that are depicted: everything that is a body, but only that, can become an image. To that extent there is a coextensiveness between imagery and corporeality. The image-theoretical slope of this argumentation is this: "All images resemble each other in that they resemble bodies."[24]

Subsequently the ban on images expanded beyond a strictly monotheistic interpretation: not only God, but also the hosts of heaven, that is, angels and heavenly powers, were not to be pictured; after all, by their very nature they could not be represented in an image because they were to be regarded as bodiless. At least that is what Epiphanius of Salamis (†403) taught; he tore down a curtain with a pictorial representation from the door of a church, justifying this destruction of foreign property by diagnosing it as a falling back into paganism, a defiance of Scripture, and an offense *contra religionem nostram*[25] (against our religion). The central argument of his discourse points to the incomprehensibility of God—called *akataleptos*—as distinct from everything that is bodily and thus extended in space in such a way that it remains essentially limited within borders.[26] God cannot be confined within boundaries and limitations, cannot be encircled by finite creatures, and therefore is bodiless and consequently superior to any image. Gregory Nazianzus (†390) spoke similarly against images of *Christ*, reasoning that the incarnate Logos shares in the divine immortality.[27] The counterargument that the Logos who has come in the flesh has assumed all the humanity and thus the human body that the painter's subject was opposed by Asterius of Amasea († ca. 410), who said that one *kenōsis* was enough for the divine Logos; one ought not to humble him again and still further by pictures that drag him down into the world of the body and the senses.[28]

3.2 Negative Evaluation of Corporeality

Although all this hints that the body was considered shameful, embodiedness as filth, and an existence determined by the flesh as theologically deficient in every respect—contrary to our contemporary and generally accepted *Zeitgeist*—we must keep in mind the systematic motif on which these expressions were founded. Its focus (particularly within the horizons of Reformed theology) was on the contrast between God's infinity and the limited nature of finite creatures. Whatever is corporeal exists within the boundaries of a closed entity and to that extent is incapable of grasping the infinite (*finitum per se ipsum non capax infinitum*). Mortality is not, in the first place, a time limit placed on temporal beings; it is already, in the present, a marker of its corporeal character, which consists of limitations and as such is inadequate in relation to the infinite (*apeiron*). As long as that motif remains central we cannot accuse such a perception of embodiment directly and unequivocally of *hostility* to the body. But things are different as soon as "the body" is associated with a particular type of sense activity, especially with imagination or fantasy, which, while they represent creativity, are not bound by any rule and can easily be accused as anomic and chaotic forces. Such an affinity with licentiousness or lack of restraint raises suspicion and colors the perception of the imaginative and the embodied. Images are then not criticized because they portray something that cannot and may not be portrayed but because the presentation through imagery as such liberates forces that preclude a disciplined life guided by reason and spirit. Imagination is not only associated with the sensual-material; its claim to new creations evokes the idea of the return of the powers of chaos. Hence for Epiphanius of Salamis the fact that painters, out of their own power of imagination, make a selection—the one this aspect, the other that aspect—and so produce a figure of the holy according to their individual phantasies (*ex idias autōn ennoias*) is the reason why he accuses them of a falling back into paganism and calls for the abandonment of images.[29] It is said to be the power of imagination that opens the door to arbitrariness—just as the fantasies of myth escape the governance of reason.

3.3 Philosophical Critique of Images (Plato)

The proximity to Platonic critique of images is revealed in the difference between *mythos* and *logos*, fantasy and rational order. For Plato (ca. 428–348 BCE) pictures are on the lowest rank in the hierarchy of being, in contrast to factual things and most certainly in contrast to what really exists, that is, the Ideas. Pictures are images of images, which brings them close to nothing compared with the ontological status of Ideas; they also remain definitively separated from the intellectual order of things. Certainly the Ideas are not mere thought structures; they are themselves forms that the soul has "seen,"[30] but access to that vision is blocked when cognition is bound to a world of shadows and images. Thus, the demiurge designs the world by means of his vision of the Ideas, while the carpenter, amid the wooden material given him and by careful orientation to the exemplary model, realizes the bedframe as well as he can and as the material permits. The painter, in contrast, stands at the lower end of this hierarchy of makers because he produces only sensory imitations of imitations.[31] As the imitations of the first order, those of the demiurge, are realized in contrast to the unity of the Idea as a multitude of appearances deviating from the original, so the imitations of the third order, that is, pictures, are only wavering deceptions, which is why illiterate people easily fall for them and do not perceive the sham or *trompe l'oeil*. To be entirely bound up in the play of shadows and, instead of perceiving reality, be compelled to exchange hypotheses about probabilities is the fate of the captives in Plato's parable of the cave—the epitome of a situation of complete simulation in the face of which only liberation and knowledge, or liberation through knowledge, can help. Remarkably enough, the things that in Plato's narrative the chained creatures drag behind them, the things whose shadows are projected on the wall, are not only vases and vessels of all kinds but also *andriantes*,[32] that is, statues. They throw the shadows whose spectacle blocks access to true reality. This is because images only project a world whose real identity is of a completely different kind.

When Plato (in *Gorgias* 463d) calls rhetoric the *eidōlon* (illusion, phantasma) of the art of governance, he is attacking the Sophists, who placed mere "science of images" in the place of knowledge, thus producing a pseudoscience that apes the art of governance but in reality devastates the *polis*. The Sophists create images (*eidōla*) by constructing projection mechanisms, whereas true knowledge leads from the image (*eikōn*) to reality and rises out of the cave into the real world.[33] Those imprisoned in the cave are chained in such a way that they are unable to turn their heads, the highest organs of reason, and so they cannot catch sight of the projection mechanism. To that extent those sitting in the cave are bound *both* in their bodies *and* in the quality of sense perception. Both aspects explain the ontological inferiority compared to the standards of the Logos and thus of human knowledge.[34]

This negative evaluation of the image in no way contradicts the interpretation of the cosmos in the *Timaeus* as a perfect *copy of the primal image* or of time as an *image* of eternity in motion, because it is not the image (*eikōn*) as such but the copy of a copy (thus the *eidōlon*) that is the reference point of the Platonic critique.[35] To that extent the point of view of manifestation, the ability-to-make-visible can modify the concept of image in a positive sense, which is why (middle) Platonism and later Neoplatonism could increasingly purify the meaning of that concept and, instead, define and value it as a concept of mere relationship[36] without sensitive elements (see §4.4). Consequent to that move the image and the plastic arts were rehabilitated. But for the moment, image, sense, and embodiedness remained linked within the thought system and were as abominable to Plato's philosophy as myths, pipe dreams, and sophism. Plato could never say that mind gains knowledge by its images[37] or that "a spiritual being can be the image of another spiritual being."[38]

3.4 Philosophical Critique of the Imagination (Descartes)

That knowledge extends only as far as our ideas are clear and definite and that human awareness is not overwhelmed with deceptions and errors is also one of the central concerns of René Descartes (1596–1650). His *Meditations on First Philosophy*[39] show how modern rationalism sought to seal off the purity of thought from the sphere of imagination (aligned with the body). In the Second Meditation ("The nature of the human mind, and how it is better known than the body") Descartes undertakes a systematic exclusion of the *imaginatio* because it entangles consciousness in worlds of images, and thus in the corporeal sphere. The constitution of the *ego cogito* (I think) as *cogito me cogitare* (I think myself as thinking) assumes that thought is withdrawn from everything that could cause the subject to fall into doubt. Such sources include, besides the prejudices of a tradition of thinking, above all the deception of the senses to which no one is immune.

The ontological difference between *res cogitans* (thinking substance) and *res extensa* (extended [i.e., material] substance), between *mens* (mind) and *corpus* (body), between thinking and extension is inextricably connected to the claim to ultimate certainty and truth, to Descartes's longing for an unshakeable foundation in knowledge. Descartes's argument for the priority of consciousness implies independence of the latter from the body. In the wake of his foundational interests, the methodical course of rational ultimate proof, the mutual independence of thought and body is indispensable for Descartes and implies that the *facultas imaginandi* (imaginative faculty) or *vis imaginativa* (power of the imagination)[40] must be completely extinguished. According to the Sixth Meditation this is *nihil aliud quam applicatio facultatis cognoscitivae ad corpus praesens* (nothing but an application of the cognitive faculty to a present body;

VI/72), which floods consciousness with imagery and leads it to premature judgments (which are therefore not controlled by rules; IV/55ff. and V/68–69). The power of imagination is not an essential part of the human mind and thus is not a necessary constituent of "me" as the *ego cogito* (VI/73): *quae in me est, prout differt a vi intelligendi, ad meî ipsius, hoc est ad mentis meae essentiam non requiri* (which I possess, in as far as it differs from the power of conceiving, is in no way necessary to my essence, that is, to the essence of my mind). It only *exists* in me, but it remains dependent on what in principle is different from consciousness: the sphere of extended things. Although for the mind, as long as it holds itself in meditative thought, nothing is more intimate than the idea of the infinite, that is, God (and although nothing else can be known that is easier and more certain), consciousness continually exchanges the truth of the infinite for sense knowledge in the service of images, which is subject to error. That is the Cartesian variant of the ban on images. Whoever holds to the second commandment will follow the path of a meditative practice that leads to the idea of God, and this way alone frees science to work methodically. Knowledge can be applied to the sphere of physical existence insofar as it treats it mathematically, that is, in purely numerical relationships. Such a science can reconstruct the human body as a machine and thus engage with bodies without falling victim to the magic of images and sense impressions.

If sensibility evokes for the human mind above all the danger of deception, this is also because finite reason is tempted to a premature readiness to judge. This is the result of a will that is keen on the senses as stimuli and enticement and does not want to miss out on anything in the game of attractions. It is the disproportionality[41] between finite reason and infinite will that, for Descartes, becomes the source of human error and wrongdoing. For the founder of modern rationalism, to make sensibility, the will, or the human body directly the seat and origin of the negative—to give a gnostic response, so to speak, to the question of the origins of evil—is as impossible as it was for Augustine, who also assigned sin not to the world of the senses but to a false usage, a disorder in the relation between what humans may need (*uti*) and what they may enjoy (*frui*).[42]

3.5 Repression of the Senses

Despite such precautions, it seems that a fundamental suspicion of everything sensual has more strongly shaped Protestant religious culture than systematic theology wanted to admit. The attitude of the Reformation toward culture, at any rate, associated image, body, and sensibility and took a view of them as highly ambivalent things wherever they aimed at a restoration of the purity of the church. The orienting model is that of a community reformed according to the word of God that, in obedience to the Holy Spirit (and in alliance with rationalism and spiritualism) strives for distance from the sensuality of images. The ban on images then appears as a directive for a *rational* worship (Rom 12:1) whose shaping power consists in its ability to neutralize the distracting and subversive power of images. Purification and abstraction, reform of the church and sanctification of the believer shed a "puritanical" light on Protestantism. Orientation to the word as rejection of sensuality and renewal of rationality creates a signature feature that Schiller characterizes in *Maria Stuart* when he has Mortimer report to the queen-designate about his experiences of education and conversion on Roman soil:

I ne'er had felt the power of art till now.
The church that reared me hates the charms of sense;
It tolerates no image, it adores
But the unseen, the incorporeal word.
What were my feelings, then, as I approached
The threshold of the churches, and within,
Heard heavenly music floating in the air:
While from the walls and high-wrought roof there streamed
Crowds of celestial forms in endless train—
When the Most High, Most Glorious pervaded
My captivated sense in real presence![43, 44]

Schiller interprets the effect of the ban on images as a suppression of the sensual. The recovery of what had been repressed drives Mortimer to conversion, to rejection of a Protestantism that says "purity of the gospel" but means "disembodying," "bodilessness," and hostility to images. To the extent that Schiller's scene is both about Marian images and the beauty of the Virgin, the scene also has sexual connotations: in the antagonism between the material image and the disembodied word and spirit, the female body represents desire, which—together with blasphemous adoration of images—becomes the characteristic expression of sin.[45] That sexual distractions aroused by images could disturb meditation as well as concentration on doctrine was Zwingli's special concern:

Here stands a Magdalene painted so whorish, that even the priests have all said again and again: How could a man take mass devoutly here? Indeed, the eternal, pure, untouched maid and mother of Jesus Christ has to show her breast....There stands a Sebastian... so cavalier, soldier-like and pimp-ish that the women have had to make confession about [it].[46]

3.6 Body as *Imago Dei*?

Such rejection of the senses as a core of interpreting the ban on images evokes resonances in the exegesis of the biblical concept of *imago Dei* (see above, §II.3.2c). Moreover, it does so with regard to the way in which the human being deserves to be called the image of God. If God is thought of as essentially spirit, then a sharing in the divine spirit (or in language, reason, the ability to call all things by their right names, etc.) could be what makes the human being the image of God—but not the human body and not even the physical feature of walking erect, though the latter was regarded in antiquity as a constitutive anthropological mark. The question whether the *imago Dei* has its appropriate place only in the human soul or (also) in the body was therefore answered, through a long tradition of interpretation, in favor of the primacy of the spiritual soul. It was first the Old Testament scholar Ludwig Köhler (1880–1956) who corrected that tradition, following Paul Humbert (and a tradition that had long existed in rabbinic interpretation), and expanding the interpretation with reference to the "upright figure of the human."[47] The traditional privileging of spirit and reason was so much a matter of course that Lutheran orthodoxy, even where it had other paths before it, swiftly returned to the usual one. Thus, Quenstedt allowed that the *imago Dei* certainly shone forth "*in corpore primi hominis* [in the body of the first human]," but only insofar as that body before the fall appears to have been incapable of suffering and so also incapable of passion. It was *impassibilitas* (impassibility; passionlessness) by virtue of which that body could be the image of the immortal God.[48]

3.7 Embodiment and Christology

Now let us consider the dualities of spirit and matter, *logos* and *sarx*, the rational and the sensual, the eternal and the temporal, God and the world, all of them involved in the reasons given for the ban on images, from still another point of view. This will allow us to take another and contrary look at the forms of reasoning about the ban on images that opens up a positive theology of the image that is genuinely Christian. As already indicated above, Christology, and especially its central focus, the theology of the incarnation, represents the strongest ground for thinking of God who comes into the world, the Logos made human, whom the New Testament identifies as "image of the invisible God" (*eikōn tou theou tou aoratou*, Col 1:15) as one that cuts the ground from under these dualisms and, consequently, undermines the ban on images motivated by them.

If redemption consists in this—that the Logos assumes human nature in all its dimensions—then "embodiment" as the goal of all God's ways[49] seems to be an excellent theological means to decipher every form of contempt for the body as a relapse into Gnostic heresy.[50] In that sense it is appropriate that the theological justification of the ecclesial image practice referred to Christology as the doctrine of the incarnation of the Logos in order to lay ground for the theology of images. Those who rejected images because of their affinity to the sense and their corporeality would then be subject to the accusation of representing a docetic Christology, that is, of regarding the body of Christ as only an appearance. Because such a heresy describes Christ in such a way that he could not be thought of either as truly human or as redeemer, it misses the basic concept and self-understanding of Christianity.[51]

Thus, every qualification of the incarnation or the death on the cross in favor of a "spiritual event" distancing them from embodiment must be rejected. Whatever the objections to the doctrine of two natures may be, its efforts to recognize Jesus's humanity without diminishment marks an indispensable aspect of Christian faith.

Still, we would be too hasty if we were to assume that this central antidocetism found in many texts of the New Testament and elaborated in the decisions of the early church was expressed, all in all, in a "sense for sensibility," in favor of the body and so also in an appreciation for the image or for images in general. We must ask why that was not the case. A seemingly easy answer would be that Christian antidocetism was exhausted in salvational realism and did not produce any feedback regarding the evaluation of the body itself. For example, the fact that, obviously, bodily focused Hellenistic culture with its multitude of stadia and statues and its frequently homosexual character appeared from the perspective of Old Testament-Jewish-Christian piety as a polytheistic moral decline against which the ban on images served as a mark of identity. Likewise, in antiquity embodiedness signified above all transitoriness and mortality, from which people hoped they had been freed. The christological emphasis on the body was therefore an exception whose uniqueness was grounded in the presence of God in Christ exclusively, so that a productive effect on the human body as such or in general was not implied. To the accusation noted above, of a liaison with Platonism (see §3 above) can be added the impression that the Lord's Supper absorbs the constitutive significance of the body, so that the sacramental and priestly representation of Christ became central to piety and interest in the body and the image remained secondary.

3.8 Christianity as a Crisis of the Body?

Hans Belting's "anthropology of the image" emphasizes that early Christology was "somatology" inasmuch as it battled for the reality of the body of Jesus and his suffering.[52] It interpreted the connections between Christology and the theology of images in light of a fundamental affinity between image and body. In terms of cultural history this affinity may be established by reference to the painted body and archaic forms of burial. The coloring of the body served purposes not only of protection, camouflage, or deterrence; it made the body—for example, through the symbolizing of blood, whether of the hunted animal or the enemy— into a vehicle of imagery and depiction. The burial of the dead was carried out as a visual staging of the corpse or used images such as the skull or death mask that are bodies, or bodies that become the images of bodies.[53] Embedding all actions in ritual enhanced this image character and gave the visualization the nature of a performance. The following aspects of rituals for the dead all rely on such an affinity between the image and the body: the power of the image to represent something or someone absent (primarily dead persons), dread of the image as dread of that presence of the ancestors, and most certainly magical practices using imagery in the narrower sense to violate the body. Power over the other is power over his or her image. According to Belting the Jewish-Christian religion led to a crisis of the body image within ancient culture; he believes that this is intensifying at the present time in the transition between photography and the arbitrary subjection of digitalized images to manipulation.[54] It seems evident that the poses taken before the camera or the many forms in which bodies are transfigured in portraits[55] suggest a general relationship between iconicity and embodiedness, between image and body, but the alteration or even loss of the traditional relationship between imagery and bodiliness is shaped by cultural contexts.

The christological basis for icons in Eastern Christianity plays an essential role in this process because it made disembodiment the meaning of depiction.[56] The original connection between image and body is detached in the wake of "Christianity's reaction against the anthropocentrism of the ancient world" and replaced by reverence to "the one, bodiless God of Jewish tradition."[57] The particular honor paid to the body of Jesus does not change anything. It even sharpens dualistic tendencies because that body alone establishes the right of the images, being itself the image of the invisible God.[58]

3.9 Preliminary Conclusion

The ban on images is deeply rooted within the historical contexts of ancient Near Eastern religions but is also shaped by the history of interpretation and the attitudes embedded within it. In that history the ban on images shows its formative organizing effect on religious ideas as a whole. Its religious and cultural efficacy does not depend on the original meaning that can be identified in various levels of the text but is coined by the constellations it conveys and the resonances it evokes. This is sharply evident in the phenomenon of embodiedness. The ban on images is not yet adequately understood if we try to grasp it solely within the horizon of the doctrine of God, thereby neglecting the anthropological consequences that result from it. (For the close connection between theology and anthropology even in the Old Testament ban on images, see above at §II.2.3–4.)

4. Ban on Images, Monotheism, and Negative Theology

The transition to monotheism in Israel's religious history did not take place as a gradual expansion and dissolution of boundaries, transforming particularism into universalism, guided by reason alone. Instead, in the crisis of the Babylonian exile (see above at §II.2.4a), a people stripped of its hopes sees its God not as defeated by other gods but as acting *sub contrario*.[59] Since the exile was regarded as the consequence of God's judgment and wrath, this showed that God is sovereign; God alone determines the course of events. Faith in the one God, before whom all other gods are shown to be nothing, achieved its significant form with the loss of the temple and the kingship. There were many temples in Babylon, and they were devoted to different gods. With the destruction of the Jerusalem temple and the collapse of the promise, monolatry had proved paradoxical. It could only be maintained by a kind of axial twist that transformed it into a specific monotheism. In that situation the ruins of the temple were reinterpreted in a context in which one could not find what was characteristic of the worship of other nations, namely, an image of God (see §II.1.1e above, with §II.2.4a). The prohibition of an image of God made a virtue of necessity and insisted on an understanding of divine law as the place where God still was to be found. Israel could live by a *spes contra spem* (hoping against hope). YHWH is unique precisely because he does not show himself through demonstrations of power, as do the other gods who are worshiped in their cultic shrines and images because they have proved victorious. To that extent monotheism and the ban on images are, so to speak, "all of a piece." When faith in covenant and election was grounded by the monotheistic belief in God as Creator, a quasi-rational enlightenment arose that mocks the efforts of other peoples who hang their hearts on idols and tin gods that cannot help anyone (see §II.2.2b above).

4.1 Hermeneutics of the Ban on Images as a Hermeneutics of Violence

If we can justify the idea that the connection between monotheism and the ban on images only became a significant mark of Old Testament Jewish religion after the exile, the origins and unique character of the image ban appear in a different light from the one shed by attempts to derive both from a cultic reform in terms of centralization, unification of order, and concentration of power.[60] According to Egyptologist Jan Assmann, the ban on images achieves its function in the rise of so-called secondary (that is, "founded") religions that establish themselves essentially as an affront to what they find in (primary) religions. Such counter-religions operate in a revolutionary fashion and appeal to a divine revelation they understand to be an altogether new beginning. According to Assmann, a strict monotheism is not grounded in the difference between unity and multiplicity, universalism and particularity, but in the guiding distinction between true and false.[61] This latter distinction reinforces the idea that the conditions existing before or independently from the revelation must simply be abandoned. We could speak of a "monopoly theism" that requires the given multiplicity of gods to submit to the One—but it is more characteristic that monotheism takes a negative (and therefore exclusive) attitude toward the other gods and therefore toward their images. In that case the ban on images is, in fact, interpreted as a call for cultic reform: "You are to destroy the images of all other cults."[62] Monotheistic religion is said to establish a religion of decision, of either/or, that is essentially a turning away from and thus a rejection of the other gods, and so of the cult of images, but whose consequence is that their adherents will be persecuted and ultimately that unrepentant "idolaters" are to be killed. The paradigmatic biblical scenes of such a monotheism of violence are the massacre of the priests of Ba'al (1 Kgs 18) and the forced divorces from participants in so-called idol cults (cf. Ezra 9:1–4; 10:1–17).[63]

That Israel's monotheism was founded by Moses, who was brought up in Egyptian wisdom (as Acts 7:22 emphasizes), according to Freud connected the Jewish ban on images with the revolution of the Amarna period brought about by Amenophis (later called Akhenaten; he was

Pharaoh from ca. 1370 to 1352 BCE).[64] Assmann is more cautious than Freud; he does not propose an immediate and direct historical relationship between the Pharaoh (whose reign and reforms were quickly suppressed in Egypt after his death) and the activities of Moses. But he does see the profound effects of a trauma[65] that lurked in the collective unconscious and erupted in its full severity in Moses.

Akhenaten (whose Hymn to the Sun was first rediscovered in 1884) had banned all images and all names of gods except the name of the one god Aten; that is, he carried out the first radical iconoclastic cultic reform known to us. The Old Testament ban on images that saw orientation to the one God (and ultimately to the priesthood representing that God) as a turning away from all "Egypt" stands for, is said to bring forth a negative attitude toward the world, and to correspond to Akhenaten's program. The alternative to monotheism would then not be—this was Assmann's original thesis—polytheism or the return of the gods in their plurality, but cosmotheism (here Assmann—not accidentally—takes up a concept shaped by F. H. Jacobi in the eighteenth-century pantheism controversy).[66] For such cosmotheism, faith in the one unique God is said to be belief in the one who is Other than the world, the One beyond all things to whom one could only belong at the price of existential alienation from the world.[67] Such a break with what is given and familiar is an act of violence toward oneself that is transformed into violence toward strangers, that is, toward the representatives of other religions.

This interpretation of the ban on images, which Assmann lays out with an eye to current religious-cultural flash points, brings into contemporary discussion a classic model of interpretation introduced by Hegel in his *Phenomenology of Spirit*. "The struggle of the enlightenment with superstition" necessarily leads to "horrors" and terror of "absolute freedom."[68] Because the Enlightenment tried to measure all forms of life by its own rational standards, while the diversity of life did not permit such rigorism, according to Assmann it made short shrift of all obstacles put in its way: the radical Enlightenment found its proper symbol in the guillotine.[69] Correspondingly, the monotheistic enlightenment always represents violence against others in the name of the one and only truth. Violence and iconoclasm[70] are the flipside of monotheism—independently of the names borne by the particular god being appealed to as the One.

The result of all this is an interpretation of the ban on images in which the issue is no longer hostility to the body but, so to speak, hostility as body, as embodiment of absolute truth and its demands. It is said that, by its nature as a structure shaped by violence, monotheism is essentially an attack on other cultures and thus can only be "implemented" as a ban on images.[71]

If we follow this line of interpretation to its conclusion, it must mean that everything that opposes the reign of the One is an image. The interpretive model is such that it cannot admit of differences between a ban on images and iconoclasm. That is its limitation, and very probably also its weakness.

4.2 Hermeneutics of the Ban on Images as Rationalistic Apologetics

As critically as postmodern authors regard terms of identity, totality, or universality, thinkers of the modern just as emphatically emphasize the correlation of philosophical rationalism and Jewish religion, and of Greek and Hebrew monotheism. Belief in the *one* God appeared to modernity as a condition under which, for the very first time, one could speak of "reason in religion," or "religion of reason" and the ban on images as the expression of a sense of the *logos*, the rational, the infinite, and the unconditioned. The fact that polytheism, while it worships gods, is unable to derive the concept of god from the multitude of their names, and thus does not conceive "God" as an idea of reason, is said to show that polytheism still lies on a lower stage of mental development in which the confusion of God with an object in nature or with one of its powerful manifestations is simply normal. Polytheism is shaped by a confusion of ultimately nonbinding cults, while the ban on images is the expression of a developing understanding of reason and universality in the field of religion.

The uniqueness of God, which can only be conceived in thought and can never be viewed in a finite object available to the senses, marks the border between confusion and clarity, between senses and reason. The ban on images is to that extent the indicator of a "religion of reason out of the sources of Judaism."[72] Deutero-Isaianic ridicule of the foolishness of idols, which, in the name of Torah and critical enlightenment, declares polytheistic religious culture outdated, is a paradigm for intellectual achievements during the so-called Axial Age (see §II.2.2b.2 above). The ban on images mutates into a rational critique of cult and religion in the name of the one, true God.

Midrash Rabbah is cited as an example of such Jewish enlightenment; it provides us with an anecdote about Abraham that is located in a field of tension between prophetic sign action, philosophical debates, and maieutic inquiry. It presents Abraham's turn to the true and only God (which also shapes the Muslim image of Ibrahim), not so much as a destroyer of idols but above all as the representative of a ploy of reason that offers chances for others to acknowledge reason and paves the way toward a rational life:

> Rabbi Hiyya said: Terah [the father of Abraham] was a manufacturer of idols. He once went away somewhere and left Abraham to sell them in his place. A man came and wished to buy one. "How old are you?" Abraham asked him "Fifty years," was the reply. "Woe to such a man!" he exclaimed, "you are fifty years old and would worship a day-old object!" At this he became ashamed and departed. On another occasion a woman came with a plateful of flour and requested him, "Take this and offer it to them." So he took a stick, broke them, and put the stick in the hand of the largest. When his father returned he demanded, "What have you done to them?" "I cannot conceal it from you," he rejoined. "A woman came with a plateful of fine meal and requested me to offer it to them. One claimed, 'I must eat first.' while another claimed, 'I must eat first.' Thereupon the largest arose, took the stick, and broke them." "Why do you make sport of me?" he cried out. "Have they then any knowledge?" "Should not your ears listen to what your mouth is saying?" he retorted.[73]

The father of Isaac appears here as a subtle enlightener who poses critical questions with Socratic irony and forces others to reflect (cf. similarly the *Apocalypse of Abraham*, cited above at §II.2.2b.1).

Eckhard Nordhofen has called comparable forms of reception of the ban on images "Jewish enlightenment"[74] and describes it as a critique of religion *avant la lettre*: "The Jewish enlightenment criticizes the making of one's own gods and condenses that critique" in the ban on images. It would understand the image of a god "as the product of human ideas, needs, and desires—in modern terms as projection."[75] Essentially, Feuerbach's theory of projection and the critiques of religion by Marx and Freud are only variants on the "basic idea of the Jewish enlightenment in the Old Testament," and on the basis of that affinity Freud called the ban on images "a triumph of spirituality over the senses."[76] Consequently it would be a curious misunderstanding for today's critique of religion to be directed against the Jewish-Christian tradition as well.[77] From this perspective theology and reason stand shoulder to shoulder with regard to monotheism, and a profound correlation between the prophets' criticism of the cult and philosophical critique of religion is supposed. The ban on images is seen as serving Christian apologetics in the form of an early dawn of enlightenment; this is especially evident when Nordhofen elsewhere cries out, concerning the senseless dancers before the "golden calf" they have produced, "How stupid, how blinded must they be when they say: these are your gods, who led you out of Egypt!"[78] (For an exegetical view of Exod 32, see above at §II.2.4b.1.)

In this interpretation the ban on images becomes the characteristic mark of an advanced, progressive, and (self-)critical religion that has left behind the atavisms of primitive religious cultures. Appearing above as the contrast between "spirit and sense," it falls here under the opposition between "rationality and hoax." The delicate problem with this interpretation may be summarized by asking whether this proposal for interpretation does not slyly shuffle the thing it is trying to interpret out of the world entirely. After all, if the image is so obviously anachronistic and the service of images, measured in terms of progress, is so completely outdated, anyone would have to be "dumb and blinded" to depend on images. Then the question is, why is there any need at all for the severity of an unceasing competition, a struggle over God or nongod? As long as we are trying to understand the Old Testament ban on images in the context of ancient Near Eastern religious history, it would be better to abandon the superior smile of our enlightened contemporaries and be clear about the fact that the biblical polemic against magic and sorcery does *not* come from a conviction that a rational person would leave such things alone since, after all, that kind of humbug is simply worthless. That may be true, but it has little to do with the hermeneutical task of reconstructing an *interpretandum*, the thing to be explained. If we are trying to do that, we must try to understand what anxiety led Israel to demand the death of sorcerers instead of simply ridiculing them.[79]

The paradigm of such a rationalistic interpretation does strike a number of intellectual sparks from the ban on images (and stands in opposition to myth and magic, belief in images and idols, fetishes and amulets, the worship of the stars and planets), but it can contribute next to nothing to historical clarification. Such a reading produces types of interpretation that are entirely directed to today's discussion. After all, if modernity can only demonstrate its normative content by assuring itself of its own concept of reason, the grooming of a rational core in Jewish prophecy (what was previously called its moral seriousness) is primarily an apologetic strategy. No matter how swiftly progress moves where it will, the "I'm already here" of a rational religion is always several steps ahead of it.[80]

4.3 Hermeneutics of the Ban on Images as Phenomenology of Alterity

Whether the ban on images represents the violence and intolerance of the monotheistic religions, an anticipated enlightenment, or an overlapping of the two as a tyranny of universalism, it always appears as an essential characteristic. It does not augment monotheism with additional attributes but emphasizes its typical features (if we may so summarize the overall position of section II). In this sense Emmanuel Lévinas calls the ban on images (emphasizing the first of the Mosaic tablets) "truly the supreme commandment of monotheism."[81] That can be said insofar as the ban on images is understood as a ban on foreign gods (see above at §II.2.3), but Lévinas means it in a more basic sense, because for him it interrupts the order of nature and fate, confronting the power of ontology and its proclivity for identity in favor of the proclamation of distinction and difference. Lévinas combines a Jewish Torah devotion, a critique of totalitarian figures, and a deconstruction of the primacy of ontology with a Neoplatonic understanding of the idea of the good. Therefore the ban on images becomes and remains representative of the true and the good, the *epekeina tēs ousias* ("otherwise than being or beyond essence"),[82] that is, simply transcending all being and every idea of being and so replacing ontology with ethics as first philosophy. In this way, in the context of twentieth-century phenomenology, the internal connection between the ban on images and the negative theology that shapes both Christian and Jewish theology was decisively renewed (see §4.5 below).

Whereas on a first tangible level the so-called golden calf, in fact an image of a bull, stands for the order of nature, for strength and fertility, and the ban on this cultic image represents faith in the one God, on a second and more general level the ban on images becomes a reminder of the freedom and sovereignty of God even toward all predicates and descriptions by which the knowledge of God identifies him. The ban on images manifests God's otherness not only compared with natural sense-oriented desires of those who had fled from Egypt but also with the human idolatry that is immanent in the worship and knowledge of God as such: the desire to lay claim to God's identity and essence and so to bring them under the sway of human concepts (see also §II.3). This suggests a hermeneutic of the ban on images that sees it as first put into effect and fulfilled when talk about God develops into a negative theology.

4.4 Negative Theology: Pre-Socratic

As early as the pre-Socratics the critique of the multiple anthropomorphisms in the mythic-poetic and religious-cultural presentations of god(s) was made a motif of negative theology (cf. §II.2.1). When Zenophanes asserted in the sixth century BCE that "among the Ethiopians the god is black and pug-nosed, among the Thracians blue-eyed and red-haired," and if the oxen or horses had hands they would equip their gods with manes and tails, he simultaneously presented the systematic counterthesis: "A god is the greatest among gods and humans, in no way existing in bodily form or in thought, like mortals."[83] Besançon calls this "the very first formulation in history of negative theology."[84]

In fact, Zenophanes supports the contrast between the one God and the many gods by tracing the latter to the multitude of human *ideas* about god and *images* of the gods, whereas the true God, without being therefore devoid of form, is not adequately portrayed by human forms. The hiatus between the depiction of the gods (in cultic images) and the being of the one God who can be grasped only in thought is certainly not the theme of a negative command here but is identified as the expression of a formal inadequacy. We may call this criticism a hermeneutics of suspicion intended to uncover a lack of awareness and a descriptive blunder. There is nothing here about blasphemy, nor is iconoclasm a side effect of this critique.[85]

With the incorporation of pre-Socratic natural philosophy into a general doctrine of being (ontology), Parmenides defined what truly exists in contrast to appearance as the One in contrast to the Many. That was the basis for the fact that today the One remains categorically separate from the multiplicity of possible predicates and thus can only be described *via negationis*. Such a discourse about God as the truly

One not only excludes individual predicates that—as in the case of "mortal"—introduce a deficiency, but also disjunctions that exhaust an entire sphere of definition: for example, the difference between "come to be/cease to be" or "past/future."[86] According to Parmenides everything that derives from the sphere of sense perception belongs among human fantasies. Thus what truly exists is pure thought (see above, §§II.2.1 and 2.2).

4.5 Transcendence as Negativity and Otherness

The point of view from which the classical predecessors of negative theology took up this philosophical idea was that this strategy touches not merely some qualities available to the senses, as a naïve anthropomorphism applies it, but precisely those characteristics of God that lie within the concept of God and are essential to it. Pseudo-Dionysius Areopagitica, who was the first to coin the term *theologia negativa*, in his work *De divinis nominibus* links the practice of excluding qualities with the Neoplatonic centering on the One (τὸ ἕν = *to hen*):

> For, as...the One above conception is inconceivable to all conceptions; and the Good above word is unutterable by word—Unit making one every unit, and superessential essence and mind inconceivable, and Word unutterable, speechlessness and inconception, and namelessness—being after the manner of no existing being, and Cause of being to all, but Itself not being, as beyond every essence, and as It may manifest Itself properly and scientifically concerning Itself.[87]

A perspective that at least includes moments of dissimilarity and noncorrespondence is the indispensable condition under which images, names, and concepts can be used. Then negative theology is first of all an attempt to keep before our eyes "the greater dissimilarity in so great a likeness,"[88] that is (to adapt Paul's expression) to speak "as though not speaking" (cf. 1 Cor 7:29–31). An awareness of this permanent reservation (which cannot be made durable by any guarantee) must accompany anything said about God. Otherwise we are forced to choose between a cultured lapse into silence (saying nothing at all) and the unstoppable misuse of the divine name. In this sense Nicholas of Cusa (1401–64) declared that negative theology is so indispensable to an affirmative speaking about God that without it what is worshiped is not the eternal God but one of God's creatures. Nicholas says explicitly that any talk about God that does not take this theoretically or practically with all seriousness falls into idolatry: "it ascribes to the image that which befits only the reality itself."[89] Altogether in the same vein Maimonides emphasizes, from the perspective of Judaism, that only a negative theology can entirely avoid idolatry.[90]

The Neoplatonic emphasis on negative theology goes along with a new understanding of the One in contrast to the Many. Multiplicity is created by the addition of one with another and then a third, and thus includes "one and another one" but precisely *not* the (true) One, which must be conceived as entirely Other than the Many. The logic of this assertion has yet another aspect. If the highest being is truly a transcendent One, we must explain why the Many came into being at all. In that case notions like superfluity or emanation are at hand, but nonetheless remain problematic if they project a change into the One, thus creating a difference within itself. The concept of depiction is highly useful for avoiding that pitfall, for depicting is a process that does not reduce or alter the being it represents. So if we distinguish the One from its image we can think of presence *and* transcendence at the same time. The unspeakable, invisible, unforethinkable (to refer to Schelling's term) One becomes, in the image, something visible, describable, and categorially determinable without, so to speak, being untrue to itself and without having its otherness diminished by such thought.[91]

When thought subject to the Neoplatonic primacy of the One attempts to adopt biblical perspectives and thus explains creation, fall, and salvation in terms of the emergence of the Many from the One and the return to it (*egressus* and *regressus*), the result may be the idea of becoming an image and, by contrast, of a gradual deimagizing: the ultimate future of the images is then a return to the undifferentiated self-transparency of the One from which they took their origins.[92]

Thus we can observe that the internal relationship between monotheism and the ban on images achieved further significance in the sharpening of negative theology. It extracts the ban on images from its original *Sitz im Leben*, that is, the context of the cult, and fundamentalizes it as a general rule for speaking about God as such. Thus the commandment not to take the name of God in vain or (in the sense of the refinement that sets another fence around the Torah) not to speak the divine name at all, parallels the attitude toward images and toward language and especially toward the word.

The ban on images, we might say, comes into its own in the absolute transcendence of the One. It is thus loosed from its historical connection to other bans that may be subsumed under the religious-historical category of taboo (from the ban on touching, invading, and entering the holy of holies or taking possession of it)[93] and is linked to the philosophical strategies of ever more exalted transcendence. The ban on images becomes the paradigm of a negative *theo*logic.

Such a reception of the ban on images also creates space, precisely within the neighborhood of (neo-)Platonism, for ethics. This is more than obvious in the work of Lévinas, to which we must return at this point (see above at §4.3). Lévinas sees the "trace of the other," that is, the presence of an alterity that opposes totality, represented in the human face. The prohibition against fixing the Other in an image or in an identity defined by us is a ban on the violence that thereby results. To that extent the subject conceived in modern philosophy as sovereign is subjected to the Other and the Other's unconditional command: "You shall not kill!" (and by such passivity is indeed *sub-iectum*).[94]

But there are other suggestions about how the ban on images may be interpreted as the basis of a material ethics. Willi Oelmüller, for example, draws a direct line from bans on worship of foreign gods, the production of idols, and the misuse of the divine name to a verdict of any religious justification of violence, the establishment of a theocracy, the sacralizing of political governance, and exclusivistic claims to truth. He also derives from the ban on images the inviolability of the human as image of God.[95] Making it a basic theological premise including universal claims corresponds to an overestimating of its moral implications.

Such a hermeneutics of the ban on images tends to see all the commandments of the second tablet of the law as implicit in the primary commandment of the first, but it fails to explain why the ban on images did *not* have any such normative consequences in the historical contexts in which it was first seriously applied. This kind of reception, impressive as it is, relies on a systematic surplus, a deeper content of meaning that gives the original text relevance even in secular contexts. To that extent the hermeneutics of the ban on images appears as a process of reception that provides new and additional meaning.

4.6 Representation of What Cannot Be Represented: Kant's Reception of the Ban on Images

The way in which Immanuel Kant interprets the ban on images in his critical philosophy can scarcely be overestimated. That human freedom cannot be demonstrated by empirical sciences, in which the universal determinism of causes must prevail, was the starting point of Kant's critical procedure of dividing *all* objects into *phenomena* and *noumena*. On the basis of that distinction freedom appeared possible (as a non-self-contradictory supposition, provided that knowledge of the chain of causal natural laws remains limited to mere appearances, i.e., phenomena). A positive theoretical basis for knowledge that would ensure freedom does not exist. But the ineluctable, practical demand of the categorical imperative helps us to overcome this difficulty. Its practical proof is offered by the moral law, making freedom the keystone of Kant's philosophy. Of course freedom remained a blank in theoretical knowledge that could not be empirically filled. In a certain sense that is why the critical orientation of Kant's philosophy depends on the conviction that ideas of reason "can never be thought as objects of the senses" and that in experience nothing can be given that covers a transcendental idea. In Kant's language that also means that "a pure concept of the understanding…can never be made into an image,"[96] and thus ideas can never be exposed in the world of the senses.

As early as his *Groundwork for the Metaphysics of Morals*, Kant borrowed a leading category of negative theology when, in speaking of the categorical imperative, he declared that we do not grasp the "practical unconditioned necessity of the moral imperative but…its *incomprehensibility*."[97] Kant ultimately made use again of this grasped incomprehensibility, which hints at the impossibility of a positive description of freedom in his *Critique of Judgement*. Aesthetic judgment, treated in part 1, is strictly distinguished from theoretical judgment as well as from the imperative of practical reason, because neither the beautiful nor the sublime is an object of theoretical knowledge. An observer can only speak of it by reference to a subjective judgment with regard to his own faculties. To call something "sublime" or to experience it as such is therefore not the result of beholding nature in its immeasurability (e.g., the starry heavens, the desert, or the sea) but comes initially from the *contrast* between something so boundless that it surpasses the ability of our senses to perceive it, on the one hand, and on the other hand the idea of freedom or of human dignity, infinitely superior to anything we see in nature. Ideas cannot be beheld directly, and they cannot be exemplified in experience. But precisely the disproportionality between the beholding of limitless space, which prima facie overpowers the human, and the idea of freedom, which asserts itself against any superior power of nature, shapes the unique character of the sublime. The highest idea that, according to Kant, the human mind can conceive, is thus neither comprehensible nor subject to depiction. But the elusiveness of a last boundary within the view of nature can be taken as representing the unrepresentable idea of freedom, or be felt as a sense of the Sublime.[98] It is then a matter of a depiction *via negationis*, an experience of difference that expands the mind[99] (although without adding anything to the contents of knowledge). The issue of a place for freedom in human consciousness, indispensable to Kant's philosophy, is thus treated by means of a negative theology. Freedom is unimaginable, but precisely in its unimaginability it can become present to the human mind as long as the ultimate concern of the latter is moral law. Against this background Kant insists that "perhaps there is no more sublime passage in the Jewish Law than the commandment: Thou shalt not make unto thee any graven image, or any likeness of any thing."[100]

The combination of negativity and unconditionedness, the commitment to a highest idea framed by a critical self-limitation of the reason presents the ban of images as a placeholder for what cannot be grasped immediately and directly. To that extent Kant's critical philosophy and his interpretation of the ban on images are mutually reflective. The connection between aesthetics, ethics, and negativity produced by this reception of the ban on images points forward to relationships among philosophical reflection on ethical experience, the development of the visual arts, and the transformation of imagery and iconoclasm into aesthetic strategies.[101] (See below, §9.)

4.7 The Ban on Images and the Media Revolution

A negative theology that not only (as we have shown above) accompanies talk about God with critical self-awareness but intends, by intensifying its negativity, to displace other forms of such talk must reject mediating figures. This constellation of negative theology, monotheism, and a ban on images transforming the exclusivity of the One culminates in the uniqueness of the negative and, as a ban on all media, ultimately leads to mystical silence. We have already encountered (above at §4.5) the conversion of such a negativity into an ethics as practical compensation for what theoretically cannot be presented in positive form.

We find this attitude articulated by focusing on the concept of discipleship of Jesus in Kierkegaard's work (which was formative for dialectical theology and for Dietrich Bonhoeffer):

> Only the imitator [disciple] is the true Christian. The admirer really assumes a pagan relation to Christianity, and this is also how admiration, in the middle of Christendom, gave birth to a new paganism—Christian art....Would it be possible for me, that is, could I persuade myself, could I be motivated to dip my brush, to lift my chisel in order to represent Christ in color or carve his figure?...No, for me it would unconditionally be an impossibility. [As it is inconceivable that someone would sharpen a knife in order to murder]...it is also incomprehensible to me from whence an artist would gain the calmness, or incomprehensible to me is the calmness with which an artist has sat year in and year out occupied in the work of painting Christ—without having it occur to him whether Christ would wish to be painted, would wish to have his portrait, however idealized it became, depicted by his masterly brush. I do not comprehend how the artist would maintain his calm, that he would not notice Christ's displeasure, would not suddenly throw it all out, brushes and paints, far, far away, just as Judas did with the thirty pieces of silver, because he suddenly understood that Christ has required only imitators....I do not comprehend it; the brush would have fallen out of my hand the very second I was about to begin.[102]

Here the ban is on aesthetic attitudes in favor of a practical maintenance of faith. Anything else Kierkegaard regards as paganism.

We have to keep this gradient in mind when discussing the observation that the victory of monotheism entails a media revolution.[103] The ban on images then appears as an early case of change in a culture's primary medium. A revolution took place, first in the transition from cultic image to written text, as vividly portrayed in the contest between the golden calf and the tablets of the law: the one God thus distinguishes himself from the multitude of gods who are only supposed to exist and are venerated in images by the fact that this God is the giver of the Torah (cf. §II.3.2a–b). At the same time pagan superstition is replaced by rational worship of God in the everyday of a moral life ("Present your bodies as a living sacrifice, holy and acceptable to God, which is your spiritual worship"; Rom 12:1). Ritual, with its decline into mere external action, is transformed in moral practice by being oriented to the good, the rational insight of the agents, or the imitation of Christ.

Formally, the obligatory nature of the law consists in the first place of being written down and thus able to be taken into account everywhere. While the image requires individual perception and presence in the cult, the text (of the Torah) is portable.[104] But above all the latter demands the proofing of copies, an understanding application, and finally a methodical interpretation so that it makes room for other affinities to rationality than the idol. Genuine fidelity to the law consists in an attitude, on the one hand, that arbitrarily does not change the letter of the law, but on the other hand by its correspondence to the eternally valid law in the practice of interpretation. Therefore the nations' worship of images is replaced by a Torah devotion of Jewish provenance focused solely on the word and the writings but fulfilled in practical action. We may say that here doing the good becomes the sole medium of God's presence and reality. It thus prepares the way for the axial emergence of universalism—in its ethical form. Contrariwise, the heritage of Greek philosophy lies in the universalism of modern science.

The statement of Jan Assmann addressed above, that secondary religions, in their dependence on a founder, are always also religions of revelation (see above, §4.1) becomes against this background a pointer to the applicability of media theory to the study of religions. Such a media theory is then transformed into a "history of cultural progress" resulting from the victorious "elimination" of images, if the change of media is viewed from a perspective according to which images made by humans are replaced by the word given only by God. Then word and Scripture become the true and only medium of revelation, whereas the image is assigned to the problematic sphere of products made by human hands. Thus we find Nordhofen writing, "When a self-made god is eliminated through insight into the conditions of its making and the nothingness of its existence, then the only counter-model to the self-made gods is the God who is self-revealed."[105]

However, using the concept of revelation one can speak only of a *change* of media, not a rejection in principle of all mediation as in the mystical tradition of negative theology. For, after all, revelation is constituted in *media* of revelation.[106] The monotheistic revolution is thus understood as the replacement of one medium (image) by another (word/Scripture), whereas the more radical negative theological way of reading the ban on images leads beyond all media. The two variants can maintain a neighborly relation to each other if they adopt the ethical paradigm and call the service of love of neighbor the sole valid representation of God.

The hermeneutics of the ban on images thus stands, as regards media theory, before the alternative of a basic kataphatic or apophatic conviction. This alternative also appears within Christian theology of images, in the difference between incarnational theology and theology of the cross: those who think within the paradigm of the "Christmas" coming of the Son into the world can derive the legitimacy of pictorial representation from the revelation of the Logos among us, and thus see the ban on images removed by the incarnation. But those who see the death of Jesus as the end of all separation—the symbol of the nothingness of all symbols, an overcoming of a cultic order that separates the hidden from the revealed—can instead aim at an expansion of the negativity grounded in the ban on images: no word, no symbol, and indeed no image can of itself and "naturally" mediate the presence of God. Only the kenotic self-surrender of the Son of God—what we may also call God's self-negation—as accomplished in Jesus's death on the cross[107] enables representations: an entirely new form of representation that includes the essential moment of negativity. Only in the mode of self-negation do symbols actually work. In a certain sense, for this position the representation of God is made possible by its limitation, precisely through the loss of God's presence. The cross represents the absence of God and nothing that could be aesthetically "pleasing," and in that sense it demystifies all images of beautiful appearance as such.

When the sign of the cross in the apse of Hagia Eirene represents the images that have been removed,[108] that contingent result of an iconoclastic power struggle is likewise a reminder of the productive power of negativity (see plate 2, Istanbul, p. I.2).

Plate 1
Christus Pantokrator, section from the dome mosaic in the
baptistry of San Giovanni, Florence, ca. 1300. © Photo:
akg-images/De Agostini Picture Lib./G. Nimatallah

I.1

Plate 2
Istanbul, Aya Irini Kilisesi—Hagia Eirene. © Photo: akg-images/Andrea Jemolo

I.2

Plate 3
Saint Veronica with the Sudarium, Master of Saint Veronica,
shroud, ca. 1420. On soft wood covered with canvas, 78
x 48 cm. Munich, Alte Pinakothek. © Photo: akg-images

I.3

Plate 4
Altarpiece of the Lutheran Hospital Church of the Holy
Ghost (Spitalkirche zum Heiligen Geist) at Dinkelsbühl,
Franconia, Germany, central nave with altar and crucifix,
1537. Photo: Thomas Scheidt/Sven Kohler/Christian Stein
© Photo: Foto Marburg/Art Resource, NY

I.4

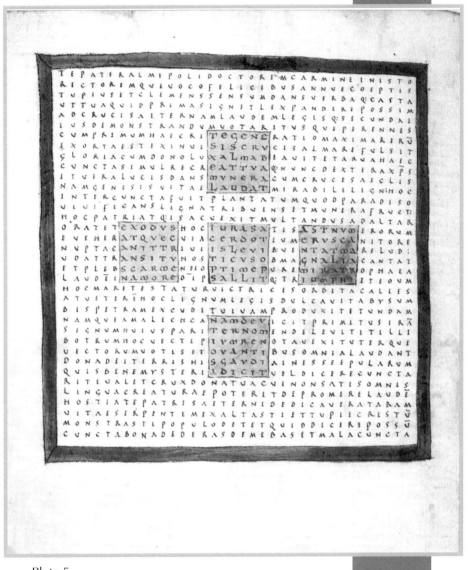

Plate 5
Rabanus Maurus (ca. 825/26), *In honorem sanctae crucis (De laudibus sanctae crucis)*. © Bibliothèque nationale de France

I.5

Plate 6
Klaus Kröger *Schriftbild* (1974). Charcoal and pencil on paper laid on canvas, 150 x 95.5 cm. © 2018 Artists Rights Society (ARS), New York/VG Bild-Kunst, Bonn; Digital Image © The Museum of Modern Art/Licensed by SCALA/Art Resource, NY

Plate 7
Rémy Zaugg, *I, the picture, see* [*Ich, das Bild, sehe*] (1998). Aluminum, varnish, silkscreen, clear varnish. 113.5 x 101.3 x 2.7 cm. © Rémy Zaugg

I.7

Plate 8a
Kazimir Severinovich Malevich, *Black Square* (Suprematist composition, 1915). Oil on linen, 79.5 x 79.5 cm, Tretyakov Gallery, Moscow. © Photo: akg-images

I.8

Plate 8b
Kazimir Severinovich Malevich, *White on White* (Suprematist composition, 1918). Oil on canvas, 79.4 x 79.4 cm, The Museum of Modern Art, NY. © Photo: akg-images/Album/Fine Art Images

Plate 9
Ad Reinhardt, Abstract Painting (1966). Gouache on photographic paper, 8 7/8 x 4 5/8 in. (22.6 x 11.7 cm). Gift of Agnes Gund. The Museum of Modern Art, New York, NY, U.S.A. © 2018 Estate of Ad Reinhardt/Artists Rights Society (ARS), New York. Digital Image © The Museum of Modern Art/Licensed by SCALA/ Art Resource, NY

I.10

Plate 10
Piet Mondrian, Composition no. 10 in Black and White
(1915). Oil on canvas, 110 x 85 cm. The Kröller-Müller
Museum, Otterlo, Netherlands. © Photo: akg-images

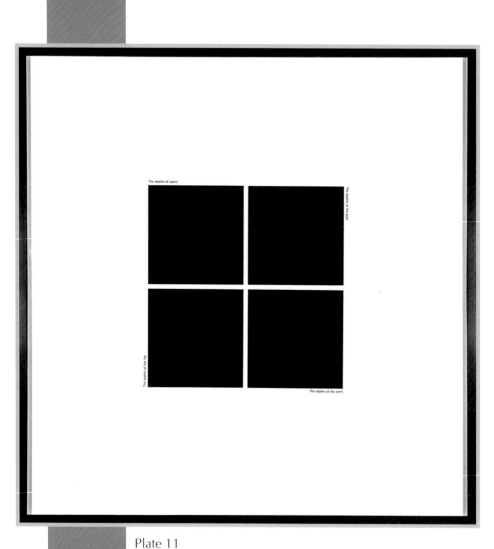

Plate 11
(double sided)
John Hilliard, *Black Depths* (1974). Two works on paper, black and white photographs and transfer script, 69 x 69 cm, Tate, UK. © John Hilliard. All Rights Reserved, DACS/ Artimage 2018. © 2018 Artists Rights Society (ARS), New York DACS, London

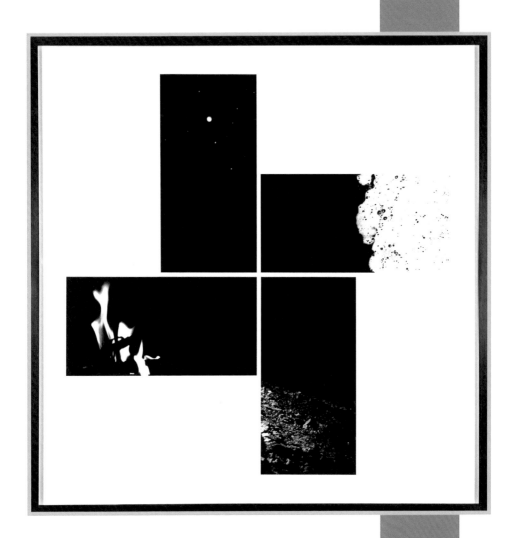

I.13

Plate 12a
Anselm Kiefer, *Bilderstreit* (1980) (artist book) © Atelier
Anselm Kiefer

I.14

Plate 12b
Anselm Kiefer, *Bilderstreit* (1977). Oil on canvas, 211.3 x 272 cm, Van Abbe Museum, Netherlands. © Atelier Anselm Kiefer

5. Invisibility or Hiddenness of God?

Up to this point we have spoken of the relationship between imagery and corporeality and of the negative attitudes toward sensation that are manifest in many interpretations of the ban on images, but we have not yet treated the larger concept that includes all three, namely, visibility. The affinities between image and body are those of visibility and therefore of the sense of sight. Defining the picture or image by using the traditional phrase *depiction based on similarity* as decisive[109] presupposes that the perception of such similarity is a function of the eye as a bodily organ. Not only is the thing seen something embodied, so also is the manner of perception. Certainly the visibility of images does not exclude the possibility that they may exist on lofty church ceilings or in remote valleys and so were evidently not intended for human sight.[110] Such images may have had apotropaic purposes, among others. The demon who saw them was to be prevented from entering the building, even if such an image event took place above or below what is visible to us. But this special function of unseen images does not change the overall subject, for "not being seen" and "not being able to be seen" do not imply invisibility.

The fact that visibility was not addressed, despite the fundamental significance of this category in what has already been said, is due to the systematic thesis that is being developed and discussed here. It has a twofold point: as regards the concept of image, it denies that "depiction based on similarity" is a necessary condition of being an image or of iconic processes. As regards the ban on images, it takes into account that the ban is not about an invisibility of God in principle but is intended to maintain YHWH's hiddenness. Section II has presented the exegetical basis for this guiding thesis. To develop it systematically requires a separate treatment

145

of the topic even though the latter is closely connected with what has already been said about corporeality and the senses.

5.1 God's Invisibility

We are thus contesting a *communis opinio* that Gottfried Boehm summarized in the formula "YHWH is an invisible God....What Moses brought down from Sinai is not an equivalent of the divine form...but rather an *imageless* message in a form *far removed from any image*."[111] In accordance with this, the divine invisibility is the basis of the ban on images and leads from what cannot be seen to what must be heard.[112] The law as God's demand is said to be the Other in respect to the image ("imageless," "far from any image"), transcending the whole sphere of figures and visible forms (as "ought" is the Other of "is"). Only in contrast to the empirical does the law correspond to Israel's God. Similarly, Calvin noted that the ban on images was directed against the "impiety of attributing a visible form to God."[113] It would be redundant to give further examples for this conviction, widespread as it is. However, we may recall that Gerhard von Rad already rejected it:

> Starting from an antithesis between visible and invisible, material and spiritual, which, while quite generally held, is quite alien to the Old Testament, the critics thought that the second commandment had to be understood as the expression of a special spirituality in the worship of God, as the signal, important overcoming of a spiritual and cultic primitivism, and so as the attainment of a decisive stage in the education of the human race.[114]

Echoing von Rad, we reemphasize our doubts about such an antithesis enjoying the status of consensus.

This model of interpretation, however, is not supported by the New Testament predicate of Christ in Colossians 1:15: "*hos estin eikōn tou theou tou aoratou* (He [the Son] is the image of the invisible God)." The concept of invisibility could become so central to the doctrine of God that this Deutero-Pauline passage is interpreted not in light of Genesis 1 but in terms of the general question of whether and how an *image of the invisible God* could be conceivable at all. One could attribute to the *logos asarkos,* as the Son begotten by the Father, a similarity of appearance with the Father on the basis of the unity of being of Father and Son.

However, the same was not true of the *logos ensarkos*, who acquires a visibility through his union with human nature in view of which being "image of God" could again become problematic. In what sense can the eternal Son be the image of the Father? Does not every answer to this question exclude a corresponding explanation for the incarnate Logos? What is worth noting is the consistency with which Origen, for example, interpreted Colossians 1:15 according to relationships that systematic theology later called "immanent trinity" when he asserted that the Logos is "the invisible [!] image of the invisible God."[115] If similarity constitutes the concept of image, and if that concept is to be used under the condition of the sameness in divine nature of Father and Son, then the concept of God's invisibility can ground the Old Testament ban on images as well as it can dominate (or really: neutralize) the New Testament's speaking of Christ as the image of God. The image may not be visible, if speaking of the *image* of God is not to be self-contradictory—or, from the opposite point of view, any visibility that belongs to the incarnate Logos must be dissolved so that the Son can be called the image *of God*. It could scarcely be possible to give clearer expression to the centrality of the category of invisibility in the theological understanding of the image (as well as the problems it creates).

But is it really any help to interpret the Johannine passage "no one has ever seen God. It is God the only Son…who has made him known" (John 1:18) in the sense of Platonic *chorismos* (separation) between the visible and the intelligible world?—and so to suggest "no one could see him because he is invisible"? And how then can we understand the biblical story in Exodus 33:18–23 (cf. §II.3.2 above), which says that God only allows himself to be seen *a tergo* (from behind) because wanting to see God face-to-face (this side of what Paul promises eschatologically) is a deadly desire? We are not posing these questions here in order to shift from the philosophical-theological concept of the invisibility of God to that of God's biblically attested visibility. That would be too simple a strategy. Instead, what we propose to test is the question whether a theological grounding or hermeneutics of the ban on images could not just as well be presented as a "refinement" or "precisioning" of God's hiddenness.[116] Perhaps the ontological paradigm of depiction on the basis of similarity and thus the impossibility of making the invisible God visible is too narrow for theology. In order to render this assumption plausible we will now clarify more fully the difference between invisibility and hiddenness and inquire into its significance for our topic.[117]

5.2 Dimensions of the Concept of Images in Luther's Theology

"That person does not deserve to be called a theologian who looks upon the invisible things of God as though they were clearly perceptible in those things which have actually happened....He deserves to be called a theologian, however, who comprehends the visible and manifest things of God seen through suffering and the cross."[118] What Luther stated in the famous Heidelberg Disputation led him later to the idea that the traditional term of the invisible church (*ecclesia invisibilis*) should be replaced and more appropriately expressed in terms of the "hidden church." This shift from invisibility to hiddenness not only betrays reservations about Platonic dualizations of reality but is so tightly linked to Luther's perspectives on justification and the theology of the cross that a Lutheran theology of images should not altogether ignore it.

The appropriate correlative for theology is not the invisible that is above all forms of perception. Such a propensity for the visible is instead characteristic of the piety of good works, for which it is essential to appear beautiful and good. We arrive at knowledge of God only when the foolishness of the cross is taken seriously, in contrast to speculative wisdom and philosophical theology. In a marked allusion to Exodus 33:23 Luther describes the knowledge required as something that takes place a posteriori, in hindsight and delay, and *sub contrario*, in contrast with suffering and the cross. The soteriological-ecclesiological consequence would be that the church is not the community of saints because new life is manifest among them, but for reasons of their faith that God is able to justify sinners in contrast to all their deeds and in contrast to the church's appearance. The church is not a *civitas platonica* nor an idea to be grasped by reason alone, nor is it an ideal in contrast to a reality that lags behind and remains somehow deviant. Precisely this coupling with the difference between ideal and reality is one of the reasons why the separation of the invisible from the visible was no longer sufficient for Luther's fundamental insight into the theology of justification. The *sanctorum communio* (communion/community of saints) is the *congregatio fidelium* (congregation of the faithful) because the saints are hidden (from one another as well as from themselves). It is therefore credited as community, contrary to the apparent state of affairs.

This jusificational perspective should be kept in mind when we attempt to interpret Luther's often-cited statement about the competition

148

between image and word: "For [real, divine] service we need no bells nor churches…images and pictures.…All these are human inventions, mere matters of taste. God does not regard them, and too often they obscure with their glitter the true service of God."[119] In this passage the Reformation's fundamental distinction between human works (here the actions performed in worship and the things present in the church building) and the righteousness that is valid before God is illustrated in a densely packed comparison in terms of image theory. As the sanctity of the inner person is not constituted by the external donning of holy robes, so true worship does not take place in works but by faith alone. Images, like church bells or gowns, are not necessary for salvation. Thus it remains a matter for human decision whether and where such things are used. That is a motif familiar to and characteristic for a Protestantism of inwardness. Still, on a second layer this motif pays attention to the ambivalence that images, as media of visibility, also serve as instruments to cover and obscure something. It is just because they strengthen visibility that they must be used in a specific way, namely, so that they no longer cover up what is taking place in a hidden way. Reading the text in that sense we are not denying that one can understand Luther's remarks also along the lines of the opposition that shaped its significance in the Confessional Age, namely the contrast between the blazing appearance of images on the one hand and the sobriety of the word on the other. But we must not necessarily read it that way, for we know that Luther not only intervened against the Wittenberg iconoclasm initiated by Karlstadt through his Passiontide sermons, defending the right of the faithful to use images; above all, he never defined the relationship of word and image antagonistically or in the sense of a dualistic devaluation of the iconic.

Thus his sermon "Von der Betrachtung des heiligen Leidens Christi" was directed against a piety of the passion that ignores "the true fruits of Christ's Passion" by merely looking at the images as a work that gives grace and trying in vain to defend themselves "with pictures and booklets" against all kinds of dangers.[120] Such all-but-magical forms of the use of images are blunders because they want to effect freedom from suffering by beholding Jesus's own suffering, which corresponds to an understanding of the Mass as a ritual that succeeds *ex opere operato* (from the performance of the act as such). However, protest against that kind of piety does not exclude usage of images.

Reformation faith, regarding the passion, aims at the relationship between knowledge of Christ and knowledge of self, namely, "that you deeply imagine and never doubt the least, that you are the one who thus martyred Christ."[121] Since at the same time the believer participates in Jesus's resurrection and its benefit (that God's righteousness is assigned to him), the human person turns into "the picture of Christ and his sufferings, be it realized in life or [for nonbelievers] in hell."[122] Thus Luther does not argue against the use of pictures of the passion but for a specific way of contemplation, through which the faithful experience resurrection to a new life, while those who persist in unbelief draw the suffering they behold onto themselves. Luther concluded, "But this kind of meditation is now out of use and very rare, although the Epistles of St. Paul and St. Peter are full of it. We have changed the essence into a mere show, and painted the meditation of Christ's sufferings only in let-ters and on walls."[123] It is not the image of the passion itself that is the object of critique but a church tradition that does not know how to use its pictures in evangelical fashion.

Therefore Luther could read Paul's description of the community as an assembly of those before whose eyes "Jesus Christ was publicly exhibited as crucified" (Gal 3:1) within the horizon of a hermeneutics of images that, while aimed at the *inner* image that transforms human beings into the image of God, does not by that attitude reject external images: "For whether I will or not, when I hear of Christ, an image of a man hanging on a cross takes form in my heart, just as the reflection of my face naturally appears in the water."[124] As natural as is a reflec-tion in water, so is seeing indispensable for all human understanding. That "we…have to grasp all things that we cannot really know through images"[125] is the hermeneutical presupposition for Luther's theology of images. It takes into account the conviction that the human being is not a purely rational being but an *animal rationale, habens cor fingens* (a rational animal with an imagining heart).[126] The ambiguities into which the human being falls and in which sinners lose themselves, but also the consolation through which the besieged conscience can bear its contradictions, are closely bound up with the tension between reason and imagination. That is, when the heart, frightened by images under-lining human sin and the death of sinners, generates forms of superfi-cial worship and works-righteousness, and perverts the "natural light of reason"[127] into mere instrumental rationality. Such a heart obscures salvation by trying to earn justification by itself and thus turns reason into a "whore." Luther's choice of terms aims at the accusation that rea-son surrenders itself to random purposes. But such misuse of reason expresses a paralysis of imagination by false use of images. It does not eliminate the constitutive relationship between reason and imagination.[128] Hence the justification of the godless changes nothing in the nature of the human heart; it is neither denatured nor replaced, but certainly the images of death are replaced by those of life.[129] The renewal of believers takes place in the exchange of images; the new life *in Christo* gains form and power over human self-centeredness. To that extent neither faith nor Lutheran theology weaken the power of imagination. The unavoidability and right of the imagination are anthropologically based and—unlike in rationalism—come to fruition. This is apparent (with consequences extending also to Lutheran churches) in the right to have images. The *theo*logical basis of that legitimacy in the narrower sense lies in the way God acts toward humans, according to Luther: "That has always been our Lord God's way, so that it is not ears alone that hear, *sed etiam oculis viderent* [but rather they conceive through the eyes]."[130]

Certainly Luther sharply criticized the use of images whenever it was an expression of works righteousness, veneration of the saints, or a self-portrait of the ecclesiastical institution in the figure of Mary. But the abolition of idolatry demanded in such contexts was never about images as such. Hence Luther never even mentioned the ban on images in his popular catechisms intended as introductions to Christianity.[131] He spoke directly against the idea "that the gospel should destroy and blight all the arts, as some of the pseudo-religious claim. But I would like to see all the arts, especially music, used in the service of Him who gave and made them."[132] The special position accorded to music in this passage is partly due to Luther's personal preference and partly to the occasion for the writing (the words are from the preface to the Wittenberg hymnal); it does not justify a suspicion that Luther's basic attitude was antipictorial. Those who hold that opinion are also inclined to suppose that the privileging of music reveals the inwardness of Augustinian piety and its orientation to rational structures of order,[133] whereas the visual arts make space for the power of anomic fantasy. Against such assessments we should keep in mind that a general rejection of the visual arts by Protestantism cannot be justified by Luther's texts.

For that reason Luther's references to the gleam of pictures and the misunderstandings thus created can be interpreted not only theologically but also as aesthetically relevant points. It would be a one-sided systematics that would regard images primarily or exclusively as copies compared to things they can never fully match. Referential imaging as relationship to an object that is recognizable in its reproduction is the concern of a special use of images. Their unique character must be conveyed from different perspectives, and here the theological distinction between what is visible and what is essentially hidden can make a contribution. If, in terms of image theory, we underestimate the internal tension between representation and absence, between givenness and withdrawal, it is no wonder that we also raise barriers to a right understanding of the preaching of the gospel. In such a case we easily fall victim to the suggestion of visibility, which recommends good works and demonstrable fruits of faith or palpable demonstrations of God's power but knows nothing about God revealing himself in the unsightliness of the Crucified. But those who hold fast to the justification of the godless, contrary to the appearance of their lives, are able to see something specific: "In a word, if you would see the holy Christian Church painted in living color and shape, comprehended in one little picture, then take up the Psalter. There you have a fine, bright, pure mirror that will show you what Christendom is."[134] Here we find a struggle over the imaginative power in a multitude of mental pictures that inwardly resonate with the visible. A hermeneutics following Luther—if we may summarize the dimensions thus presented—has little reason to interpret the ban on images as a basic motif for a theological theory of images.

5.3 The Ban on Images and the "Image of God"

The ban on images as a prohibition of the worship of foreign gods is primarily directed not outward (see §II.2.2b.2) but inward: it defends the transcendence of God above all as his unavailability that applies to Israel itself. This insight is crucial in every instance in which the apparent nearness of God was celebrated in the temple cult or in synagogal worship, or when it was recalled in the giving of the law, the exodus from Egypt, or the dedication of the temple (see §II.2.2a–b). That, at any rate, is how interpreters have perceived it historically. God's freedom and difference are to be made secure in the face of all human attempts to instrumentalize God or to objectify him, and so the dialectic between gift and withdrawal, nearness and distance, or revelation and hiddenness is to be maintained. It is not God's invisibility that is to be protected by the ban on images; it is resistance to transparency.

This interpretive perspective points to an analogy between the ban on images interpreted along these lines and the internal relationship between an understanding of the human being as image of God and human dignity as guaranteed in constitutional law. Even if that relationship is not to be read as legitimizing the secular law of the state on the basis of religious convictions, but instead the openness of the constitution to alternative interpretations is to be kept in view, it is at this point that people like to emphasize the relationship between theology and law, something that likewise sheds light on the reception of the ban on images.

Theology in our time does not see human beings in the horizon of the creation myths of ancient Near Eastern religious history and their biblical echoes, any more than it still posits a cosmological basis for the exceptional position of humans. Theology nowadays considers humanity's definition as image of God as linked to processes of erudition and human *self-determination*,[135] that is, within the horizon of freedom. The human being is not only a being open to the world (Max Scheler) and the undetermined animal (Friedrich Nietzsche) but has to do with openness above all in self-understanding (Helmuth Plessner). Just as God is indefinable, so impossible is it to locate human beings definitively within the fixed boundaries of a given identity.[136] Since it recognizes that individual existence cannot be viewed in any other way than as possessing the right of free self-determination, contemporary Lutheran theology acknowledges the relativizing of all state authority over the inviolable dignity of the human being, as secured by the Constitution. It regards that dignity as the expression of the relationship between God and the human being in which the unity of God's revealedness and hiddenness is the foundation of the image-of-God character of humans. Human beings are inviolable precisely in the sense that they incorporate and represent a transcendence no one else has a right to disprove. In that sense the category of image-of-God defends the inaccessibility of the human being as the ban on images defends the transcendence of God. Or, to use the words of Gerhard Ebeling,

> The God who has made human beings in the divine image is the same [God] whose revelation...makes known the mystery of divine hiddenness, without eliminating it....Human beings correspond in that they themselves are first revealed and come to the truth because their lives are hidden in God....The hidden God and the hidden human being...correspond.[137]

153

Ebeling reads the theological category of *absconditas Dei* and Plessner's expression *homo absconditus*[138] in the sense that the ban on images and the concept of image-of-God belong together.

Even though there may be historical doubts about this interpretation because it overlooks the terminological difference between *ṣelem* and the concept of *pesel* on which the Decalogue focuses, it has its place in the context of questions of reception history (but cf. also §II.3.2c). It nonetheless applies where ideas of transcendence and hiddenness are treated with regard to negativity, that is, as directed against immediate givenness. It is not a positive endowment (such as speech, reason, or upright posture) that makes human beings the image of God but God's special relationship to them, which excludes an understanding of subjectivity as a form of arbitrary domination over the self. It may also be said that as little as human beings are able to penetrate the being of God, they are equally impenetrable to themselves. It is in this correlation that we encounter the ban on images and the human as image of God. We need to say something briefly about the consequences.

5.4 "Images Let Us See"

The sciences of images emerging from the so-called *iconic turn* differ no more clearly from traditional philosophies of imagery on any point than with regard to their assessment and treatment of the concept of depiction. When Hans Belting declares that "simple mimesis was never the be-all and end-all of picture-making,"[139] we may read this statement first as a mere restriction of the traditional paradigm. But if we are to understand that images make visible what cannot be seen without them, their achievement is more comprehensive than mimetic depiction. To formulate in Ernst Cassirer's terms, their function is not merely copying of existing things but "configuring *towards* being."[140] After Kant proclaimed the Copernican revolution, philosophy could no longer make use of the concept of depiction; the result was a crisis of representation. Cassirer reacted against it, using Wilhelm von Humboldt's concept of the inner form of language, that is, signs, images, words, and symbols do not identify and represent a world that is already complete without them but rather are means to open up reality and give access to it. The symbolic forms articulate meaning and establish determinateness of being. Even when we cannot deny that we in fact use images as depictions, it does not follow that such use is the most elementary and primary or that it defines the basic function of images. To that extent the current consensus (as expressed, e.g., by Gottfried Boehm),[141] says that images do not reflect or depict but rather make visible. That formula may be traced historically to the words of Paul Klee ("art does not reflect the visible; it makes visible")[142] or Martin Heidegger ("The essence of the image is to let something be seen. But the depictions and copies are themselves mutations of the real image, which…allows us to see the invisible").[143] That point of view is the watershed between a traditional concept of the image and one that is refined transcendental-philosophically or media-theoretically.

Images reveal and conceal; they draw boundaries between the visible and the unseen. They open our eyes and offer ways of seeing, but their strategies for visualization at the same time close off other possibilities. The revolutionizing of painting by the introduction of central perspective—scarcely accidentally—has introduced one of the most important concepts of the critique of knowledge that has shaped both modernity and postmodernity. We cannot get rid of the idea that *perspectives* must be adopted in order to see something. This idea has shaped our understanding of knowledge and science. Its flipside, however, should not be forgotten: to share a perspective often means to "overlook" something. With the diversion of the view other things withdraw (what is in the background, outside the frame, or blurred does not come into sight). That conviction does not run into arbitrariness of each perspective or the indifference of all standpoints, but it calls for a change of perspective as working on the limitation of human insights, even though a total view, a *view from nowhere*, cannot be achieved.[144] To that extent every *por*trayal is likewise a *be*trayal; every image is the suppression of another way of viewing. Therefore (to put it perhaps somewhat dramatically) the donative character of the image (the gift of the image to *let* us see), its opening of the visible,[145] cannot be thought of independently of the withdrawal it expects of the viewer.[146] Luca Giuliani begins his book *Image and Myth*[147] with a motto from William J. T. Mitchell that pointedly summarizes this matter: "We can never understand a picture unless we grasp the ways in which it shows what cannot be seen."[148] The makers of images (in the widest possible sense of the word) hence work to "portray the unportrayable."[149] They present what cannot be seen in the midst of the visible. We will come back to that from the viewpoint of time and representation in the next section. But it should be clear in what sense images are phenomena of transcendence in which the thresholds and borders between the visible and the unseen (thus not necessarily the invisible) are established, and where they are also transgressed.

An interpretation that shifts from the invisibility of God to the dialectic of revelation and hiddenness sheds new light on the ban on images showing that it need no longer be regarded as exclusively icono-clastic or necessarily critical of imagery. The negation of imagery has been emphasized one-sidedly in the history of reception, but the ban on images can also increase self-awareness of the picture-making animal, can sharpen and strengthen the competence of image-making. Such impulses are released above all when the idea of God is shifted within the horizon of negative theology. The challenge of this move comes to the fore in image theory.

6. The Power of Images: Making Present and Intensifying Presence

We have spoken above about the power of images from the point of view of representations of rulers and the stabilization of power in the context of political iconography. In this chapter, I return to the power of images, which is factually presumed in those phenomena. Previously we were concerned with images of power; now it is time to speak of the power of images understood as their ability to create a solid presence.

6.1 Ambivalent Presentations

According to Gottfried Boehm the power of the image "awakens out of the ability to make present an impalpable and distant being, lending it a presence such that it is able to fill the space of human attention to the full."[150] There can be no doubt: images are attractive and, as "eye-catching," they appeal for our attention. This is true not only of erotic images, though it is especially clear in their case. The strategy of over-powering, with which advertising creates such an allure for the sake of preserving market share, is certainly also recognizable in images of pure violence from whose brutality we recoil in horror and try to turn our eyes away[151]—and, depending on one's personal sensitivity, also in documentations of real violence, though more from their staging and self-staging.[152] Their revolting character is, we may say, a counterpart to what is "eye-catching," a rearrangement of the power of the image within the same household. When Boehm says that such power "awakens out of" the image, he leaves open the question of what part of the process is due to the image and what to the subjective "economy of attention" (Georg

157

Franck),[153] that is, the disposition of the viewer. When, finally, people speak of the "enchantment" of pictures or, in a religious-historical context, of the "magic of the image" and the "spell" they exude, it is as if this were an objective force with which the image is atmospherically laden. It is then an easy step to see the ban on images as breaking through such power of appearance and to refer its freedom-preserving sense not only to the sovereignty and transcendence of God but also to the freedom of the recipients: while images captivate, God's word makes free. But at this point we should also consider that such a contraposition, despite its *particula veri*, remains inadequate, and that the hermeneutics of the ban on images can profit from a more profound set of reflections produced by recent image theories.

6.2 Folding Together of Presence and Absence

Everyone who uses photographs as an aid to memory will admit that "presence and absence are inextricably intertwined in the riddle of the image."[154] We hold present and "fast" in the image what in the course of time moves away or from which we are forced to separate spatially. The image represents, it makes present what is not given here and now.[155] As mentioned above (§3.8), to the extent that making present is making present *again* (*re*-presentation), a cultural-historical perspective is once more useful here, because images played a central role in the cult of the dead (and they still do). The layout of graves and the production of mummies were image practices;[156] sculptures—frequently used as burial objects—and the iconic representation of an entire army[157] all express the enduring power of the imperial ruler that accompanies him even in death. In pre-Christian Rome, masks of dead ancestors, often represented by actors,[158] were carried in funeral processions so as to depict the community between the living and the dead. Wisdom 14:15–16 probably has corresponding practices in view when it says that, when his son died prematurely, a father had an image made in which the deceased—in the view of the text—was worshiped as a god or at least was kept present in the context of ritual celebration. Even though one can only speculate about the meaning and function of the cave paintings of Lascaux, Altamira, and elsewhere it seems clear that—whether as part of the magic of the hunt, a cult, or the taming of panic—they made present what was absent.[159] Even the auto-icon commissioned by Jeremy Bentham (1748–1832) to be made from his corpse, not as a wax figure but as a mummy, aimed at the desire to be present beyond death in "a man who is his own image," and thus *in corpore* to participate in university conferences."[160]

Such an image practice can only be understood if it has a basis and reference point in the image, or at least in what is believed about the image. We may think of the constitutive distinction between the medium and what it shows, between the visual and what it makes visible. With regard to these two moments of the image, the real presence of the one in the other is claimed. The archetype is present in the representation, the thing itself is in the image; what is shown is present in the showing in whatever way conceivable. When in view of this structure, Boehm speaks of iconic difference,[161] it consists precisely in the enabling of a presence that is established, so to speak, by the image. Images join presence and absence; they are not only external signs standing for what is absent. Their function in the cult of the dead is probably the product of that structure.

6.3 Presence and Magic

If we think about what is visible in and through the image as a power dwelling within it, the phenomenon of presence-in-the-image can make sorcery and magic with images understandable. As Ernst Cassirer repeatedly emphasized, sorcery and magic make use of the uniqueness of the symbolic form as the link between sense (meaning) and sensory experience, representing a union of intellectual and material that appeared to the archaic mind's immediate grasp as indifference and concrescence. In sorcery performed with images and signs, according to Cassirer, the image is *not yet understood as an image*, the sign *not yet as sign*; rather, in the contiguity of image and thing, the one is incorporated in the other. The image of the enemy is damaged, the buffalo dance is performed because the battle with the enemy or the hunting of the buffalo begins in the image itself.[162] In this sense the image is not a reproduction but a first incorporation of the enemy. The overcoming of such perspectives of the mythical consciousness is the beginning of an awareness of cultural mediation in which human beings discover themselves as *animalia symbolica*—a process to which religions' awareness of difference (as expressed in the Jewish ban on images, but not only there) made a significant contribution. Hans Jonas also describes the fact that only human beings are in a position to grasp images *as images* and so to move from distance to the presence of the given thing as what is characteristic of humans as *homines pictores*: the ability to distinguish type and token, form and matter; thus to differentiate what presents itself to the eye from what is visible within it constitutes human freedom.[163]

6.4 (Re)presentation and Image

Such a focus on freedom also shapes Sartre's phenomenology of imagination,[164] which is mentioned here because it describes the uniqueness of representation in images within the notion of absence. Helpful for an initial approach is the observation of the contexts within which a concept has developed, for the basic term *Vorstellung* as translation of *representatio* or *idea* corresponds, since Locke and Hume, to "image" in both English and French—a word that clearly indicates the significance of image processes in the construction of knowledge. The notion has also been incorporated into German in recent years through the common use of the expression *mental images* (see §II.2.4 above). For David Hume ideas are weak images of strong impressions that the senses mediate. As such they are in a position to represent in weakened form, in other words to make present what the "impression" has left behind.[165]

Sartre then investigates the relationship of these images to what we otherwise call pictures, from photo and caricature by way of pantomime to dream images,[166] all from the governing point of view that an image of his friend Pierre can make present (*rendre présent*) his face and thus Pierre himself during his absence.[167] Sartre's point is that imagination relates directly to "Pierre" in a way analogous to perception; although positing him as absent, it does so in such a way that the mental act and the object are no less internally connected than in the case of perception. The internal unity of act (*noēsis*) and object (*noēma*) consistently characterize consciousness. Against this background Sartre—similarly to Cassirer—posits a thesis regarding the derivative character of magic in archaic religions involving imagery based on the uniqueness of human consciousness:

The subject has ontological primacy. But he incarnates himself, he descends into the image. This explains the attitudes of primitive people towards their portraits and certain practices of black magic (the effigy of wax pierced with a pin, the wounded bison painted on the walls to make the hunt more fruitful). It is not a question, moreover, of a way of thinking that has disappeared today. The structure of the image remained, with us, irrational.[168]

Thinking the image *as image* is said to be a secondary achievement of a consciousness that has become reflective. It is more basic to see Pierre in a painting: "the picture [*shows*] Pierre, though Pierre is not there."[169] The power of imagination, which according to Kant is a hidden artistry in the depths of the human soul that mediates concepts and intuitions,[170] in a sense brings forward presence under the condition of the absence of what is pictured. The coupling of image and presence, according to Sartre, is so fundamental that, he says, the mental image of Pierre disappears as soon as Pierre himself is present.

The later writings of Ludwig Wittgenstein also speak of a unique presence of the thing in the image. While his *Philosophical Investigations*[171] sharply criticize the image theory of his earlier *Tractatus logico-philosophicus* (1918), in which he had asserted that "the problems [in philosophy] have in essentials been finally solved" (i.e. by him),[172] he later draws the consequences for our topic as they are implied in his turn from ideal language philosophy to ordinary language philosophy. Wittgenstein comments on the relationship between God and images, and above all on the idea of representation.

For the earlier position of the *Tractatus* the category of images contains not only paintings, photos, and drawings, but also maps, three-dimensional models, sculptures, and musical scores, even gramophone records.[173] All of these, after all, are depictions that create a relationship between the image and the thing, each by its specific method of projection. Wittgenstein assumes that an image can only reflect reality to the extent that the two have a common form.[174] Therefore he developed a logical atomism according to which a meaningful proposition is an image of a singular fact. The world is everything that is the case, namely, the totality of facts, not of things; the world divides into facts corresponding each to one and only one proposition, and truth or falsehood depends on a comparison with reality.[175] Sentences (pictures) can only be true if there is an isomorphic relationship between their form and that of the world. This leads to assertions that revise what has previously been called the traditional concept of representation under the conditions of logical atomism. "In the picture and the pictured there must be something identical in order that the one can be a picture of the other at all."[176] And: "What the picture must have in common with reality in order to be able to represent it after its manner—rightly or falsely—is its form of representation."[177] The aim of Wittgenstein's *Tractatus* was to identify the realm of meaningful propositions and so to draw a clear boundary between what one can say and what one must remain silent about. The latter, however, can show itself beyond all possibilities of articulating it adequately in propositions.[178] Wittgenstein is referring to what he called "the Mystical," a sphere including everything of importance for humans, be it in ethics, religion, or concerning the meaning of life.

Wittgenstein's *Philosophical Investigations* criticizes these basic assumptions of the *Tractatus*, which had become programmatic for the Vienna Circle, as "grave mistakes"[179] and, in particular, rejects the idea of a single form of representation. The argument is now this: just as it is impossible to reduce the multitude of games to a single common form (e.g., ball games) that makes them all to be games, so it is impossible for one identical form of representation to encompass the nature, uniqueness, and laws of images. It is true that we learn to use images as representations, which we regard from the point of view of similarities, for example when presenting photographs of our holidays to friends. But we must abandon that very notion, or at least set it aside as not being basic when, for example, we look at Michelangelo's paintings on the ceiling of the Sistine Chapel. They show us God, but differently from the way in which our family albums show us our aunts. Wittgenstein emphasizes that Michelangelo did not assume that God looks as he is represented in the picture, precisely *not* because he thought God has a different appearance—as if, for example, his painterly technique were not well developed enough to present a correct image—but because Michelangelo is using the image in a different way.[180] The logic of the relationship of similarity that makes the image a representation of reality can be suspended without the image's ceasing to be an image. The image shows God, and it does so in a form that according to Wittgenstein could certainly be expressed by saying "God is in the picture."[181] For in painting the gesture of the creating God awakening Adam to life, the artist shows everything that is important in the relationship between God and human beings. The rule under which this picture is viewed and understood can, of course, only be grasped by knowledge about beliefs of Jewish-Christian religion and about the way in which religion orients the lives and actions of believers, both Christian and Jewish.

Such a description may also, under some conditions, include the issue whether the statement "God is in the picture" implies an offense against the biblical ban on images. But that question cannot be answered on the basis of a general ontology of the image. "What is the case" can only be recognized in the practice of religion and its way of life. Whether an image is worshiped or only honored, what expectations are laid upon it and how actions are oriented to it—all this must be described in order to understand the significance of images in religion. A theological interpretation of the ban on images can thus not be founded on the basis of representation, possibly enhanced with a conceptual definition of the idea of God. Instead, understanding the prohibition requires a judgment in light of other religious convictions. The hermeneutics of the ban on images turns from semantics to pragmatics. Its key issue becomes the usage of images.

6.5 Preliminary Conclusion

We may say in summary that images make what is absent to be present and that this representation can be experienced, depending on the type of image, as an intensification or increase of presence. Visibility in the image can exalt the intensity of what attracts the eye, even to the point at which looking at the picture is experienced as "pausing" and "lingering"[182] or as a "blink of the eye" or a "decisive moment."[183] The fact that the practice of devotion may be pursued as meditation on an image or as prayer-through-viewing is thus rooted in the abilities of the image itself. There is need for a closer investigation of the temporal structuring of images and contemplation, including the question whether images can initiate a time of their own (cf. also §II.3.2a–b). Boehm speaks of an "indwelling temporality" in images that challenges an understanding of their character as process.[184] The image requires a figuration, "a genesis, that is, time, which it makes to be and to appear as what it respectively is and appears to be."[185] "Temporal reconstruction of the image"[186] is a category of aesthetic reception, though of course it is also correct to note that the *production* of the image has its own temporality. Visualization, consequently, becomes a basic concept that seeks to understand the image not according to the model of "all at once,"[187] and not under the paradigm of a *nunc stans* as a fixed hub in the (rolling) wheel of time. Rather than thus deriving the image from stopped movement, from a frozen moment, we may instead discover in the image itself the borderline character of such figurations of time. The moment is what it is because it passes. Likewise, iconic representation cannot exclude the temporal uniqueness of perception; rather, it repeats it.[188] The connection between time and the power of imagination, which we encounter in Kant (especially emphasized in Heidegger's interpretation of the chapter on schematism in the *Critique of Pure Reason*), is the philosophical-historical background to such considerations.

At any rate, where an immediate identity between an image and what it makes visible impresses reception, a specific power in the *image* seems at work. The limit concept of iconic representation is the glance under a spell, in which the viewer seems to be overpowered by the image.[189] But understanding the image *as image* means escaping the spell and entering again into the process of melding representation and reception, which is temporally structured (see above, §6.3). Following Kant's terminology one could say that aesthetic intuition tends toward totality, a *simul totum*. This is a pure threshold because human knowledge is always coined by the discursive mind. That is precisely how it differs, as finite knowledge, from the *intellectus divinus*. We could also say that every act of contemplation realizes that one cannot achieve what the image promises.

6.6 Concentration of Presence and Availability

When Old- and New Testament criticism of cultic images repeatedly denounces the fact that they are nothing but things made by human hands, the issue is the rejection of the suggestion of power. Reference to the origin of the cultic image in the craftsperson's work and drawing parallels with the production of other useful objects leads religious ideas back from the presence of the deity to the ground of human acting. We are reminded of the craft underlying the image, ignored or forgotten. Such criticism no longer understands the ritual by which the image is made as something that gives the image a theophoric quality. The focus of attention in the prophetic criticism lies not on the function of manifesting the presence of a god but on the uncovering of the ignorance in the human process of representation. The prophetic voices do not reproach the cults of foreign gods for the seductiveness of the images due to their palpability and physicality but for the lack of reflection on one's own activity in creating the representation.

A reflective process of interpretation comes to the fore and takes the place of an understanding of the golden calf simply as a symbol of Canaanite nature- and fertility cult, an image of the power that Yʜwʜ seems to lack here and now and that therefore causes the people to seek another god. The image of the calf or bull can certainly be thought of as representative of the God who led Israel out of Egypt, but no one should think that the presence of this God can be compelled by means of the image and make God available for human purposes: such a presence would preserve neither the freedom of divine hiddenness nor the hiddenness of our own freedom.[190] It is not the iconic representation as such, but the suggestion that God might be subject to availability that is the primary point of view from which the ban on images is to be understood.

This leads us to the way in which Karl Barth interprets the ban on images in §17 of his *Church Dogmatics*. Whereas God's self-revelation is God's own free work of grace, owing nothing to the creature, *religion* is characterized by being the kind of unbelief in which the human "attempts…to justify and to sanctify himself before a capricious and arbitrary picture of God."[191] Even if we may think that the relationship between revelation and religious experience cannot be adequately described along these lines, still the systematic point of this interpretation of the ban on images is clear. Barth associates the Reformation thesis of the futility of any human self-justification, the critique of Deutero-Isaiah on *homo faber*, who even makes his own gods, and the projection thesis that is part of Feuerbach's critique of religion. The image concretizes a relationship to the self that remains, in principle, in conflict with what can be understood as transcendence in the strict sense. The human being who seeks to assure righteousness before God through works of the law is like the makers of idols, who fall short of what they seek. God's revelation contradicts those arbitrarily fashioned images, but it does not impose aniconism with violence since it does not ignore that the human being is the kind of creature that needs images. It is not a turning away from images but a critical self-awareness (including the awareness of the gap between human action and God's difference) that then becomes the point. The consequence is that just as it is faith alone that allows human beings to achieve a good work, so a sense for the sovereignty of God also liberates human use of images. Thus must the argument be developed— even against Barth's own statements.

6.7 Image and Sacrament

What we have called an iconic intensification of presence also sheds light on the relationship between image and sacrament. Faith in the presence of Christ in bread and wine (however it may be described) creates a competition with the power of images to make present, as we have described above. At the same time, and in reverse, the presence of Christ celebrated in the Lord's Supper opens up not only image-critical but also image-productive dimensions.

Both the affinities identified above between image and corporeality (cf. §3) and the iconic interpenetration of presence and representation are challenges to the development of eucharistic theology. The problems are already evident before doctrines about the real or the spiritual presence of Christ in bread and wine are completely developed, since the basic dimensions of the sacramental celebration show that breaking and distribution of the bread, as well as the passing of the wine, are actions with a clearly iconic quality. Beyond that, they also recall various scenes in the narrated story of Jesus while interpreting his suffering and death as the offering of his life "for us." Bread and wine are themselves not arbitrary conventional signs that can be interpreted nominalistically or replaced by other signs. They are elements that, through their institution by word, are elevated above all other objects and acquire sacramental character. They become saving media of the presence of Christ. The Eucharist, or Lord's Supper, does not point to something or someone absent; it celebrates the presence of Christ in the community, and in such a way that in the communion the assembly of believers knows itself to be the body of Christ. True presence and even—in Luther's terms— real presence of the body of Christ are the main thing of the sacramental celebration; not images.

Paul's paraenesis of the Lord's Supper already introduced this paradigm of a competition (between images and sacrament) when arguing that those who belong to the table fellowship of the Christian community cannot take part in the pagans' service and worship of idols (thus 1 Cor 11 culminates in v. 14 even though v. 30 might sound like a reversal). Recalling Israel's time in the wilderness, Paul emphasizes to the community how impossible and categorically excluded is any kind of participation in the cult of foreign gods on their part. It is true that the pagan idols may reveal a seductive power (concretely: pleasure in eating meat from the market that is culturally associated with pagan sacrificial feasts), but under the sign of the one, true God such gods are degraded to nothings (and demons). Paul associates the ban on images and the Eucharist in a systematic constellation that becomes part of Christian tradition, independently of the question whether the law of the old covenant (and so the ban on images in the Decalogue) is obligatory for Christians or not.[192]

Thus it is no surprise that theological arguments for iconoclasm insist that only bread and wine can be regarded as the true image of Christ; icons cannot. That was the statement of the anti-iconic declaration of the "Headless Council" of Hieria ("Mock Council of Constantinople," 754), which furnished the Emperor Constantine V with legitimation of his iconoclastic policies. Its conclusions were rejected, or corrected, by Nicaea II (Second Council of Nicaea, 787), but also by the General Synod of Frankfurt under Charlemagne in 794.

The competition between image and sacrament continued, however. Within it, in the Western church, questions of participation in salvation or damnation, godly and ungodly were transformed in the course of the struggle over the obligatory representation of God. The development of medieval eucharistic theology, in the form of the doctrine of the real presence of Christ in bread and wine—rejecting a "merely" symbolic representation—not only had dimensions of the search for "real" salvation in the context of the history of devotion; it also reflected the power politics at work in the debate over competing claims to representation. Those who fought for the real presence of Christ in bread and wine defended the significance of the priestly representation of God (even before there was a fully developed doctrine of transubstantiation), and so relativized the claims of political rulers to embody God or to being anointed as agents of the Spirit. Actions in worship and in the church in general could not be merely symbolic in the sense that the mundane side (i.e., the realm of political leadership) could then have claimed to be the sole reality. The rejection of the power of images is a relativizing of the power of the ruler who is projected in them. For it is only the sacrament of the altar that makes present the power of the One before whom all knees must bow. To that extent eucharistic theology is determined neither by concern for certainty of salvation alone nor by speculative interest in realism. It is, above all, a matter of political theology.

Rethinking the image, it is striking that the expectation that the power of the image would create a powerful presence was absorbed by the sacramental event. The host became an image, the only image in which the presence of Christ is given and salvation may be received. Different from ordinary bread, of course, even if the host remains a tiny disk,[193] anything but attractive for the senses. Image and the aniconic, figural representation and sacramental form are thus interwoven. Likewise, the recollection of the consumption of the golden calf (ground up by Moses before all the people, Exod 32:20), required by the imposition of the ban on images, furnishes a contrasting motif to the saving reception of the body of Christ.

Belting emphasizes that the competition between image and sacrament over the privilege of true presence and transforming power had consequences for the understanding and production of images. What images lost in the denial of their power of representation, by the solitary positioning of the sacrament, they compensated for, so Belting thinks he can show, by an escalation of realistic depictions.[194] Increasing their power to impress became the program of images that, while not forbidden, had been deposed from their rank in the hierarchy of representation by the sacrament. In this respect also a hermeneutics of the ban on images may as well accept the fact of dialectic, for it is true that the deposed images developed a richer life in the shadow of their negation and demystification.

The competition between image and sacrament may prove more enduring than the much-invoked principal and fundamental opposition between image and word,[195] to which we will now turn.

7. Seeing versus Hearing, Image versus Word: Protestant Constellations of a Theology of Images?

Again and again we encounter attempts to trace competing religious or alternative ontological positions regarding the world to different privilegings of the two principal human senses. So one often reads that the difference between seeing and hearing governs the antithesis between a Catholic Church oriented to the visibility of its offices, the elevation of the host, the monstrance and Corpus Christi processions, colorful robes, and a liturgy that appeals to the senses (and therefore is fit to encounter the new media), and a Protestantism that attends only to the word and *obedience* to God, with its worship space organized as a lecture hall, bound likewise to an antiquated cultural medium (the book) and an individual, inner-directed reading.[196] Such a schematic contrast is just as appropriate for flagging a basic Western constellation of Greek-pagan and Jewish-Christian shaping as alternatives between two different worldviews: one that founds its ultimate and highest certainty in visibility, in the *logos* as the sum of having-seen, and consequently in rational *insight* into the order of what is always the same, and another that is characterized by faith in one God whose law opens itself only to those who will listen, while the world appears as a constantly changing, contingent order in which humans ultimately cannot find a home.[197] To put it succinctly: "If Hellas is called the 'eye of the world,' Israel can be said to be 'the ear of the world.'"[198]

The subject for discussion in the present context is not the reliability of such contrasting structures for confessions or cultures but only the question whether these attributions are part of the history of the reception of the ban on images. Even so, turning away from the image is recognized as the mark that singles out Judaism among ancient cultures (see above, §II.2.2a). As has been shown in the section on exegesis, the form-critical embedding of the Decalogue (and thus also the ban on images) in the narrative of the revelation of God on Sinai/Horeb represents an important precondition for the complex of ideas being discussed here (see above, §II.3.2a–b). However, it would be impossible to reconstruct the genesis of such classifications without taking into account the social- and religious-historical strategies of inclusion and exclusion in perceptions of Judaism and also its members' own self-description.

It is not especially surprising that the contrast between seeing and hearing is also a subject of interest to current Old Testament research:

> Even in his appearing, God himself was not visible but only audible. Thus this example not only gives hearing a priority over sight in regard to the idea of God but creates within that idea an actual opposition between hearing and seeing, word and image, even though immediately before this the text spoke of phenomena in Nature accompanying the theophany. Even if those effects of YHWH's appearing are perceptible, God himself remains "formless," not subject to representation; he approaches humans only through his voice.[199]

To the extent that this voice primarily articulates itself in prohibiting images, the consequence for the interpreter is plain: the imageless revelation of the God so resistant to visibility is, tendentiously, not a theophany but a "theo-phony,"[200] and demands listening to the law as the counter to Greek-pagan-polytheistic concentration on the magic of visual appearances.

The *particula veri* (particles of truth) in this suggestion were sketched in the section on Luther (see above, §5.2). It consists in a command to distance oneself from appearances in favor of the nonapparent character of the Word that has come into the world and that absolves human beings despite the visible evidence of their sins, by the power of faith in the voice of the Good Shepherd. In this sense Luther could say that the kingdom of Christ is a hearing kingdom, not a seeing kingdom: "for the eyes lead and draw us not there, where we can find and learn to know

Christ, but the ears must do it; but also such ears as hear the word from the lips of the little children and nurslings."[201]

In its constitution the kingdom of Christ stands in contrast with the world whose order must be established and maintained by the use of violence,[202] and in opposition to unbelief, which is unable to recognize the glory of God in the cross.

Thus for Luther the opposition of seeing and hearing has a specific location and context. As far as I can see, Luther never explains it in terms of the ban on images, nor does he import it into general discussions of his understanding of images—to say nothing of using it to describe common cultural attitudes toward the world. When Luther speaks of the ban on images it is mainly within the horizon of the current question about the binding character of the law for evangelical faith, that is, in contrast to the radical positions adopted by Karlstadt and others, and in clear rejection of their opinions. For Luther the ban on images remains an internal matter for Judaism. The law of God whose political use is indispensable for Christians also contains neither a ban on images nor instructions for the use of images; it leaves the matter open and allows for images and for doing without them.

A Protestant hermeneutics of the ban on images and (included within it) of imagery should therefore not be paralyzed by the contrast "seeing versus hearing." It will not, for this reason, include the power of the image in the Sinai pericope under the above-quoted concept of mere "*phenomena accompanying* the theophany," but will treat such a definition rather as collateral damage by a cultural model that we cannot take seriously. Instead we should look for new paths enlightened by scholarship regarding images that lead to a point where neither the Reformed nor the Lutheran interpretation of image and ban on images is convincing.

The observation that Calvin, in a rigorous expansion of his suspicion of images (in worship), advocated an "aesthetics without images," whereas Luther defended the "image without aesthetics,"[203] separates the traditions and is likewise subject to a double-deficit diagnosis: Reformed theology continues to abominate images, whereas Luther's rehabilitation of them is inadequate because it regards the image as illustration and decoration of Scripture, that is, in a literary sense.[204] According to Cottin, there is no aesthetics of the image to be found in Protestantism. If this contrast between the two Reformers is in itself schematic and dualistic, we may still conclude from the deficiencies it notes that the contrast between seeing and hearing does not exhaust the Protestant perspective. It must be restricted to the respective contexts into which the Old Testament or the theology of the Reformation introduces it, but it cannot serve as the organizing principle for Protestant theology of the image (and the word) overall. A simple theological attention to metaphorology forces us to revise these contrasts (see above, §II.3.1).

8. Christological Rehabilitation of Images: Systematic Considerations on the Ban on Images in Ancient Christianity

The Byzantine iconoclastic controversy was also an expression of a problem within an empire that—dependent as it was on religious-political unity—had to achieve integration of both Judaism and emerging Islam within a Christian context. Whereas the use of images, at home in monasticism, shaped Christians' devotional practice, military circles and the Byzantine court in particular were interested in a unified imperial order. In this especially sensitive area, change of rulers and imperial succession involved more than a century of constant unrest over policy regarding images in the wake of religious-political U-turns.

In the Latin West these struggles over images were perceived primarily in terms of a violent iconoclasm and an imperial policy forbidding images, and at the same time were part of the interest in retaining the West's own practice regarding images, which had become a matter of course. The Western church had remained in the background with regard to the special liturgical place of icons and the ultimately victorious dogmatizing of devotion to them. The violent intensity of the strife within the Eastern church remained foreign to it. This was certainly due as well to the way in which the Western church treated the whole subject.

8.1 Didactic Rehabilitation of Images

From the perspective of the Western church the letter written in October 600 by Pope Gregory the Great (b. 540; reigned 590–604) to

Serenus, the bishop of Marseilles, remained the defining word with which church practice defended itself against the charge of violating the ban on images. Serenus, influenced by the strict spirit of ascetic piety, had not only forbidden an appeal to the saints for protection against the pestilence that was raging in the port city of Marseilles, a place foreign to him, marked by a colorful syncretism and terrified of the plague; he had even caused the *sanctorum imagines* (pictures of the saints) to be destroyed.

Gregory criticized the rigorism and mindless zeal of the iconoclasts while acceding to the theological conviction that worship of images was impossible. Nevertheless, he transformed the theological problem, we might say, into one of religious teaching and achieved some clarifying formulae suitable for easing the furor over images. He called on the bishop to see reason and justified the use of images by the uneducated:

> To adore a picture [*picturam adorare*] is one thing, but to learn [*addiscere*] through the story of a picture what is to be adored is another. For what writing presents to readers, this a picture presents to the unlearned who behold, since in it even the ignorant see what they ought to follow; in it the illiterate read. Hence, and chiefly to the populace [*gentibus*], a picture is instead of reading.[205]

Images, accordingly, are media by which biblical teaching can be illustrated for the people: for example, they can internalize "what they ought to follow" from a picture of the Good Samaritan. As *biblia pauperum* (Bible of the poor) the wall paintings are educational provisions for content that is opened to the learned in other ways. This assessment may also be affected by, or make use of, the idea that images more enduringly touch the affective center of human experience than *logos* and *ratio* ever can.[206]

It is worth noting that from such a perspective the image is thought of as a medium for subjective use and not as a manifestation of holiness immanent within it.[207] To that extent the image remains dependent on Scripture or *sacra doctrina* and receives its justification and legitimacy from there.[208] The usefulness of images was discussed without reference to a presence of the holy or of God in them. The operative logic here: when images are disempowered in this way they can safely be left to the people who need them.

Arguments of this kind gave the Latin church the freedom to use images and to legitimate the practice against the attacks of the iconoclasts. But insofar as it made images nothing but instruments and aids to preaching it undermined their proper but ambivalent potential: in this instrumentalizing perspective the images were simply not considered as places of aesthetic-religious experience, as vivid communication of their own truth, or as the presence of God. This move to the secondary aspect has been succinctly articulated by one of our contemporaries in a paraphrase of the decree of the Second Council of Nicaea: "These images already possess a catechetical character; they should be an aid to understanding the message that is received, addressed by God to his own.... By fulfilling this instructive function the images continually point to something other and higher than themselves."[209] Anything that fulfills a purely servant function as a means to understanding remains, whereas any sense for images is set aside. Once images have been trivialized to that level it requires no effort to legitimize them, but this instrumental reading uses a strategy of neutralization.

Accordingly, most reflection on the limits to the legitimate use of images proceeds on the ethical level. One may neither adore an image nor subject oneself to its power; one must distinguish between what belongs to God and what to the image (ultimately between Creator and creature). The internal connection between God's self-representation ("I am the LORD, your God") and the prohibition of images is preserved as long as *latreia* (= *adoratio*) is reserved to God alone. On this condition, it is not necessary to forbid *timē* (= *veneratio*) of the image. Bowing down before a picture, kissing it or placing candles before it, and so on, can be an expression of human surrender to God and God alone, while the image evokes or occasions a remembrance of God, to whom alone belongs all worship and who cannot be captured by any image. Wherever the West took a position on the Byzantine battle over images through the reading of conciliar texts and other written expressions, a central issue was always how Greek *proskynesis* would be translated into Latin. The kind of reverence indicated by this word would determine the legitimacy of a pious practice—a striking example of Wittgenstein's thesis that the limits of language represent the limits of a world.

8.2 Theological Perspectives

John of Damascus († before 754) gave a more profound theological grounding to the legitimacy of images in his three "Treatises on the Divine Images";[210] in particular he disputed the applicability of the Old

Testament prohibition for theological judgment on images. The ban could not be obligatory for Christians because they no longer live under the law—a reasoning in which Paul's treatment of the command for male circumcision was used as a model for theological hermeneutics. The author was not impressed by the fact that Paul, who in Romans 1 presupposes a horror of idols, was being used by the opponents of images as the prime New Testament witness for the contempt for images. John saw that ban as addressed only to the Jews, and given in a situation in which, during their flight from Egypt, they had not altogether escaped the endemic idolatry of the place. Their golden calf was therefore the expression of their falling back into slavery, and this had to be forbidden.

The applicability of the ban in John's own time, however, had come to grips with a new situation and a new threat. For God "himself…was the first to make images and let them be seen,"[211] by ordering that the ark of the covenant be surrounded by cherubim. But above all John grounds the legitimacy of images through a definition of the concept: "The image…is the likeness [*homoiōma*] and example [*paradeigma*] and type [*ektypōma*] of something in that it shows in itself what it represents."[212] This definition is based on distinctions and interprets the image as a manifestation of an internal difference. It may well be the definition's strength that it is able to derive from the unique character of the image the usage that distinguishes legitimate veneration of images from idolatry. After all, the danger of idolatry first arises when the relationship between the image and what it points to (according to the standards of a Neoplatonic idea of participation) is neglected and the immediate presence of the invisible prototype is assumed, with the result that the representation itself appeared as a holy object in which the divine was manifested.[213] But the image need not create such a suggestion of presence; it can just as easily be used according to the degree of distinction that lies within itself.

As we have emphasized above (§4.5), a Neoplatonic concept of imagery can receive contrary accents. Depending on one's choice, the emphasis may fall on the presence of the prototype (archetype) in the representation, or on the difference and withdrawal of the One.

8.3 Participation in the Holy

If the image participates in the reality it reflects—if imagery is even a form of emanation from the One (God)—there is support for the idea that there are also images that neither arise by nature nor are made by human hands (*non-manu-factum*). Belief in such *acheiropoetic*[214] images combines the idea of participation with the thought of supernatural origin such as is immanent in belief in miracles. The presence of the divine in the image is then either guaranteed or attested through its miraculous origin. Coming from God himself, *theographos* (written by God) or being *theoteuktos* (made by God) pointedly means an origin that excludes human activity or any natural cause. Such an abrogation and denial of any kind of mediation is found not only in the theology of images but also in the doctrine of Scripture, if it falls captive to the notion of verbal inspiration.

Through an orientation to divine origin and miraculous creation, Veronica's veil received the designation *vera icon*, for in it the creation of an image of Jesus was believed to be the direct continuation and immediate result of Christ's passion, as Jesus leaves an image of his face in the cloth given to him (cf. plate 3, p. I.3, *Saint Veronica with the Sudarium*).[215] Similarly with the pericope of the woman with a hemorrhage: it was in the moment when she touched his holy body that healing power went out from it, without the intervention of a deliberate decision on Jesus's part to help the woman (Mark 5:25–34; for Paul cf. Acts 19:12). In Veronica's veil the haptic grounds the visual; the touching of the body creates visible traces and realistic depiction. We could also say that belief in relics here gives a foundation for the high estimation of images and transforms the desire for the visible into an interpretation of the image.[216] The true image is the supernatural one that arises entirely without human action. It was only in that exaggerated form that the understanding of worship attacked by the Reformers arose (whether as critique of church practice, in the disenchanting actions of members of the Enlightenment, or in iconoclasts imitating Boniface): an understanding that transforms the image of the holy into the holy image. Where such faith in images was widespread we do not lack accounts of the miraculous powers emanating from the images; they are as common as stories of the miraculous discovery of an image that are woven into sagas or of the weeping and bleeding of pictures damaged by the hands of unbelievers. Such narratives take up motifs we encounter both in the Old Testament stories about the ark of God (1 Sam 5) and in myths about the miracles wrought by images and sculptures.

Whether in popular or refined philosophical/theological versions, belief in images regards the holy picture not as an object one looks at but as a divine reality to which one is exposed (cf. §II.1.1b on the corresponding ideas in the ancient Near East). They are therefore not *made* by an artist; they arise so to speak in the artist and through her or him (*passivum divinum*) in a religious act that is highly in need of purification and asceticism, contemplation and prayer. In the icon, the divine touches the world. It is the window open to a higher reality.

8.4 Theology of the Image and Christology

Against this background it is understandable why the quarrel that began with the question of the applicability of the ban on images developed into a battle over Christology and was ultimately decided on those terms. From the time of the first opponents of images, the idea of a presence of God in the image established a competition between the image experience and faith in Christ. Only the one Son of the Father could be regarded as the true image of God (Col 1:15), the place of divine presence. Those who sought it elsewhere drew suspicion upon themselves and were accused of confusing the mortal with the eternal and thus dishonoring God's divinity. But on the part of the iconophiles—who, because they did not *worship* icons, should not be labeled iconodules—it was precisely thanks to the incarnation of the Logos that mortality was put on the path to immortality. The presence of the spirit of Jesus in the church sanctified everything the church does, and it primarily inspired and transformed worship services. Could one then fail to believe that the "dawn of eternity" shone forth from the icon? The basis for this belief was the incarnation of the Son of God, and the icon par excellence was thus the image of Christ.

The relationships among the idea of participation, theology of images, and Christology are also evident in the fact that both sides could make the argument that the image of Christ is *Christ himself*. We find this supported by Emperor Constantine V as well as by John of Damascus.[217] Those who saw the basis for the ban on images in the encroaching attempt to draw boundaries around the infinite God who cannot be confined ran into difficulties in the realm of Christology. Neither the model of "because Christ is of divine nature he must not be depicted" nor the contrary motto "because he is (nothing but) human he may be depicted" was convincing. In questions of image theology one could acquire the odium of a christological heretic, but one could also be suspected of a one-sided accentuation if one saw everything human so

flooded with the brilliance of divine presence that there was nothing left
to paint. Between monophysitism and Nestorianism, between Alexandrian and Antiochene traditions the attitude toward images was bound
up with doctrinal decisions about Christology. Theology of the image
became a chapter in Christology.

If the ban on images was seen as an implication of God's being God,
the theological value of images was in turn founded on Christology, the
notion of God's becoming human. But there was another side to this
connection with Christology, because, to the extent that this reasoning
was applied, it appeared that not only were images permitted but images
of Christ were the hallmark of an orthodox dogmatics, which is to say
that correct doctrine positively commanded them. Orthodoxy was thus
proved to mean devotion to icons.

Nicaea II, the so-called seventh ecumenical council, accordingly concluded in the fall of 787 that

> as the figure of the honored and life-giving Cross, so the venerable
> and holy images, the ones from tinted materials and from marble
> [!] as those from other material, must be suitably placed in the
> holy churches of God, both on sacred vessels and vestments, and
> on the walls and on the altars, at home and on the streets, namely
> such images of our Lord Jesus Christ, God and Savior, and of our
> undefiled lady, or holy Mother of God [this is included against
> Nestorius], and of the honorable angels, and, at the same time, of
> all the saints and of holy men.

In the conciliar text the following three are explicit: the theological
arguments of John of Damascus and Basil the Great, the distinction
between adoration and veneration, and the conviction that veneration
of the image is for the sake of the primal image (archetype). Accordingly
anyone who casts aside any pictorial representation that has been conse-
crated by the church is a heretic.[218]

The christological implications of image theology were evident
again when the Reformed tradition, whose Christology was always
based on the absolute distinction between divine and human natures,
distanced itself from images. By contrast Lutheranism, which was
closer to the Alexandrian tradition, did not develop such a *reservatio
mentalis*. But what is crucial is that the role of images in worship was
discussed primarily on the level on which it had been regarded since the

time of Gregory the Great in the West: as a practice to be accepted for the sake of the uneducated. Against this line of compromise, Reformed Protestantism insisted on a restoration of pure biblical teaching. Thus the Heidelberg Catechism responded to the question "But may not images, as books for the laity, be permitted in the churches?" with a clear denial: "No: for we must not be wiser than God, who desires that his Christianity be instructed not by dumb idols but by the living preaching of his word."[219]

Those who regard the matter in that way overlook the complex and deep-seated relationships between the image question and Christology, the affinity between image and body, the rejection of all dualisms that might shape theology and anthropology. The fact that Christology likewise demands a decision about the hermeneutics of images may be regarded as a theological achievement of the Eastern church. Of course, it only applied this point to the special world of icons and never thought of drawing consequences from the legitimacy of images of Christ for visual perception in general or for the legitimacy of other images. For us, however, it seems we should once again expand the theological attention for imagery within the horizon of the history of interpretation of the ban on images.

9. Aesthetics within the Horizon of a Ban on Images

In the critical theory of the Frankfurt School the ban on images acquired a history of reception that adopted perspectives from negative theology in the form of a "negative dialectic" and a corresponding "aesthetic theory." That in turn sheds light on iconoclastic strategies in modern art for which the ban on images offers a hermeneutical key. Therefore it is appropriate for a hermeneutics of the ban on images to broaden our perspective as we conclude our essay.

9.1 Prohibition of Images in Critical Theory

As early as their book *Dialectic of Enlightenment*, Theodor Adorno (1903–69) and Max Horkheimer (1895–1973) made "the prohibition against calling on what is false as God" a motto of their critique of bourgeois society. It is said that the fundamental wounds of bourgeois society, proceeding by means of the culture industry from alienation to anti-Semitism, result from a twisting of truth into lies, something that allows only for a damaged life. It is said to be part of the dialectic of modernity that it fails to recognize the kind of enlightenment that myth already provided, and as a result turns its enlightenment into mythology.[220]

This diagnosis presumes the central significance of the combination of the Platonic critique of images and the biblical critique of idols in the self-description of modern science. Francis Bacon (1562–1626) called the biases and related delusions of traditional opinions (as found in language, in theological dogmas, or in the teachings of philosophy) "idols." They are deceptions[221] like those that, according to Plato, the Sophists duped their captives into believing in the reality of shadows, and at the same time they are idols that, in the name of divine truth, must be struck down. The sin of unfreedom and the process of becoming accustomed to error work together, hand in hand. Human beings can only realize their destiny to rule over nature if they learn to describe and explain nature, using the methods of exact science.

Still, the one-sidedness with which the modern sciences push the process of disenchantment motivated by this self-image into a naive positivism only serves to turn the impulse of the Enlightenment into its opposite. Adorno and Horkheimer describe the transition from the methodical mathematicization of knowledge to a technical relationship to nature, paired with a will to exploit nature but also involving the direction of all social relations toward calculation and instrumental rationality.

It is forgotten that the biblical creation accounts were themselves forms of demythologization, though of course they were the kind that did not sacrifice truth and reason to universal predictability. Poetry and art, or thought accustomed to both, perform a corresponding resistance to positivism. Whereas the rationality of the mathematical natural sciences knows only the application of empty forms to a reality that they construct according to the measure of their arbitrary purposes, ancient myth, like the religion of the word, pointed to the internal relationship between thought and reality, language and truth.

Against this background the authors take up the central content of Judaism, with a subtle emphasis on its negative theological character.

> In the Jewish religion…the bond between name and being is still recognized in the ban on pronouncing the name of God. The disenchanted world of Judaism…allows no word that would alleviate the despair of all that is mortal. It associates hope only with the prohibition against calling on what is false as God, against invoking the finite as the infinite, lies as truth. The guarantee of salvation lies in the rejection of any belief that would replace it: it is knowledge obtained in the denunciation of illusion.… The justness of the image is preserved in the faithful pursuit of its prohibition.[222]

The connection between the ban on uttering the name of God and the prohibition against making an image of God for oneself is thus also something that can be accomplished, from a philosophical perspective. Driven from paradise, accepting death and despair as the signs of human finitude, the Jewish religion adopts the *via negationis*: it sees through all positive promises of salvation as being empty, poor affirmations of what is, and guards against confusing the finite with the infinite. Negation and contradiction become the typical forms of remembering the realm of freedom that renounces every belief in a salvation already arrived or a reconciliation already accomplished—especially when the concept of reconciliation is used to romanticize existing circumstances. To avoid such a justification of what exists, as Hegel projected it in his apotheosis of the Prussian state as reason made actual and rational reality, nothing would suffice but a movement of thought that contains all syntheses and thus remains a negative dialectic. Bans on the name and on images, but also the conviction that the Messiah has not yet come: both worked as barriers against the drift of Christian certainty of incarnation toward an absolutizing of the finite even to the point of dissolving eschatology into the present. "Therefore, I see no other possibility than an extreme ascesis toward any kind of revealed faith, an extreme loyalty to the prohibition of images, far beyond what this once originally meant."[223]

From this perspective the situation is such that Christianity, with its belief in the incarnation of God, had revived idolatry, whereas the genuine Jewish combination of prohibitions on speaking the name and making images, expectation of the messiah to come and memory of sacrifices, constitutes the root of a critical theory of society. To that extent the ban on images is an essential paradigm within which the future content of religion can be philosophically reconstructed. What is hermeneutically noteworthy is that in this perspective the ban on images is received primarily as a prohibition against falling back or regression. Regression to the false gods that only promise salvation and thus promote the stabilization of alienation appears as the thing that *absolutely* must be avoided.

Whether, beyond the portrait of negativity founded on the prohibition of images, some view of redemption may surface is something that should be discussed within the horizons of Adorno's aesthetics. There is no room for that here, but in conclusion, and in transition to what follows, we should point out that the visual arts have not capitulated to the ban on images; they asserted themselves precisely through the development of iconoclastic programs of imagery. The negation of the image can itself be set into pictures, and the destruction of the images can be used for the building up of new ones. The following sections will be about that.

9.2 Image-Producing Dimensions of Reformation Theology

The relationship between Reformation theology and the visual arts appears to have been shaped (and, on the whole, damaged) by the central positioning of the word in opposition to the practices of the Roman Catholic Church in regard to images, which roused the suspicion of magical practices. The reaction was expressed most dramatically in the removal and destruction of images in the Reformed churches influenced by Zwingli and Calvin. However, against this assessment in recent years it has repeatedly been objected that Protestantism can also be understood as a trigger for new practices regarding images. (In the Reformation period that is true for Dürer as well as for Cranach, and it is not unfair to think of modern art as influenced by this development.) The following aspects, which we will offer with the necessary brevity and without claiming to be comprehensive, are relevant for a hermeneutics of the ban on images.

(a) Luther's position, developed in response to the Wittenberg attack on images, caused the word to "vanquish"[224] the image, so we constantly hear, but it did not mean defeat of images; rather, they were valued as *adiaphora* (things theologically and morally indifferent). The magical defect is not founded in the image itself but in the false beliefs and superstitions of those who use images wrongly. In and of themselves images and other art objects are neither holy nor sinful but are "worldly things" that can be used with sense and understanding. Referring to Luther's corresponding explanations in the sermons for *Invocatio* ("images are neither this nor that, neither evil nor good, we may have them or not, as we please").[225] Werner Hofmann asserts, "Modernity begins with this charter"[226]—whereby he apparently means an epoch as designated in art history while at the same time insinuating a certain legitimacy and a feeling of starting afresh. The autonomy of modern art appears as the result of an unburdening of images from both the claims and the censure of religion. To that extent Hofmann promotes a theory of modernity that applauds "gaining freedom through Reformation-grounded worldliness and human reason." This idea also appears in many of the coauthors in *Luther und die Folgen für die Kunst*.[227]

(b) This general assessment is associated with the more specific thesis that Luther's insistence on the role of images paved the way for an aesthetics of reception. (Hofmann speaks of an "aesthetics of the beholder"). What the artistic work is or represents is determined by the perspective of the viewer.[228] With reference to the importance of the act of seeing for the meaning of the work (seeing is always "seeing something as something" [see §6.5 above]), Hofmann explains the new forms in which image and religion were associated in the aesthetic experience of modernity. When Caspar David Friedrich could say of the presence of the cross in his pictures that some saw that cross *as consolation*, others as simply a cross,[229] according to Hofmann the freedom of reception comes to the fore.

(c) Such a "switch" in meaning showing up in this historical context is in fact a unique character of aesthetics itself. Likewise, when a "found object" by Marcel Duchamps (e.g., his famous montage of a wheel on a footstool) is received *as* art, the freedom of regard is presupposed. Hence Hofmann says regarding the constitution of art in the eye of the beholder that "it all began with Luther. His devaluation of images swung back into an upward valuation; restriction proved to be liberation."[230] According to this interpretation Luther's theological confrontation with the question of images, and especially his distinction between law and gospel, achieves a very broad significance for the modern understanding of images and therefore for the history of art as a whole. The iconoclasm attached to the ban on images and its return to life during the Reformation led to a ferment in the production of pictures.

(d) Zwingli and Calvin banned images from the churches, but they permitted them in private and public places (in homes, in the city hall, and consequently also in museums). In doing so they de facto promoted new programs in art, because in these new places and contexts the focus shifted to motifs from family life and city history, depictions of citizen or council gatherings, and studies of animals and landscapes. Insofar as pictures were not made for the sake of ostentation but for the study of nature or for private or public memorialization, they were useful and therefore legitimate even for purists. In the wake of such secularization theories (which indeed have systematic pitfalls),[231] it follows that art made a turn from the spiritual to the secular, from a worship function to autonomy, even to *l'art pour l'art*. In tendencies to a bourgeois character in the depiction of biblical scenes, increasingly common and approved in this development, we can, of course, read not only the power of transformation but also the ambivalence of such tendencies.[232]

(e) If the sharp opposition between the intellectual and the sensual, the spiritual and the fleshly, God and image in Calvin's thought led to the restrictive rule that only such things as one could see with one's eyes might be painted, following that one-sided rule *in the long run* promoted a trend to realistic painting. The verdict against imagination and fantasy shaped, for example, the Calvinist-influenced Dutch realism and can even be demonstrated in van Gogh's early work.[233]

(f) The fact that Luther permitted his own translations of the Bible to be printed with a rich variety of woodcuts corresponded to a didactic-illustrative narrowing of the idea of images, the foundation and limitations of which we recalled above (§8.1). Under the preeminence and governance of the word, pictures took on the function of depicting significant moments in biblical narratives. The long-term consequence of such a new functionalization was productive in the development of so-called historical painting. Here *narratio* and *factum* defined the status and significance of the image.[234] In this sense, even the later Zwingli could arrive at an affirmative view of images—to the extent that it was guaranteed that the images were only painted "in historical fashion," that is, that they were created as depictions of historical events.[235]

(g) Countering the overwhelming sensuality of works by Catholics (e.g., Rubens), a Protestant culture of images insisted on the clarity of the word and the purity of the senses (e.g., Rembrandt). In the later development of the arts this tendency was more and more obviously dominant and favored a clearer form. The basic rationalistic side of Protestantism advanced the inclination to abstraction and reveals a distant influence even in the art of Piet Mondrian (see §9.3 below).

(h) Finally, the domination of word over image led ultimately to programs of imagery that made the word itself into a picture. One Reformation example is the altarpiece of the Lutheran Spitalkirche at Dinkelsbühl, which shows only the words of institution and the Decalogue, but does so with pictorial means: "a picture made up entirely of writing"[236] (cf. plate 4, p. I.4).

As early as Rabanus Maurus (ca. 825/26) we find figurative poems (*carmina figurata*) in which image and word, or more precisely image and writing are fused together (cf. plate 5, p. I.5).[237] The collection begins with a picture of Christ in cross form, with outstretched arms, but representing for the observer (reader) an approaching Christ. His whole body consists of letters—unmistakably a programmatic affirmation that Christ can be depicted while at the same time translating the conviction that the picture serves to point to the real mystery of faith. That conviction, however, is represented by the picture. We can find examples in our own time in Klaus Kröger's tablets with writing (cf. plate 6, p. I.6); in oil paintings in which quotations from Sacred Scripture (e.g., from the Synoptic apocalypse) appear as if engraved; in pictures depicting walls recalling the "writing on the wall" (*mene tekel*; Dan 5:1–30) or scratches on prison walls. In this way texts are aesthetically transformed into images.

To the dominance of the word over the image responds, in dialectical reversal, the word in the image and as image. The difference between word and image is erased, maintained, and overcome as the unique character of painterly method develops. A new concept of the image arises in and with the text.[238] Corresponding works can also be found in the art of the Swiss Rémy Zaugg (cf. plate 7, p. I.7), who was influenced by the theology of Karl Barth.

Jochen Gerz, in his pictures displayed at St. Etienne, 1973–75, also deserves notice. The ten pictures in the exhibition represent ten statements (in analogy to the Decalogue), but they were not immediately accessible in the exhibit space; they could only be "deciphered" by technical means that produced a tablet of bans on images from "do not look at me" through "do not compare me" to "make for yourself no image of me."[239]

These are only a few pointers to the aesthetically productive sides of the contrast between word and image.

9.3 Iconoclasm as Aesthetic Strategy

The assertion that modern aesthetics developed its own hermeneutics of the ban on images in working on and with the image cannot here be attested through intense analyses informed by art history. A few references to artists who claim such a connection for their works must suffice.

(a) Kazimir Malevich (1878–1935), with his *Black Square* (1915; cf. plate 8a, p. I.8) and *White on White* (1917; cf. plate 8b, p. I.9) advanced the development of abstract art as separating from existing objects available to be depicted and making structures, forms, and colors independent, in the sense that the image "shows nothing more." This results in images that disappoint the viewer's expectations. The observer is then invited "further into the empty wilderness"[240] in which the creative and the destructive, being and nonbeing coincide: "I have transformed myself *in the zero of form*."[241] This *transformation*, which dissolves the form and returns to primal formlessness, seeks an ultimate *reductio in nihilum* (reduction to nothing) that offers no hope of a *creatio ex nihilo* (creation from nothing) unless it be one embedded in the artistic work itself. Malevich's *Black Square* was perceived as an expression of nihilism (in Nietzsche's sense): as the experience of a loss but at the same time also as a revaluation of all previously accepted pictorial values. But when Malevich presents his black square in a place reserved for Russian Orthodox icons as part of a history of devotion, when he hangs his picture not on the display wall of the museum but in the upper corner of the room, he creates a unity of abrogation and confirmation of the image. The picture that no longer shows anything then represents, *via negativa*, the God whose death Nietzsche's Zarathustra announced.[242] In his essay "Gott ist nicht gestürzt! [God is not overthrown!],"[243] Malevich accordingly speaks of a movement of transcendence that leads beyond the picture by way of the picture. In fact, he thereby lays claim to a structure Paul Tillich articulated in speaking of "the God above God."[244] God's transcendence can be experienced precisely where concrete images of God are themselves transcended.

(b) Ad Reinhardt (1913–67) integrates a black cross into a black plane; it evades the superficial glance just as such a glance avoids the inner dynamics of the colored plane in Malevich's *Black Square* (cf. plate 9, p. I.10). Reinhardt's picture shows a cross by hiding it, as though it were to match the dialectics of revelation and hiddenness, God's nearness and distance, presence and withdrawal. Reinhardt described his work of reduction or negation of painterly means and methods as "the last painting":[245] the blackness of the painting expands a medium that drives back visibility, a darkening that belongs both to the Synoptic passion account and to the Last Supper. Negation is the medium of transcendence. Reinhardt's self-commentary explicitly adopts the terminology of negative theology:

Self-transcendence
revealed yet unrevealed
Undifferentiated unity, oneness, no divisions, no multiplicity
No consciousness of anything
No consciousness of consciousness
All distinctions disappear in darkness
The darkness is the brilliance numinous, resonance[246]

Recollections of the act of creation, the connection between the ban on images and the understanding of God, as well as a theology of the cross lead to a last picture that definitively leaves behind everything traditionally pictorial.

(c) We may say that John Hilliard's *Black Depths* (cf. plate 11, p. I.12–13) is related, or part of the same family. Hilliard combines four black square photos in such a way that a cross appears in the space between them.[247] From the negation of representation—the photos show nothing—emerges the symbol of the cross, as if a distant echo of ancient iconoclasts who removed the picture of *Christus Pantokrator* from the apse of the Eirene church and replaced it with a black cross.[248]

(d) Piet Mondrian's (1872–1944) variant on abstract images introduced geometric signs or symbols in strict binary order and regarded these as the refusal of a direct representation of what is available to the senses. Not only God but the visible world itself withdraws from direct representation. Mondrian's picture *Pier and Ocean* approaches the event by a roundabout path of logical construction (cf. plate 10, p. I.11). The image is simultaneously translated into figures accessible to thought and diagrammatic structures. Thus a field of horizontal and vertical symbols in countless variations represents the structure and dynamics of the surface of a body of water, such as revealed by the ocean. Even what is available to the senses manifests itself only by way of its opposite or by way of turning it upside down as if it were a looking-glass world. The *Gestalt* we see refuses direct copying and permits itself to be presented only in the abstract form of a binary code. In it alone, it is visible. What the picture presents, it transforms into otherness.

Whereas Calvin called for artists to show modesty by painting only what can be seen (see above, §9.2), Mondrian's work was dominated by the conviction (influenced by Madame Blavatsky's theosophy) that one cannot even paint what one sees. The very idea of a visible world requires spiritualizing; whatever we see has already passed beyond the limits of particularity and so meets the universal for reason of its abstract formal language. Imagery will be "pure" when it leads from the sensible-concrete to the spiritual-universal. Works like *Composition I-A* (1930) or *Composition in Red, Blue, and Yellow* (1937–42) leave behind the objective painting with which Mondrian began and develop pictures into a system of ordering, with balances between forms and colors. Grids form the means of depiction; they not only surround planes but again and again allow lines to extend endlessly (into infinity), so that the otherwise enclosed planes of color open out beyond the existing frame. Thus the pictures fence out all objects of sense perception and at the same time represent a movement of transcendence. Mondrian indicates his proximity to the ban on images (or at least to its rationalistic interpretation; cf. §3.5 above) when in his sketchbooks for 1913/14 he asserts, "If one does not represent things, a place remains for the Divine."[249]

(e) Decidedly iconoclastic is the love for images in the work of Arnulf Rainer (b. 1929). He distorts images by overpainting, whether initial monochrome partial covering or mauling the image (often a photo of himself) with black chalk marks that render the original grotesque (cf. *Braune und Blaue Flamme* [Brown and blue flame] and *Rotbraun-Kreuz* [Red-brown cross]). At the same time the damage done to the picture yields a new and different picture: destruction of the image is at the same time its building up.[250] The religious-theological background is not only relevant where Rainer concentrates on the cross. Instead, Rainer interprets the destruction of the image (especially the self-image) as *mortificatio*, a becoming-formed as Christ. In analogy to Karlstadt, the *rejection of images* (see §3.1 above) appears as a destruction of the flesh, the old Adam. When later, in place of the aggressive black, a "colorful angelic garment" pours over Rainer's pictures, the artist regards it as corresponding to resurrection.[251]

Be it noted: this is not about illustrations for a dogmatic theology of the cross or artistic decoration of churches. Rainer stresses the rejection of his works by churches and affirms his ongoing "annoyance with the theologians,"[252] but also the rage that seeks expression in his works. But it is evident precisely in this distance from the internal world of the church that the dispute over images and iconoclasm can be not only about theological positions but also a contemporary aesthetic strategy. This should not be forgotten by a hermeneutics of the ban on images that reckons with the virulence of pictures.

(f) I would like to end this section with a reference to Anselm Kiefer, who explicitly connected the Byzantine quarrel over images with the means employed by the images themselves. This is worked out in a series of images under the title *Bilderstreit* (lit.: "Battle over images"/ Iconoclastic controversy). In a 1977 version (cf. plate 12b, p. I.15), the names of the controlling figures in the debate on the side of the Eastern Church (Empress Eirene as well as John of Damascus and his iconoclastic opponents) are integrated into the picture. They are grouped around a palette as painters use it that dominates the picture and at the same time is surrounded and threatened and thus held in check by tanks. In other versions the only text shown is the title (cf. plate 12a, p. I.14), but the image is understandable even without it (cf. plate 12b, p. I.15). In this series the painter's palette is recognizable, even though sometimes it is blending into something like a human face or a mask. Some of these pictures are composed of a variety of different media: we find photos, partly overpainted, partly overlaid with other materials. In the 1977 version discussed, Kiefer sketches the contours of a painter's palette in black, at its center the photo of a sculpture by Michael Heizer (*Rift*) can be discerned. The martial-appearing tanks aim at this center. Flames and black spots look like craters from artillery shells on the battlefield of the painter's palette,[253] which at the same time has taken the form of a target.

Finally, let me refer briefly to the interpretations by Hofmann and Taylor. The one interprets the earlier, the other the later version.

Hofmann, in line with his interpretation of Protestantism, emphasizes the relationship between word and image: the image is accessible in the first instance through an understanding of the names and their historical significance. The palette has been hit by the shots fired by the anti-image forces and the color flows from it like blood. The battle destroys the possibility of painting and the painter is shown as helpless before this strife between ideologies that has driven him from the field. The picture is said to be "a new kind of historical image that (as in the Middle Ages) serves the purpose of a mutual commentary between word and image."[254]

Taylor, in contrast, centers his interpretation on relationships to Kiefer's pictures of Aaron and his work on the Holocaust: "Kiefer realizes that idolatry is not only a religio-aesthetic issue, but, perhaps more important, a political problem."[255] The picture shows the ravaging and destruction (*Shoah*); the blazing fires recall war, but also places of sacrifice and especially the crematoria at Auschwitz. "Kiefer's artistic wager is that what cannot be thought can be figured by a certain disfiguring....He neither erases nor absolutizes figure but uses figure with and against itself to figure the unfigurable."[256] The image makes use of displacement and distortion, constituting presentation by the detour of negation because it thematizes what explodes every measure of the human imagination. The theological battle over the right of images is once again, in the interpretation of this postmodern American theologian, related to the problem of depicting what is beyond depiction. But for Taylor it is not only about God's divinity; it is about the crisis of representation that is part of remembering the Shoah.

9.4 Once Again: The Representation of What Cannot Be Represented

Adorno's dictum that no more poetry can be written after Auschwitz because the shadow of the incommensurable and unbearable makes that lovely form impossible affects the plastic arts as well. Gerhard Richter's breaking off his work on a picture of Auschwitz belongs in that context, as does Joseph Beuys's assertion that Auschwitz points to "what cannot be represented," a horror that stands contrary to the picture and its media and precisely in doing so shapes the memory of it. Jean-Luc Nancy, in his *Forbidden Representation*, offers an extended discussion of the connection between the biblical ban on images and this crisis of pictorial representation, though he summarizes in conclusion, "The confusion gets even more difficult when attempts are made to establish connections with what we call the biblical prohibition on representation."[257]

If we assert that the pictures we have discussed are "images of image-lessness,"[258] they are part of the history of reception of the ban on images.

9.5 The End of the Image?

At this point we may recall Hegel's distinction among art, religion, and philosophy as three spheres belonging to what he called *Geist* (spirit) or the Absolute. He assigned art to the senses, religion to imagination, and philosophy to the realm of concepts, and he tried to conceive the relations among these three forms in terms of their common object. Accordingly, both art and philosophy have the Absolute, and therefore God, as their object, though not in specific religious form. Religious form surpasses the form of art, and is in turn elevated into the form of the concept.

When Hegel praises art within this architectural structure for setting "truth before our minds in the mode of sensuous configuration," he is at the same time characterizing the limitations that call for elevation: "For us art counts no longer as the highest mode in which truth fashions an existence for itself." He grounds this statement by saying, "In general it was early in history that thought passed judgement against art as a mode of presenting the Divine; this happened with the Jews and Mohammedans, for example, and indeed even with the Greeks." Of course, that is an interpretation of the ban on images. Hegel then assures us that Christianity, after its imageless beginnings, later encouraged art, but that stage ended with the inward-turning spirituality of the Reformation. The deeper spirit thrust the form of external sense experience from itself as a serpent sheds its old skin:

> We may well hope that art will always rise higher and come to perfection, but the form of art has ceased to be the supreme need of the spirit. No matter how excellent we find the statues of the Greek gods, no matter how we see God the Father, Christ, and Mary so estimably and perfectly portrayed: it is no help; we bow the knee no longer.[259]

The references above to the afterlife of the ban on images in today's art (§9.3) show that Hegel's remarks on the end of art did not mark a breakdown of aesthetic work and experience; at best they were an occasion for liberating new and more radical forms of imagery. Because Hegel's thesis regarding the significance of the ban on images points to the disempowerment of the image brought about by Protestant inwardness, it may serve as the transition to our closing reflections—more as dissent than as continuation.

10. Concluding Reflection on the Systematic Section

The long path followed by the history of interpretation and reception that has been traveled in this third section in seven-league boots leaves us before the task of arriving at an appropriate understanding of the ban on images, even though it is far distant from the original contexts portrayed in section 2. It is only in this way that the cultural sedimentation of meaning can be described; it gives growth to layers of meaning that are more than a mere accessory or tertiary addition to a supposedly original meaning. The positivistic claim to refer to the true core of the one primal fact would lead to simplicity. Instead, interpretation and reception are part of the making of texts because the text itself has achieved its characteristic form through a long process of transformative tradition, redaction, and theological reflection. As the exegetical section of this volume proceeded in the crabwise way of the spirit from what came later in order to inquire about things that had been reshaped to make them what they are, so also the systematic observations held to the most elaborated models of interpretation, often structured by clear oppositions. The intent was to reconstruct, based on their presuppositions and conclusions, how the paradigms of interpretation have changed. The "object" to be understood is not the absolute clarity of the only adequate, original meaning, but the changes in meaning.

(a) Instead of assigning the ban on images to the primary layer of the biblical text or making it the ultimate foundation stone of Jewish religion, we have to look—adopting a metaphor shaped by Cornelius Castoriadis[260]—at the magma whose permanent flow generates meanings that it simultaneously shifts into a change of meaning. Even speaking of the aniconism of the early Jewish cult or the reference to the absence of an image of God in the Jerusalem temple (see above, §II.1.1c) already

194

describes these phenomena in terms of other historical evidences stemming from other contexts. All we know for the moment is that the ban on images was articulated later, and in combination with other identity strategies (male circumcision, the uniqueness of YHWH, the idea of covenant), and so became a mark of Jewish/Old Testament religion.

The ban on images acquired its dynamic by modifying multiple dimensions of meaning, imbued with figures of imagination and memory in altered contexts. What has emerged is framed by oppositions. The transcendence of God versus the freezing of a given cultic object, infinity versus finitude, isolation versus concrescence, unlimitedness versus determination, spirit versus body, rationality versus sensuality, freedom versus servitude, miraculous origin versus production by one's own power, revelation versus projection, purity versus susceptibility to temptation, otherness versus sameness, but above all Creator versus creature: oppositions such as these do not arise from a secondary interpretation of the biblical texts; rather, they constitute the nutrient solution within which the ban on images crystallized (see above, §II.2.3–4).

Hence it is appropriate that in the context of Christianity (more precisely: in the light of a faith in the God of Israel that appealed to Jesus of Nazareth and was christologically-soteriologically shaped) this shift in meaning continued. On the way to its trinitarian outcome, this changing meaning fell under an increased influence of philosophical critique of images and a Neoplatonic theology of the image. The legitimacy of the image, despite banning and denial, was disputed and even strengthened by an incarnational Christology. If the ban on images was a mark of Jewish identity, so the reintroduction of what was excluded could fulfill a parallel function for Christians. That a ban on images is no longer valid for Christianity—or even that God's glory is pictured in Christ—shaped (and shapes) self-awareness, all the more since those who favored images and were at first persecuted, ultimately won the victory. It was not the exclusion of the heretics that shaped the formation of Christian devotion but the futility of all attempts to forbid images.

(b) The hermeneutics of the ban on images sketched here developed between the poles of God's transcendence and otherness, with an inclination to negative theology on the one hand and, on the other, an anthropology of the *imago Dei* with an affection for *animal symbolicum and homo pictor*. In this field of tension not only are questions about images likewise questions of faith;[261] so also theories of image are theologies (even if they sometimes seem weak or apparently trivial). Christology was and is the organizing center of these tensions and at the same time fulfills the function of a media theory.[262]

(c) The so-called *iconic turn* in cultural studies and the revival of philosophical theories of the image introduce a new horizon for theology. It is not only a theoretical challenge but indicates a significant change in image praxis. Parallel to the digitalizing of the worlds of imagery and their enduring worldwide accessibility, the ambivalence of the imagery increases. The divide between religious and secular reception of images, between the cultic image and the art image, is more and more frequently traversed. The potential for exciting the public through imagery is felt throughout the world; less and less often do images remain private. The sexual exploitation of children has become a problem of imagery, so that there are any number of reasons to call again for a ban on images. Even in the present, humanity proves itself in the context of a struggle over images.

(d) As regards the concept of the image, the overcoming of its definition in terms of depiction is probably the most important tendency in scholarship. This tendency eliminates the competition between image and speech, between the visible and reason, and between image and word that became prominent in so many struggles over the appropriate form of representation. That competition is being resolved through a new attention to the ability of the image to make visible something that would otherwise remain unseen or be overlooked. Images are media that draw boundaries between the visible and the forbidden even when they are used for purposes of depiction.

(e) The ambivalence of images includes not only successful representation but also despair over the "dilemma [caused by] our sense of sight, [which allows us to perceive things] but at the same time…restricts and partly precludes our apprehension of reality."[263] Hence the tension between representation in images and the transcendent God should be thought of not only as one of inappropriateness and discrepancy as a long tradition; there are also affinities between a culture of images and Protestant faith. These should be developed in an anthropology of the image that would take seriously the character of the human that Luther identified as a tension between *ratio* (reason) and *cor* (heart), between *intellectus fidei* (the mind of faith) and *vis imaginativa* (the power of imagination).

(f) This task correlates with a tendency observable at the present time to transpose the Bible's forbidding the making of images into a contrary commandment: "You *shall* make images for yourself!"[264] or at least to interpret our cultural situation in such a way. The plural (images) reveals a theological assessment of what was fearful about the image and why the tradition considered it forbidden: the enchanting power that does not leave a space for otherness and variation, a power to bring about just one picture that counts. Correspondingly, Bruno Latour declares, "Thou shall not freeze-frame any graven image!"[265] Thus there is some reason to suppose that a hermeneutics of the ban on images can lead not only to a *theo*-anthropology of image but also to a theology of culture.

IV

Prospect

When work began on the present publication, we could not yet foresee how current the question of images, and with it those concerning the significance of the ban on images, might yet become. With the attacks in Paris in January 2015, for the first time in our present age a boundary was crossed: it could now happen that militant Islamists might destroy not only the images created by ancient cultures and other religions—as in the case of the Taliban's destruction of the statues of the Buddha—but that artists in the middle of Europe might be murdered because they had created images that were felt to be blasphemy and provocation. As Horst Bredekamp said in an interview in the *Süddeutsche Zeitung*, with this event the question of how we deal with images has, after so long a time, once more become a life-and-death issue.[1] The new iconoclasm that does not draw the line at the body and life of *Homo pictor* is an existential challenge to the most important heritage of the Reformation and the Enlightenment: the ability to achieve distance that alone makes possible the freedom of art, of both its making *and* seeing. Bredekamp refers to his *Theorie des Bildakts*:[2] "In order to preserve a space for our freedom we must insist on the distance between image and body, image and God. As the murder of the artists in Paris has shown, that is now the most important commandment of the Enlightenment: a question of life and death. This connection has been repressed, distorted, and made toothless for a long time. We must face the question of a culture of images."[3] The new quality of those questions may by no means be traced only to the opposition between cultures and religions, the "clash of civilizations" between West and East, Christianity and Islam. However, it does constitute a challenge to Western societies, precisely in this context and probably for the foreseeable future.

The Hermeneutics of the Ban on Images

As Silvia Naef emphasizes, Islam—unlike Judaism and Christianity—contains no explicit ban on images; there are only some ambiguous texts in the tradition that historically have been interpreted with various degrees of rigor.[4] They have in common their distancing from a reverence for images that threatens to "defile" the religious sphere. In that regard the reaction of fundamentalist Islamism to the caricatures of Muhammad stands within a much broader context of what is sensed as endangering the "holy"; within Islam's sphere of influence this is also connected to the fact that because of the dominance of Western culture,

> while there has been a swift "increase" of images during the last two hundred years, connected especially with the newer techniques of reproduction, the place of the image in society has not fundamentally changed: the image remains, as before, excluded from religious praxis but is permitted in the secular sphere. Instead of speaking of a "ban on images" we might better talk of the circumstance that in Islam the image performs particular functions that are distinct from those Christianity has known and still knows.[5]

Naef points out that the Islamic traditions are in this respect closer to ancient Jewish theory and praxis in dealing with images than to those of Christianity.[6] In Judaism and Islam it is not the image *as such*, but rather the possibility that it could be religiously revered that leads to its exclusion. A corresponding way of dealing with images was *one* (though not central) element of "correct" religious praxis: images had to be excluded or made invisible during prayer because they could divert and lead astray.[7] This involves an understanding of images—scarcely reflected in Islamic sources—that attributes a significant power to them. This is obviously true in particular of the extreme variants of the idea of images in Islamic circles that attribute a reality to the image (in particular as it affects human beings) that acknowledges no distance at all. Bredekamp emphasizes this: "The new perpetrators make no distinction between the image and God, the image and the body. They identify the drawings of the Prophet with the Prophet himself."[8] This is not simply about a premodern concept that might give rise to feelings of superiority. The virtuosic iconic staging, for example, of destructions of images in Syria and Iraq by the so-called Islamic State shows, in its own way, that the medial power of images (in this case the deliberate presentation of an attack on the heritage of world cultures) strikes a nerve in our own culture of imagery, which is in the midst of such rapid change.

In the world-embracing digital internet, every image is immediately available. With the limitless presence of pictures, our ability to distinguish and interpret fades "in face of the image." As the systematic-theological part of this volume has shown (cf. esp. §III.2–3), what is immediately obvious in the iconic staging of political power or in pictures presented for the purpose of erotic stimulation—namely, that there is a presence of the image that does not (or should not) allow for distance—shapes ordinary digital culture as well. Here Bredekamp points, for example, to the "selfie movement" (in which there is often no longer any distinction between the self and the staging) and to the "journalism of the moment" with its suggestive immediacy of live photos that explain nothing but—especially in the case of catastrophes and wars—belong to an aesthetics of overpowering: "What we need in the media, instead, is room for reflection, not an absence of any distance from the event."[9]

It is also an interest of both parts of this book to work out a "hermeneutics of the ban on images" through biblical-exegetical and systematic-theological reflection, a hermeneutics that will strengthen our ability to forge a responsible and discriminating engagement with images. In the face of imagery as an anthropological phenomenon of great symbolic force and enduring asynchronicity, Christian theology today is especially challenged to contribute to a better understanding of images in light of the biblical ban on them in the context of other biblical texts.

This should take place through a historical *and* systematic-theological examination of contexts of origin and forms of reception of the ban on images. The authors' task was to present by way of examples the multiple layers of interpretation from the perspective of Protestant theology. The twofold approach stands as an example for discipline-spanning cooperation on such themes in theology, whose complexity cannot be grasped from a *single* point of view or by a *single* method. This is also evident in the confrontation with knowledge drawn from the study of art and philosophy, which, from the viewpoint of both authors, is necessary to the theological task of producing an adequate hermeneutics of the ban on images.

In view of the age and origins of the ban on images, there cannot be a "final" explanation (which as such is simply impossible) through the reconstruction of "origins" or "original intents." Instead, the group of problems revealed itself as one that can be described with historical precision only under the conditions of ancient Israel's explicit monotheism from the exilic period onward. In that light an approach through an "archaeological" inquiry seemed appropriate; we could thus question backward from the late polemical texts of the Old Testament against images to the (exilic) Decalogue and possible older elements (aniconism in Jerusalem, prophetic critique of images). It is clear that Hellenistic and Roman authors were correct in associating the aniconism of ancient Jewish religion (we are not speaking here of a "ban") very closely with its special monotheism. In fact, the ban on images in the Decalogue is not independent; it is to be seen as a concretion and focusing of the first commandment (to worship YHWH alone). In this connection, then, Jan Assmann's thesis—despite justified criticism on particular points—remains interesting, namely, that iconoclasm, in light of the distinction between God and the world, is *theo*clasm and ultimately is aimed against "cosmotheism" that (for anthropological reasons) cannot be eliminated.[10] But we must still insist that, while the Jewish religion retained a tradition of a semantics of violence against images/idols (cf. Deut 7, and elsewhere), because of the history of Judaism—differently from Christianity and Islam—this did not lead to iconoclastic actions.[11]

Under the conditions of a christologically transformed idea of images, alongside the affirmation of images in Christianity there has repeatedly been a violent eruption of efforts to remove them, for example in Egypt under the rule of the Eastern Roman Empire (with regard to the witnesses to Pharaonic culture) and in the later Byzantine iconoclastic movement or during the Reformation (then internally directed). In the systematic-theological section of this book the reasons offered for these movements and the counterarguments have been opened up and examined in correlation with newer theories of the image. That section likewise does not follow a chronological scheme; it does not "tell" a story. Rather, it makes clear how, in light of the fundamental and anthropological (and theological) significance of the question of images, conflicts and attempts at resolution follow one another without any expectation of offering a conclusive clarification. In Johann Gustav Droysen's sense, the presentation untangles the snarl of interpretations of the ban on images in the history of Christian thought and separates them in orderly fashion.[12] Important here is the guiding thesis worked out by exegesis and the history of religions: the concept of image implied by the biblical ban on images and the history of its reception, beginning already within the Old Testament itself, cannot be grasped in terms of the powerful theory of similarity and imitation. Instead, that theory has aided in the devaluation of the image, making it "merely an image."

Instead, newer proposals in the theory of images since Heidegger, and especially since the *iconic turn* in philosophy and cultural studies associated with Hans Belting and Gottfried Boehm, start with an understanding of the image that begins by recognizing a specific presence of the image itself. Re-presentation is not set aside but it no longer obeys the logic of *mimesis* of a higher reality (Plato's theory of the original and the copy). The special presence of the image lies, instead, in its intensification through *presentation*:[13] the image displays something by "displaying itself," that is, by "offering itself to be seen." Genesis *as* image *in actu et in mente* is both a productive and a receptive action; the making and seeing of images work together.

The point of such a concept does not lie in a presence that simply brings the viewer under its spell and erases all differences, as one might suppose in light of the phenomena revealing the power of images in everyday culture mentioned above. Even when passive experiences before and with an image bring forth things that are essential in terms of the anthropology of images,[14] still the "copresence" of the viewer (Gottfried Boehm)[15] in the act of perception is also shaped by *differences*. In the image something appears in a specific way so that its presence causes what is absent to be "there" and active *as such*. There is a hidden space of the inexpressible in the image itself, an "iconic opacity."[16] The presence of the image is thus also its withdrawal; it underlies time, the perception of which is marked by a constant movement into the past, so that it cannot be fixed in place. The anti-image dwells within the image; affinity to the ban on images and to a "negative theology" is not foreign to an image thus understood.

Finally, against this background, a second aspect of the guiding thesis regarding the detachment of the paradigm of representation through the model of presence (and withdrawal) is significant for both approaches represented in this book. The biblical ban on images was not about preserving God's invisibility (or avoiding every notion of violence) but in the precise sense of the word it was about God's *hiddenness*, even in connection with God's revelation. The dialectical dynamic of appearance and concealment, presence and withdrawal represents—in its ineluctable temporal dimension—an important, if not, in the authors' opinion, the most important boundary definition for thinking about images in theology and philosophy. The *theologia crucis* can stand as representative of the line of interpretation thus given, the interpretation of what is ultimately noninterpretable.

The play of withdrawn transcendence in the image—often primarily in the form of a "negative theology"—likewise shapes any number of images in contemporary art, if we view them in light of the statements of artists such as Gerhard Richter. The systematic-theological section ended with a look forward to such theological and christological dimensions in modern works of art. These indicate that images and ban on images are still "stacked on one another," like faith and God in Luther's writings.[17] Also in contemporary art the fundamental tension of the image, made explicit in the ban, has not dissipated but instead has changed. Today it underlies new challenges to thought. Work on "the question of a culture of images"[18] must become even more intensive and interdisciplinary—also because of the current relevance of the subject and its serious significance. A "hermeneutics of the ban on images" appears to be not only a *desideratum* of theology (e.g., in view of an image-theoretical Christology or doctrine of the sacraments) but also an important link to media theory, aesthetics, and the hermeneutics of culture. Only in that way can the art of right discernment (still a theological virtue, after all!) successfully enter into the current debates over the "flood of images" in which awareness of the image—and thus of the relevance of the ban on images as the necessary distancing from the image—threatens to perish:

> The hostility of the media industry to images remains unbroken, not because it forbids or puts obstacles to images; on the contrary, because it sets loose a flood of images tending basically to suggestion, images as substitute for reality, the criteria of which have always been to conceal the boundaries of their own image-character. The much-lauded new age of the image—after that of Gutenberg—is iconoclastic, even when its enthusiasts do not notice the fact. That, of course, is not to say that strong pictures cannot be produced through reproductive—or simulative—techniques. The history of photography, film, or the beginnings of video art have given adequate evidence that they can. But making use of these new techniques to strengthen the image presumes building up the iconic tension in controlled fashion and making it visible to the beholder. A strong image lives from this twofold reality: showing

something, even faking something, and *at the same time demonstrating the criteria and premises of the experience.*[19]

It will be a crucial task for a hermeneutics of the ban on images to keep in mind a sense of the boundaries of the visible that accompany the image and so to build up and preserve the ability to maintain a distance from every kind of ideologization of images themselves.

Notes

I. Introduction

1. Richard M. Rorty, ed., *The Linguistic Turn: Essays in Philosophical Method, with Two Retrospective Essays* (Chicago: University of Chicago Press, 1967).

2. Gottfried Boehm, "Zu einer Hermeneutik des Bildes," in *Seminar: Die Hermeneutik und die Wissenschaften*, ed. Gottfried Boehm and Hans-Georg Gadamer (Frankfurt: Suhrkamp, 1978), 444–71, at 444.

3. Boehm, "Zu einer Hermeneutik," 457.

4. Boehm, "Zu einer Hermeneutik," 456.

5. Cf. Boehm, "Zu einer Hermeneutik," 469.

6. See, e.g., Jochen Hörisch, *Die Wut des Verstehens: zur Kritik der Hermeneutik* (Frankfurt: Suhrkamp, 1988).

7. "Time does not wear away instances of pregnance, it brings things out in them—though one may not add that these things were 'in them' all along." Hans Blumenberg, *Work on Myth*, trans. Robert M. Wallace, Studies in Contemporary German Social Thought (Cambridge, MA: MIT Press, 1985), 69.

8. Emmanuel Lévinas, "Phenomenon and Enigma," originally published in French in *Revue de Métaphysique et de Morale* 62 (1957): 241–53. English in Emanuel Lévinas, *Collected Philosophical Papers*, Philosophica 100 (Dordrecht and Boston: Nijhoff, 1987), 61–70, at 68.

II. Exegetical and Religious-Historical Perspectives

1. The notes—in accord with the character of an essay—offer, besides direct references for quotations, only a limited selection of literature for further exploration. When there is reference in parentheses

to other parts of section II, this will be without repetition of the Roman numeral, but such reference will be made in cases of allusions to section III.

2. On this cf. Klaus Schmidt, *Sie bauten die ersten Tempel. Das rätselhafte Heiligtum der Steinzeitjäger. Die archäologische Entdeckung am Göbekli Tepe* (Munich: Beck, 2006); James Mellaart, *Çatal Hüyük: A Neolithic Town in Anatolia* (New York: McGraw-Hill, 1967).

3. See Ernst Cassirer, *The Philosophy of Symbolic Forms*, vol. 2, *Mythical Thought*, trans. Ralph Manheim (New Haven, CT: Yale University Press, 1955), 103, where he attributes "a primordial mythical-religious feeling" to the symbolism of the threshold. Cf. also Kurt Hübner, *Die Wahrheit des Mythos* (Munich: Beck, 1985).

4. Cf. Hübner, *Wahrheit*, 163–67; Mircea Eliade, *Patterns in Comparative Religion*, trans. Rosemary Sheed (New York: Sheed & Ward, 1958), 367–85. On the problematic and indispensable character of the category of the "holy," see Carsten Colpe, *Über das Heilige. Versuch, seiner Verkennung kritisch vorzubeugen* (Frankfurt: Hain, 1990).

5. See Jan Assmann, *The Search for God in Ancient Egypt*, trans. David Lorton (Ithaca, NY: Cornell University Press, 2001), 30–35. On Egyptian temples in general, see Dieter Arnold, *Die Tempel Ägyptens. Götterwohnungen, Baudenkmäler, Kultstätten* (Zürich: Artemis & Winkler, 1992); see also Dieter Arnold et al., *The Monuments of Egypt: An A–Z Companion to Ancient Egyptian Architecture* (London: Tauris, 2009); Dieter Arnold et al., *Temples of Ancient Egypt* (Ithaca, NY: Cornell University Press, 1997); Dieter Arnold, *Temples of the Last Pharaohs* (New York: Oxford University Press, 1999); Dieter Kurth, *The Temple of Edfu: A Guide by an Ancient Egyptian Priest* (New York: American University in Cairo Press, 2004).

6. The path of the deities, especially during festivals, is more likely to move from inside to outside (see n. 14 below).

7. Cf. Friedhelm Hartenstein, *Die Unzugänglichkeit Gottes im Heiligtum. Jesaja 6 und der Wohnort JHWHs in der Jerusalemer Kulttradition*, WMANT 75 (Neukirchen-Vluyn: Neukirchener Verlag, 1997); Bernd Janowski, "Die heilige Wohnung des Höchsten. Kosmologische Implikationen der Jerusalemer Tempeltheologie," in Janowski, *Der Gott des Lebens*, Beiträge zur Theologie des Alten Testaments 3 (Neukirchen-Vluyn: Neukirchener Verlag, 2003), 27–71, at 35–41.

8. Cf. Robert Koldewey, *The Excavations at Babylon*, trans. Agnes Sophia Johns (London: Macmillan, 1914), 183–97, 204–14, 327; Wilfred

George Lambert, *Babylonian Creation Myths*, MesCiv 16 (Winona Lake: Eisenbrauns, 2013), 199–200; Hansjörg Schmid, *Der Tempelturm Etemenanki in Babylon*, BaghF 17 (Mainz: von Zabern, 1995); for summary, see Ernst Heinrich, *Die Tempel und Heiligtümer im Alten Mesopotamien*, Denkmäler antiker Architektur 14/1–2 (Berlin: de Gruyter, 1982); Stefan M. Maul, "Das Haus des Götterkönigs. Gedanken zur Konzeption überregionaler Heiligtümer im Alten Orient," in *Tempel im Alten Orient*, ed. Kai Kaniuth et al., CDOC 7 (Wiesbaden: Harrassowitz, 2013), 311–24.

9. On this, see Kurth, *Temple of Edfu*; also his *Treffpunkt der Götter. Inschriften aus dem Tempel des Horus von Edfu* (Düsseldorf: Artemis & Winkler, 1998); Arnold, *Tempel*, 98–102; Emma Brunner-Traut et al., *Ägypten. Kunst- und Reiseführer mit Landeskunde*, 4th ed. (Stuttgart et al.: Kohlhammer, 1982), 694–98.

10. Assmann, *The Search for God in Ancient Egypt*, 31.

11. Dieter Arnold, "Naos," in Arnold et al., *The Monuments of Egypt*, 158.

12. Arnold, *Tempel*, 32.

13. For this "countertemple," see Arnold, *Temples of Ancient Egypt*, 181. For the "ears" on the external wall, see Hartwig Altenmüller, "Gott und Götter im alten Ägypten. Gedanken zur persönlichen Frömmigkeit," in *JHWH und die Götter der Völker. Symposium zum 80. Geburtstag von Klaus Koch*, ed. Friedhelm Hartenstein and Martin Rösel (Neukirchen-Vluyn: Neukirchener Verlag, 2009), 17–58, at 32–33.

14. See Jan Assmann, ed., *Das Fest und das Heilige. Religiöse Kontrapunkte zur Alltagswelt*, Studien zum Verstehen fremder Religionen 1 (Gütersloh: Mohn, 1991), including Assmann, "Der zweidimensionale Mensch: das Fest als Medium des kollektiven Gedächtnisses," 13–30; Assmann, "Das ägyptische Prozessionsfest," 105–22. For Mesopotamia, see Beate Pongratz-Leisten, *Ina Šulmi Īrub. Die kulttopographische und ideologische Programmatik der akītu-Prozession in Babylonien und Assyrien im 1. Jahrtausend v. Chr.*, BagF 16 (Mainz: von Zabern, 1994).

15. For Gen 28:10–22, see Erhard Blum, *Die Komposition der Vätergeschichte*, WMANT 57 (Neukirchen-Vluyn: Neukirchener Verlag, 1984), 7–35; Friedhelm Hartenstein, "Wolkendunkel und Himmelsfeste. Zur Genese und Kosmologie der Vorstellung des himmlischen Heiligtums JHWHs," in *Das biblische Weltbild und seine altorientalischen Kontexte*, ed. Bernd Janowski and Beate Ego, FAT 32 (Tübingen: Mohr Siebeck, 2001), 125–79, at 156–60.

16. Cf. Adam Falkenstein and Wolfram von Soden, *Sumerische und akkadische Hymnen und Gebete*, BAW.AO (Zürich: Artemis, 1953); Marie-Joseph Seux, *Hymnes et prières aux dieux de Babylonie et d'Assyrie*, IAPO (Paris: Cerf, 1976); Jan Assmann, *Ägyptische Hymnen und Gebete*, 2nd ed., OBO (Fribourg: Universitätsverlag; Göttingen: Vandenhoeck & Ruprecht, 1999); Otto Kaiser, ed., *Lieder und Gebete I–II*, TUAT II/5–6 (Gütersloh: Mohn, 1989/1991); Bernd Janowski and Daniel Schwemer, eds., *Hymnen, Klagelieder und Gebete*, TUAT n.s. 7 (Gütersloh: Gütersloher Verlagshaus, 2013); Alan Lenzi, ed., *Reading Akkadian Prayers and Hymns. An Introduction*, ANEM 3 (Atlanta: SBL, 2013).

17. Cf. Lambert, *Babylonian Creation Myths*; Otto Kaiser, ed., *Mythen und Epen*, TUAT III/3–6 (Gütersloh: Mohn, 1993–97); Bernd Janowski and Daniel Schwemer, eds., *Weisheitstexte, Mythen und Epen*, TUAT n.s. 8 (Gütersloh: Gütersloher Verlagshaus, 2015).

18. Arvid S. Kapelrud, "Temple Building: A Task for Gods and Kings," *Or*, n.s. 32 (1963), 56–62; cf. Victor A. Hurowitz, *I Have Built You an Exalted House: Temple Building in the Bible in Light of Mesopotamian and Northwest Semitic Writings*, JSOT.S 115 (Sheffield, UK: JSOT Press, 1992); Richard S. Ellis, *Foundation Deposits in Ancient Mesopotamia*, YNER 2 (New Haven, CT: Yale University Press, 1968). For palace building, see Sylvie Lackenbacher, *Le palais sans rival. Le récit de construction en Assyrie* (Paris: La Découverte, 1990). In the ancient Near East and Egypt, the building of a temple was always a combined action that played itself out simultaneously on the levels of the human and the world of the gods and was shaped by the corresponding rituals.

19. Cf. Mark E. Cohen, *The Canonical Lamentations of Ancient Mesopotamia* (Potomac, MD: Capital Decisions, 1988); Thomas Podella, *Ṣôm-Fasten. Kollektive Trauer um den verborgenen Gott im Alten Testament*, AOAT 224 (Kevelaer: Butzon & Bercker/Neukirchen-Vluyn: Neukirchener Verlag, 1989).

20. See Hans Sedlmayr, *Die Entstehung der Kathedrale*, Herder Spektrum 4181 (Freiburg et al.: Herder, 1993 [1950]), 104–5; Arnold Angenendt, *Geschichte der Religiosität im Mittelalter* (Darmstadt: Primus, 1997), 432–39. For ancient Egypt, taking the temple of Satis at Elephantine as an example, built around a natural cave in a cliff and expanded more and more through the centuries, see Assmann, *The Search for God in Ancient Egypt*, 39–40.

21. For interdisciplinary overviews of the subject, see, e.g., Hans-Joachim Klimkeit, ed., *Götterbild in Kunst und Schrift*, Studium Universale

2 (Bonn: Bouvier, 1984); Brigitte Groneberg and Hermann Spiecker-mann, eds., *Die Welt der Götterbilder*, BZAW 376 (Berlin: de Gruyter, 2007); Maria Michela Luiselli, Jürgen Mohn, and Stephanie Gripentrog, eds., *Kult und Bild. Die bildliche Dimension des Kultes im Alten Orient, in der Antike, und in der Neuzeit*, Diskurs Religion 1 (Würzburg: Ergon Verlag, 2013).

22. On this, see Arnold, *Temples of Ancient Egypt*, 22, with an example of a falcon god. For Egyptian images of gods, see, e.g., the exhibition catalogue, *Gott und Götter im Alten Ägypten*, by Sylvia Schoske and Dietrich Wildung (Mainz: von Zabern, 1992); David Lorton, "The Theology of Cult Statues in Ancient Egypt," in *Born in Heaven, Made on Earth: The Making of the Cult Image in the Ancient Near East*, ed. Michael Brennan Dick (Winona Lake, IN: Eisenbrauns, 1999), 123–210.

23. For the various media used to shape the concepts and the imagery of the gods, in terms of the example of Greece but also with transcultural significance, cf. Burkhard Gladigow, "Präsenz der Bilder—Präsenz der Götter. Kultbilder und Bilder der Götter in der griechischen Religion," in Burkhard Gladigow, *Religionswissenschaft als Kulturwissenschaft*, Religionswissenschaft heute 1 (Stuttgart, et al.: Kohlhammer, 2005), 62–72; Gladigow, "Epiphanie, Statuette, Kultbild. Griechische Gottesvorstellungen im Wechsel von Kontext und Medium," in Gladigow, *Religionswissenschaft*, 73–84; Verity J. Platt, *Facing the Gods: Epiphany and Representation in Graeco-Roman Art, Literature and Religion*, Greek Culture in the Roman World (Cambridge: Cambridge University Press, 2011).

24. Angelika Berlejung, *Die Theologie der Bilder. Herstellung und Einweihung von Kultbildern in Mesopotamien und die alttestamentliche Bilderpolemik*, OBO 162 (Fribourg: Universitätsverlag; Göttingen: Vandenhoeck & Ruprecht, 1998), 58. Emphasis in original.

25. See Friedhelm Hartenstein, *Das Angesicht JHWHs. Studien zu seinem höfischen und kultischen Bedeutungshintergrund in den Psalmen und in Exodus 32–34*, FAT 75 (Tübingen: Mohr Siebeck, 2008), 26–52.

26. For the division of building façades by means of niches as "from the earliest prehistory...an infallible sign of cultic character," see, e.g., Anton Moortgat, *Die Kunst des Alten Mesopotamien, Sumer und Akkad* (Cologne: DuMont, 1982), 24.

27. Cf. Berlejung, *Theologie der Bilder*, 58–61.

28. Elena Cassin, *La splendeur divine. Introduction à l'étude de la mentalité mésopotamienne*, CeS 8 (LaHaye: Mouton, 1968); Cf. also Willem

H. P. Römer, *Numinose Lichterscheinungen im alten Mesopotamien. Eine terminologische und religionsgeschichtliche Betrachtung*, JARG 1 (Saarbrücken: [S.I.], 1973), 65–122; Shawn Z. Aster, *The Unbeatable Light: Melammu and Its Biblical Parallels*, AOAT 384 (Münster: Ugarit-Verlag, 2012).

29. Berlejung, *Theologie der Bilder*, 59.

30. William Robertson Smith, *Religion of the Semites*, new ed. (New Brunswick, NJ: Transaction, 2002 [1894]), 208.

31. For the relief at Sippar, see Berlejung, *Theologie der Bilder*, 141–49; Hartenstein, *Angesicht*, 44–45; Ursula Seidl, "Das Ringen um das richtige Bild des Šamaš von Sippar," *ZA* 91 (2001): 120–32.

32. Cf. the translation by Walter Farber in *Texte aus der Umwelt des Alten Testaments*, 2. *Religiöse Texte 3: Rituale und Beschwörungen* I, ed. Otto Kaiser, TUAT II/2 (Gütersloh: Mohn, 1988), 227–32.

33. A. Leo Oppenheim, *Ancient Mesopotamia: Portrait of a Dead Civilization*, ed. Erica Reiner (Chicago: University of Chicago Press, 1977), 183–98; see also Wilfred George Lambert, "Donations of Food and Drink to the Gods in Ancient Mesopotamia," in *Ritual and Sacrifice in the Ancient Near East*, ed. Jan Quaegebeur, OLA 55 (Leuven: Peeters, 1993), 191–201; from an Old Testament perspective Friedhelm Hartenstein, "'Brote' und 'Tisch des Angesichts'—Zur Logik symbolischer Kommunikation im Tempelritual," in *"Einen Altar von Erde mache mir....." FS Diethelm Conrad*, ed. Johannes F. Diehl, Reinhard Heitzenröder, and Markus Witte, Kleine Arbeiten zum Alten und Neuen Testament 4/5 (Waltrop: Hartmut Spenner, 2003), 107–27.

34. See Brigitte Menzel, *Assyrische Tempel 1. Untersuchungen zu Kult, Administration und Personal*, StP 10/1 (Rome: Biblical Institute Press, 1981), 289.

35. Cf. Dietz Otto Edzard, "Die Einrichtung eines Tempels im älteren Babylonien. Philologische Aspekte," in *Le temple et le culte*, ed. Emeri Johannes van Donzel et al., CRRA 20 (Leiden: Nederlands Historisch-Archaeologisch Instituut te Istanbul, 1975), 156–63; Barthel Hrouda, "Le mobilier du temple," in van Donzel, *Le temple*, 151–55.

36. Cf. Marti Nissinen et al., *Prophets and Prophecy in the Ancient Near East*, SBL Writings from the Ancient World 12 (Atlanta: Scholars Press, 2003), 147–48 (No. 101: Assurbanipal, Prism B v 15–vi 16, ll. 49–71).

37. See Angelika Berlejung, "Kultische Küsse. Zu den Begegnungsformen zwischen Göttern und Menschen," *WO* 29 (1998): 80–97.

38. For corresponding Babylonian texts with regard to the "exile" of the statue of Marduk, see Christina Ehring, *Die Rückkehr JHWHs. Traditions- und religionsgeschichtliche Untersuchungen zu Jesaja 40,1-11, Jesaja 52,7-10 und verwandten Texten*, WMANT 116 (Neukirchen-Vluyn: Neukirchener Verlag, 2007), 135–56.

39. Berlejung, *Theologie der Bilder*; cf. also Christopher Walker and Michael B. Dick, "The Induction of the Cult Image in Ancient Mesopotamia: The Mesopotamian *mīs pî* Ritual," in *Born in Heaven*, ed. Michael B. Dick, 55–121 (see n. 22 above).

40. Cf. the associated prayer of raising the hands/invocation (ŠU. ÍL.LÁ) in the ritual of washing the mouth (*mīs pî*) in Berlejung, *Theologie der Bilder*, 200, 49–51, esp. 11. 77–81 (see below).

41. Cf. Angelika Berlejung, "Geheimnis und Ereignis. Zur Funktion und Aufgabe der Kultbilder in Mesopotamien," in *Die Macht der Bilder*, ed. Ingo Baldermann et al., JBTh 13 (Neukirchen-Vluyn: Neukirchener Verlag, 1999), 109–43; Angelika Berlejung, "Der Handwerker als Theologe. Zur Mentalitäts- und Traditionsgeschichte eines altorientalischen und alttestamentlichen Berufsstands," *VT* 46 (1996): 145–68.

42. Berlejung, *Theologie der Bilder*, 200.

43. Berlejung, *Theologie der Bilder*, 276.

44. Jan Assmann, *Maʾat. Gerechtigkeit und Unsterblichkeit im alten Ägypten* (Munich: Beck, 1995), 195, referring to the performative act of recitation (here the hourly ritual to support the progress of the sun).

45. Cf. Walter Burkert, *Griechische Religion der archaischen und klassischen Epoche*, 2nd ed., RM 15 (Stuttgart: Kohlhammer, 2011), 140–46 on temple and cultic image.

46. Fritz Graf, "Der Eigensinn der Götterbilder in antiken religiösen Diskursen," in *Homo Pictor*, ed. Gottfried Boehm, Colloquia Raurica 7 (Munich: Sauer, 2001), 227–43, at 234 (emphasis supplied).

47. On this cf., e.g., Jean Bottéro, *Mesopotamia: Writing, Reasoning, and the Gods* (Chicago: University of Chicago Press, 1992), 216–17; Manfred Krebernik, *Götter und Mythen des Alten Orients* (Munich: Beck, 2015), 54–56; Brigitte Groneberg, *Die Götter des Zweistromlandes: Kulte, Mythen, Epen* (Düsseldorf: Artemis & Winkler, 2004), 240–55; Walther Sallaberger, "Pantheon, A. I: Mesopotamien," *RIA* 10 (2004): 294–308; for Egypt, Erik Hornung, *Conceptions of God in Ancient Egypt: The One and the Many*, trans. John Baines (Ithaca, NY: Cornell University Press, 1982), esp. 217–50; for more detail from the perspective of religious studies, see

Fritz Stolz, *Einführung in den biblischen Monotheismus*, Series Theologie (Darmstadt: Wissenschaftliche Buchgesellschaft, 1996), 32–61.

48. See the index entries for this keyword in Henri Frankfort, *Kingship and the Gods: A Study of Ancient Near Eastern Religion as the Integration of Society and Nature*, 5th ed. (Chicago: University of Chicago Press, 1965).

49. On this, see Gebhard J. Selz, "'The Holy Drum, the Spear, and the Harp': Towards an Understanding of the Problems of Deification in Third Millennium Mesopotamia," in *Sumerian Gods and Their Representations*, ed. Irving L. Finkel and Markham J. Geller, CM 7 (Groningen: STYX, 1997), 167–213; Barbara N. Porter, "Blessings from a Crown, Offerings to a Drum: Were There Non-anthropomorphic Deities in Ancient Mesopotamia?" in *What Is a God? Anthropomorphic and Non-anthropomorphic Aspects of Deity in Ancient Mesopotamia*, ed. Barbara N. Porter, Transactions of the Casco Bay Assyriological Institute 2 (Winona Lake, IN: Eisenbrauns, 2009), 153–94.

50. Berlejung, *Theologie der Bilder*, 276.

51. Berlejung, *Theologie der Bilder*, 278.

52. Cf. Ursula Seidl, *Die babylonischen Kudurru-Reliefs. Symbole mesopotamischer Gottheiten*, OBO 87 (Fribourg: Universitätsverlag; Göttingen: Vandenhoeck & Ruprecht, 1989).

53. Thus the idea that the biblical prohibition of images should be viewed against the background of Babylonian *symbols* of god, as Tallay Ornan suggests, seems very far-fetched (see §2.4a below); cf. Tallay Ornan, *The Triumph of the Symbol: Pictorial Representations of Deities in Mesopotamia and the Biblical Image Ban*, OBO 213 (Fribourg: Academic Press; Göttingen: Vandenhoeck & Ruprecht, 2005). For the relationship between human and symbolic figures as representations of a deity, see Tallay Ornan, "In the Likeness of Man: Reflections on the Anthropocentric Perception of the Divine in Mesopotamian Art," in Porter, *What Is a God?*, 93–151.

54. Cf. Tryggve N. D. Mettinger, *No Graven Image? Israelite Aniconism in Its Ancient Near Eastern Context*, CB.OT 42 (Stockholm: Almqvist & Wiksell, 1995), 20, with n26; Mettinger, "Israelite Aniconism: Developments and Origins," in *The Image and the Book: Iconic Cults, Aniconism, and the Rise of Book Religion in Israel and the Ancient Near East*, ed. Karel van der Toorn, CBET 21 (Leuven: Peeters, 1997), 173–204, at 187.

55. Cf., for an overview, Krebernik, *Götter und Mythen*, 44–46; Hornung, *Conceptions of God*, 85–89; Burkhard Gladigow, "Zur Konkurrenz

von Bild und Namen im Aufbau polytheistischer Systeme," in *Wort und Bild. Symposion des Fachbereichs Altertums- und Kulturwissenschaften zum 500-jährigen Jubiläum der Eberhard-Karls Universität Tübingen*, ed. Hellmut Brunner et al. (Munich: Fink, 1979), 103–22.

56. On this, see Hartenstein, *Angesicht*, 45–46; Seidl, *Kudurru-Reliefs*, 124–25, 130; Frans A. M. Wiggermann, "The Staff of Ninšubura: Studies in Babylonian Demonology II," *JEOL* 29 (1985): 3–34, at 10–11; Ornan, *In the Likeness of Man*, 114; Zainab Bahrani, *The Graven Image: Representation in Babylonia and Assyria* (Philadelphia: University of Pennsylvania Press, 2003), 185–201.

57. See Hartenstein, *Angesicht*, 46, with n163.

58. On this, see n. 31 above.

59. See esp. the important monograph by Tryggve N. D. Mettinger, *No Graven Image?* See also his *Israelite Aniconism* and "JHWH-Statue oder Anikonismus im ersten Tempel? Gespräch mit meinen Gegnern," *ZAW* 117 (2006): 485–508; see further Ronald S. Hendel, "Aniconism and Anthropomorphism in Ancient Israel," in van der Toorn, *The Image and the Book* (see n. 54 above), 205–28; Brian B. Schmidt, "The Aniconic Tradition: On Reading Images and Viewing Texts," in *The Triumph of Elohim: From Yahwisms to Judaisms*, ed. Diana V. Edelman, CBET 13 (Grand Rapids: Eerdmans, 1996), 75–105. In the field of comparative religions, see also Hans-Martin Barth and Christoph Elsas, eds., *Bild und Bildlosigkeit. Beiträge zum interreligiösen Dialog*, Rudolf-Otto-Symposium 1993 (Hamburg: Rissen, 1994).

60. For Mesopotamia and Syria/Phoenicia, see Astrid Nunn, "Bildhaftigkeit und Bildlosigkeit: ein Widerspruch?" in *Von Göttern und Menschen. Beiträge zu Literatur und Geschichte des Alten Orients. FS Brigitte Groneberg*, ed. Dahlia Shehata et al., CM 41 (Boston: Brill, 2010), 132–68; for Palestine, with important distinctions, see Bernd U. Schipper, "Kultbilder im antiken Israel. Das Verhältnis von Bild und Kult am Beispiel der anikonischen Kultobjekte," in Luiselli et al., *Kult und Bild*, 163–80.

61. On this, see Mettinger, *No Graven Image?* 69–79, referred to by Silvia Naef, *Bilder und Bilderverbot im Islam. Vom Koran bis zum Karikaturenstreit* (Munich: Beck, 2007), 29–32; the stone cult in pre-Islamic times was already discussed by Julius Wellhausen, *Reste arabischen Heidentums* (Berlin: de Gruyter, 1961 [1897]), 101–3.

62. Cf. Albert I. Baumgarten, *The Phoenician History of Philo of Byblos: A Commentary*, EPRO 89 (Leiden: Brill, 1981), 16, 182, 202; see the quotation of Philo in Eusebius of Caesarea, *Praeparatio evangelica* I, 10, 23.

63. Nunn, "Bildhaftigkeit und Bildlosigkeit," 134.

64. Nunn, "Bildhaftigkeit und Bildlosigkeit," 142.

65. Thus Annemarie Schimmel, *Die Zeichen Gottes. Die religiöse Welt des Islam*, 3rd ed. (Munich: Beck, 2002), 24 ("the black stone—a meteor—in the southeast corner of the Ka'abah"); but see Wellhausen, *Reste*, 73–74, and A. J. Wensinck, "Ka'ba," *Handwörterbuch des Islam* (Leiden: Brill, 1941), 236–44, neither of which says anything about a meteor (according to Wensinck, it may be lava or basalt; "Ka'ba," 237), but both emphasize its pre-Islamic function as a stone image/idol of a god (p. 243).

66. On this, see Monika Bernett and Othmar Keel, *Mond, Stier und Kult am Stadttor. Die Stele von Betsaida (et-Tell)*, OBO 161 (Fribourg: Universitätsverlag; Göttingen: Vandenhoeck & Ruprecht, 1998), 45–94 (probably a symbol of the moon god).

67. For the interpretation, see Bernett and Keel, *Mond, Stier und Kult*, 1–44.

68. Cf. Helga Weippert, *Palästina in vorhellenistischer Zeit*, Handbuch der Archäologie Vorderasien II/1 (Munich: Beck, 1988), 282–83.

69. Jens Kamlah, "Temples of the Levant: Comparative Aspects," in *Temple Building and Temple Cult: Architecture and Cultic Paraphernalia of Temples in the Levant (2.-1. Mill. B.C.E.)*, ed. Jens Kamlah, ADPV 41 (Wiesbaden: Harrassowitz, 2012), 507–34, at 525 (with the two examples just cited from Hazor and Bethsaida).

70. Cf., similarly, the argumentation of Schipper, "Kultbilder," esp. 174–77.

71. On this, see previously Karl-Heinz Bernhardt, *Gott und Bild. Ein Beitrag zur Begründung und Deutung des Bilderverbotes im Alten Testament*, Theologische Arbeiten II (Berlin: Evangelische Verlagsanstalt, 1956), who thoroughly reviews the older theses on the origins of the prohibition of images (see 96–98 for the "cultural poverty of the wilderness period") and himself identified the "practical lack of images" (149) with older nomadic traditions of Israel (with the ark [see below] as an "itinerant sanctuary without images") while also linking the "uniqueness" of the Sinai tradition to the possible beginnings of the prohibition of images. For the fundamental significance of "things" bearing numinous features from the perspective of ethnology and history of religions, cf. Karl-Heinz Kohl, *Die Macht der Dinge. Geschichte und Theorie sakraler Objekte* (Munich: Beck, 2003).

72. Cf. Othmar Keel, "Warum im Jerusalemer Tempel kein anthropomorphes Kultbild gestanden haben dürfte," in Boehm, *Homo Pictor*, 244–82 (see n. 46); Othmar Keel, *Die Geschichte Jerusalems und die Entstehung des Monotheismus*, 2 vols., OLG IV/1-2 (Göttingen: Vandenhoeck & Ruprecht, 2007), esp. 1:294–307; Tryggve N. D. Mettinger, *The Dethronement of Sabaoth: Studies in the Shem and Kabod Theologies*, CB.OT 18 (Lund: Gleerup, 1982), 19–37; Jens Kamlah, *"Und es herrschte Friede zwischen Hiram und Salomo." Studien zum Tempelkult in Phönizien und in Israel/Juda* [forthcoming in the series ADPV]; for the broader religious- and architectural-historical context of the Jerusalem temple, cf. the contributions of the Tübingen meeting regarding the temple in Kamlah, *Temples*, especially Kamlah's summary on the "Sacred Focal Point: Cult Statue, Cult Image or Cult Symbol" (524–26): "With regard to the Iron Age temple at Jerusalem, this archaeological evidence (i.e., the Phoenician *naiskoi* and sphinx throne [FH]) leads—in comparison with the description of the cherubim inside the shrine (1 Kgs 6:23–28)—to the conclusion that the shrine (*dᵊbîr*) contained an empty sphinx throne (cherubim throne), thus an iconic cult symbol, as sacred focal point" (526).

73. On this, cf. Othmar Keel, *Jahwe-Visionen und Siegelkunst. Eine neue Deutung der Majestätsschilderungen in Jes 6, Ez 1 und 10 und Sach 4*, SBS 84/85 (Stuttgart: Katholisches Bibelwerk, 1977), 15–45; Othmar Keel, *Geschichte Jerusalems*, 1:294–333; Mettinger, *No Graven Image?*, 81–113; Martin Metzger, "Jahwe, der Kerubenthroner, die von Keruben flankierte Palmette und Sphingenthrone aus dem Libanon," in his *Vorderorientalische Ikonographie und Altes Testament. Gesammelte Aufsätze*, Jerusalemer Theologisches Forum 6 (Münster: Aschendorff, 2004), 112–23.

74. For this image, cf. Keel, *Geschichte Jerusalems* 1:302, 304, with fig. 191; Ronny Reich, *Excavating the City of David: Where Jerusalem's History Began* (Jerusalem: Magnes, 2011), 215, fig. 146 (photo).

75. On this, cf. Weippert, *Palästina*, 604–7.

76. See, for a summary, Bernd Janowski, "JHWH und der Sonnengott. Aspekte der Solarisierung JHWHs in vorexilischer Zeit," in Bernd Janowski, *Die rettende Gerechtigkeit. Beiträge zur Theologie des Alten Testaments 2* (Neukirchen-Vluyn: Neukirchener Verlag, 1999), 192–219; Keel, *Geschichte Jerusalems* 1:273–86; Martin Leuenberger, "Die Solarisierung des Wettergottes Jhwh," in his *Gott in Bewegung.*

Religions- und theologiegeschichtliche Beiträge zu Gottesvorstellungen im alten Israel, FAT 76 (Tübingen: Mohr Siebeck, 2011), 34–71.

77. Cf., e.g., Mettinger, "Dethronement," 80–123, and most recently Thomas Wagner, *Gottes Herrlichkeit. Bedeutung und Verwendung des Begriffs kābôd im Alten Testament*, VTSup 151 (Leiden and Boston: Brill, 2012).

78. Cf. Herbert Niehr, "In Search of YHWH's Cult Statue in the First Temple," in van der Toorn, *The Image and the Book*, 73–95; Christoph Uehlinger, "Anthropomorphic Cult Statuary in Iron Age Palestine and the Search for Yahweh's Cult Images," in van der Toorn, *The Image and the Book*, 97–155; Christoph Uehlinger, "Bilderkult III. Bibel," *RGG*⁴ I (1998): 1565–70; Matthias Köckert, "Die Entstehung des Bilderverbots," in Groneberg and Spieckermann, *Welt der Götterbilder*, 272–90; Matthias Köckert, "Vom Kultbild Jahwes zum Bilderverbot. Oder: Vom Nutzen der Religionsgeschichte für die Theologie," *ZTK* 106 (2009): 371–406. For important dissenting voices, cf. only Mettinger, *No Graven Image?*; Keel, "Warum," esp. 260–77; Keel, *Geschichte Jerusalems* 1:305–7; Eckart Otto, *Deuteronomium 1,1—4,43*, HTKAT 8.1 (Freiburg et al.: Herder, 2012), 563–64 (and see further below at n. 145).

79. See also Keel, "Warum," 262–64, 280 (on the ark and the stone[s]).

80. Keel, "Warum," 263. (Notes in square brackets by FH.)

81. In this context Mettinger speaks of a mental "'basileomorphic' *image of God*" in ancient Israel. Cf. his "The Elusive Essence: Yhwh, El and Baal and the Distinctiveness of Israelite Faith," in *Die hebräische Bibel und ihre zweifache Nachgeschichte. FS Rolf Rendtorff*, ed. Erhard Blum et al. (Neukirchen-Vluyn: Neukirchener Verlag, 1990), 393–417, at 396. Emphasis in original.

82. Jean-Pierre Vernant, "Corps obscur, corps éclatant," in *Corps des dieux*, ed. Jean-Pierre Vernant and Charles Malamoud, Le temps de la réflexion VII (Paris: Gallimard, 1986), 19–45 (= Jean-Pierre Vernant, "Mortals and Immortals: The Body of the Divine," in Jean-Pierre Vernant, *Mortals and Immortals: Collected Essays* [Princeton, NJ: Princeton University Press, 1992], 27–49); Cf., for the ancient Near East, Porter, *What Is a God?*; for the OT, Hartenstein, *Angesicht*, 15–26.

83. Jean-Pierre Vernant, *Zwischen Mythos und Politik. Eine intellektuelle Autobiographie* (Berlin: Wagenbach, 1997 [French 1996]), 250.

84. Vernant, *Zwischen Mythos und Politik*.

85. On this, see, besides Hartenstein, *Angesicht*, and Aaron Shart, "Die 'Gestalt' YHWHs. Ein Beitrag zur Körpermetaphorik alttesta-

mentlicher Rede von Gott," *TZ* 55 (1999): 26–43, now more recently Benjamin D. Sommer, *The Bodies of God and the World of Ancient Israel* (Cambridge: Cambridge University Press, 2009); Andreas Wagner, *Gottes Körper. Zur alttestamentlichen Vorstellung der Menschengestaltigkeit Gottes* (Gütersloh: Gütersloher Verlagshaus, 2010); Andreas Wagner, ed., *Göttliche Körper—Göttliche Gefühle. Was leisten anthropomorphe und anthropopathische Götterkonzepte im Alten Orient und Alten Testament?* OBO 270 (Fribourg: Universitätsverlag; Göttingen: Vandenhoeck & Ruprecht, 2014).

86. Classic on this point: Ludwig Köhler, *Theologie des Alten Testaments*, 3rd ed. (Tübingen: Mohr [Siebeck], 1953), 6: "It is at this point that we recognize the function of the anthropomorphisms....The human figuration is not a humanization. They did not work that way, except in cheap polemics. Instead, they were meant to make God accessible to humans....They represent God as a person....Because the OT speaks of him in anthropomorphisms, its god appears as the personal and living God to those who encounter him willingly and actively, one who affects and approaches human beings."

87. See, respectively, Hartenstein, *Angesicht*; Klaus-Peter Adam, *Der königliche Held. Die Entsprechung von kämpfendem Gott und kämpfendem König in Psalm 18*, WMANT 91 (Neukirchen-Vluyn: Neukirchener Verlag, 2001).

88. On this, see Hornung, *Conceptions of God*, esp. 125–30; Claude Traunecker, *The Gods of Egypt*, trans. David Lorton (Ithaca, NY: Cornell University Press, 2001), 42–56. From the French original, *Les dieux d'Égypte* (Paris: Presses universitaires de France, ©1992).

89. Hornung, *Conceptions of God*, 252. Notes in brackets by FH. The phrase "multiplicity of approaches" is quoted from Henri Frankfort, et al., *The Intellectual Adventure of Ancient Man* (Chicago: University of Chicago Press, 1946), 16.

90. For these, see now Lambert, *Babylonian Creation Myths*, 147–68.

91. Cf. the famous passage in the *Enuma elish*, Tablet V.1–2: "He (i.e., Marduk) made the stations for the great gods; The stars, their images, as the stars of the Zodiac" (Leonard W. King, *Enuma Elish: The Seven Tablets of Creation* [New York: Cosimo Classics, 2010 {orig. 1902}]), 79. See, as essential to this idea, Francesca Rochberg, "'The Stars Their Likenesses': Perspectives on the Relation between Celestial Bodies and Gods in Ancient Mesopotamia," in Porter, *What Is a God?*, 41–91.

92. See the influential essay by Benno Landsberger, "Die Eigenbe-grifflichkeit der babylonischen Welt," *Islamica* 2 (1926): 355–72 (repr. *Libelli* 142; [Darmstadt: Wissenschaftliche Buchgesellschaft, 1965], 1–18).

93. Cf. Stolz, *Einführung*, 163–87, esp. 174; also his *Weltbilder der Religionen. Kultur und Natur, Diesseits und Jenseits, Kontrollierbares und Unkontrollierbares*, Theophil 4 (Zürich: Pano, 2001), 139–61.

94. Clement, *Strom.* 5.14.109.1: "One god there is 'midst gods and men supreme; in form, in mind, unlike to mortal men." See http://www .newadvent.org/fathers/02105.htm (accessed April 13, 2021).

95. Clement, *Strom.* 5.14.109.2 (see n. 94).

96. Clement, *Strom.* 5.14.109.3.

97. Clement, *Strom.* 7.4.22, in Fenton John Anthony Hort, trans., *Clement of Alexandria, Miscellanies Book 7* (New York: Macmillan, 1902), 37. Available online at http://www.westcotthort.com/books/Hort _-_Clement_of_Alexandria_-_Miscellanies_Book_VII_(1902).pdf.

98. *Theosophia* 68, in Philip Wheelwright, *Eraclitus* (Princeton, NJ: Princeton University Press, 1959), v. 75. Online at https://archive.org/ stream/heraclitus00whee/heraclitus00whee_djvu.txt.

99. This is the well-founded proposal of Laura M. Gemelli-Marciano, ed., *Die Vorsokratiker 1* (Berlin: Akademie Verlag, 2011), 268, 407–8.

100. For what follows, cf. Martin Hengel, *Judaism and Hellenism: Studies in Their Encounter in Palestine during the Early Hellenistic Period*, trans. John Bowden (Philadelphia: Fortress Press, 1974), 255–309 (on the *Interpretatio Graeca* of Judaism); Othmar Keel, "Warum," 246–52; Peter Schäfer, *Judeophobia: Attitudes toward the Jews in the Ancient World* (Cambridge, MA: Harvard University Press, 1997), 34–65.

101. Cf., e.g., Herbert Niehr, *Der höchste Gott. Alttestamentlicher JHWH-Glaube im Kontext syrisch-kanaanäischer Religion des 1. Jahrtausends v. Chr.*, BZAW 190 (New York: de Gruyter, 1990); Eric E. Elnes and Patrick D. Miller, "Elyon," *DDD*[2] (1999), 293–99.

102. So Schäfer, *Judeophobia*, 35.

103. Cf. Schäfer, *Judeophobia*, 35–36; Hengel, *Judaism and Hellenism*, 331n123, "end of the fourth century"; cf. Walter Spoerri, "Hekataios 4," *KlPauly* 2 (1967): 980–82.

104. Cf. Schäfer, *Judeophobia*, 86; François Lasserre, "Strabon," *KlPauly* 5 (1975): 381–85.

105. On this, see, e.g., Konrad Schmid, "Himmelsgott, Weltgott und Schöpfer. 'Gott' und 'Himmel' in der Zeit des Zweiten Tempels," in

Der Himmel, ed. Martin Ebner et al., JBT 20 (Neukirchen-Vluyn: Neukirchener Verlag, 2006), 111–48; Sebastian Grätz, "*Jhwh,* der Gott des Himmels. Erwägungen zu einer alttestamentlichen Vorstellung," in *Ex oriente Lux. Studien zur Theologie des Alten Testaments. FS Rüdiger Lux,* ed. Angelika Berlejung and Raik Heckl, ABG 39 (Leipzig: Evangelische Verlagsanstalt, 2012), 407–17; Friedhelm Hartenstein, "JHWH, Erschaffer des Himmels. Zu Herkunft und Bedeutung eines monotheistischen Kernarguments," *ZTK* 110 (2013): 383–409.

106. Cf. Wolfgang Röllig, "Baalshamem," *DDD²* (1999): 149–51, as well as Herbert Niehr, "JHWH in der Rolle des Baalšamem," in *Ein Gott allein? JHWH-Verehrung und biblischer Monotheismus im Kontext der israelitischen und altorientalischen Religionsgeschichte,* ed. Walter Dietrich and Martin A. Klopfenstein, OBO 139 (Fribourg: Universitätsverlag; Göttingen: Vandenhoeck & Ruprecht, 1994), 307–26.

107. For the state of research, see Rachel Hachlili, *Ancient Synagogues— Archaeology and Art: New Discoveries and Current Research,* Handbook of Oriental Studies 1, The Ancient Near East, vol. 105 (Leiden: Brill, 2013).

108. Cf. Schäfer, *Judeophobia,* 39, 226n35; Hengel, *Judaism and Hellenism,* 338–39.

109. Schäfer, *Judeophobia,* 17–21; cf. H. Wolfgang Helck, "Manethon," *KlPauly* 3 (1969): 952–53; for the citations of Manetho in Josephus, cf. Dagmar Labow, *Flavius Josephus, Contra Apionem Buch I. Einleitung, Text, Textkritischer Apparat, Übersetzung und Kommentar,* BWANT 167 (Stuttgart: Kohlhammer, 2005), 53–98, esp. the excursus on Manetho on 58–70. For this work in English, see *The Works of Josephus,* trans. William Whiston (Peabody, MA: Hendrickson, 1987), *Against Apion* I.14–16, 26–35, 773–812, at 778–80, 787–93.

110. Cf. Schäfer, *Judeophobia,* 36–38 (Varro); 31–33 (Tacitus); 42–45 (Celsus); Keel, "Warum," 247–48 (on Tacitus); 250 (on Varro).

111. Schäfer, *Judeophobia,* 34.

112. For the temple-dedication prayer in 1 Kgs 8 in light of the idea of heaven, cf. Hartenstein, *Unzugänglichkeit,* 225–26; Bernd Janowski, "'Ich will in eurer Mitte wohnen.' Struktur und Genese der exilischen *Schekina*-Theologie," in Bernd Janowski, *Gottes Gegenwart in Israel. Beiträge zur Theologie des Alten Testaments* (Neukirchen-Vluyn: Neukirchener Verlag, 1993), 119–47, at 129–30; for the expansive cosmology of Isa 66, see Matthias Albani, "'Wo sollte ein Haus sein, das ihr mir bauen könntet?' (Jes 66,1). Schöpfung als Tempel JHWHs?" in

Gemeinde ohne Tempel = Community without Temple: zur Substituierung und Transformation des Jerusalemer Tempels und seines Kults im Alten Testament, antiken Judentum und frühen Christentum, ed. Beate Ego, Armin Lange, Peter Pilhofer, and Kathrin Ehlers, WUNT 118 (Tübingen: Mohr Siebeck, 1999), 37–56.

113. See Marcus Tullius Cicero, *De natura deorum: Academic*, trans. Horace Rackham, LCL 268 (Cambridge, MA: Harvard University Press, 1979).

114. Tacitus, *Historiae* V,5,4. Quoted from *The Annals & The Histories*, ed. Moses Hadas, trans. Alfred Church and William Jackson Brodribb, Modern Library Classics, rev. ed. (New York: Random House, 2003), 565; cf. Keel, "Warum" (see n. 72), 247.

115. Cf. Schäfer, *Judeophobia*, 15–33 (on the expulsion from Egypt); for Tacitus, see 31–33. See also Keel, "Warum," 247.

116. Hecateus; cf. Schäfer, *Judeophobia*, 25.

117. This is the general consensus in OT exegesis; on this cf., e.g., Jörg Jeremias, *Theologie des Alten Testaments*, GAT 6 (Göttingen: Vandenhoeck & Ruprecht, 2015), 371: "Tightly aligned with the prohibition of foreign gods, in God's address, is the prohibition of images, which after the 1st commandment is the weightiest and most consequential rule in the Decalogue"; Jan Assmann, *Exodus. Die Revolution der Alten Welt* (Munich: Beck, 2015), 265: "The second commandment, the prohibition of images, is to be understood as forbidding cultic images. In that sense it is connected to the prohibition of foreign gods."

118. See also the course of the discussion in Keel, "Warum."

119. Cf. Belkis Philonenko-Sayar and Marc Philonenko, *Die Apokalypse Abrahams*, JSHRZ V/5 (Gütersloh: Mohn 1982), 415–60; Emil Schürer, Geza Vermes, et al., *The History of the Jewish People in the Age of Christ (175 B.C–A.D. 135)*, III/1 (New York: Bloomsbury T&T Clark, 2014), 288–92; Quotations from *Apoc. Ab.* are based on Alexander Kulik, *Retroverting Slavonic Pseudepigrapha* (Atlanta, GA: Society of Biblical Literature, 2004 and Leiden: Brill, 2005), available at https://www.marquette.edu/maqom/kuliktranslation.html. See also the older translation by Paul Rießler, *Altjüdisches Schrifttum außerhalb der Bibel* (Augsburg: B. Filser, 1928), 13–39, 1267–69; for an interpretation, cp. Beate Ego, "Abraham im Judentum," in *Abraham im Judentum, Christentum und Islam*, ed. Christfried Böttrich, Beate Ego, and Friedmann Eissler (Göttingen: Vandenhoeck & Ruprecht, 2009), 11–61.

120. *Apoc. Ab.* 1:1–2. Kulik writes "destroying" where older translations have "planing." "Destroying" seems hard to justify in the context.

121. On this, see Ego, "Abraham im Judentum," 33–34.

122. For the polemic/critique of images in these early Jewish texts (and *Apoc. Ab.*), cf. the still-valid summary in Horst Dietrich Preuss, *Verspottung fremder Religionen im Alten Testament*, BWANT 92 (Stuttgart: Kohlhammer, 1971), 260–68.

123. For the critique of idols in Pss 115 and 135 (and Hab 2:18–19), see Berlejung, *Theologie der Bilder*, 400–401; for Ps 135, see esp. Judith Gärtner, *Die Geschichtspsalmen. Eine Studie zu den Psalmen 78, 105, 106, 135 und 136 als hermeneutische Schlüsseltexte im Psalter*, FAT 84 (Tübingen: Mohr Siebeck, 2012), 318–72, esp. 335–36, 352–62 (for comparison with Ps 115); for the polemic against cult images in the LXX version of Ps 115, cf. Erich Zenger, "Götter- und Götterbildpolemik in Ps 112—113 LXX = Ps 113—115 MT," in Zenger, *Der Septuaginta-Psalter. Sprachliche und theologische Aspekte*, HBS 32 (Freiburg et al.: Herder, 2001), 229–55, esp. 236–45 (on Ps 115 MT); for Hebrew Ps 115, see Frank-Lothar Hossfeld and Erich Zenger, *Psalms 3*, trans. Linda M. Maloney, Hermeneia (Minneapolis: Fortress, 2011), 201–12.

124. Biblical quotations, unless otherwise noted, are from the NRSV.

125. Cf. Gärtner, *Die Geschichtspsalmen*, 360: "By culminating [its list] with the breath of life Psalm 135 emphasizes that a truly living breath can only come from Yʜwʜ, the creator of heaven and earth." See further Friedhelm Hartenstein, "Exklusiver und inklusiver Monotheismus. Zum 'Wesen' der Götter in Deuterojesaja und in den späten Psalmen," in *Ich will dir danken unter den Völkern. Studien zur israelitischen und altorientalischen Gebetsliteratur. FS Bernd Janowski*, ed. Alexandra Grund, Annette Krüger, and Florian Lippke (Gütersloh: Mohn, 2013), 194–219, at 213–14.

126. For the subject of "blessing" in the Psalter, see the overview by Martin Leuenberger, *Segen und Segenstheologien im alten Israel. Untersuchungen zu ihren religions- und theologiegschichtlichen Konstellationen und Transformationen*, ATANT 90 (Zürich: Theologischer Verlag, 2008), 449–50; for Psalm 67, cf. Frank-Lothar Hossfeld and Erich Zenger, *Psalms 2: A Commentary on Psalms 51—100*, trans. Linda M. Maloney, Hermeneia (Minneapolis: Fortress, 2005), 149–57; Hartenstein, *Angesicht*, 196–98.

127. Cf. Hartenstein, "Exklusiver und inklusiver Monotheismus," 206–7.

128. For these much-discussed texts, see Preuss, *Verspottung*, 192–237; Reinhard G. Kratz, *Kyros im Deuterojesajabuch. Redaktionsgeschichtliche Untersuchungen zu Entstehung und Theologie von Jes 40–55*, FAT 1 (Tübingen: Mohr Siebeck, 1991), 192–206; Berlejung, *Theologie der Bilder*, 369–91; Michael Brennan Dick, "Prophetic Parodies of Making the Cult Image," in Dick, *Born in Heaven, Made on Earth*, 1–53; Jürgen Werlitz, *Redaktion und Komposition. Zur Rückfrage hinter die Endgestalt von Jesaja 40–55*, BBB 122 (Berlin and Bodenheim: 1999), 40–53, 221–37; Sven Petry, *Die Entgrenzung JHWHs. Monolatrie, Bilderverbot und Monotheismus im Deuteronomium, in Deuterojesaja und im Ezechielbuch*, FAT 2nd ser. 27 (Tübingen: Mohr Siebeck, 2007), 105–240; Christina Ehring, *Rückkehr*, 262–67; Sonja Amman, *Götter für die Toren*, BZAW 466, 2015.

129. For Isa 44:9–20(21–23), see, besides the literature listed in n. 128, the thorough treatment by Ulrich Berges, *Jesaja 40–48*, HTK.AT 37 (Freiburg et al.: Herder, 2008), 332–62.

130. See Friedhelm Hartenstein, "Personalität Gottes im Alten Testament," in *Personalität Gottes*, ed. Wilfried Härle and Reiner Preul, MJT 19 (Leipzig: Evangelische Verlagsanstalt, 2007), 19–46, at 41–42; Hartenstein, "Exklusiver und inklusiver Monotheismus," 205–7.

131. For Jer 10:1–16, see Preuss, *Verspottung*, 166–70; Helga Weippert, *Schöpfer des Himmels und der Erde. Ein Beitrag zur Theologie des Jeremiabuches*, SBS 102 (Stuttgart: Katholisches Bibelwerk, 1982), 34–37; Berlejung, *Theologie der Bilder*, 392–99; Dick, "Prophetic Parodies," 17–20; for a full treatment, see Georg Fischer, *Jeremia 1–25*, HTK. AT 38 (Freiburg et al.: Herder, 2005), 373–99.

132. For this monotheistic "core argument," cf. Hartenstein, "JHWH, Erschaffer des Himmels."

133. On this, see Weippert, *Schöpfer*, 34–35.

134. For depictions of Zeus on coins, cf. Diana V. Edelman, "Tracking Observance of the Aniconic Tradition through Numismatics," in Edelman, *The Triumph of Elohim*, 185–225; Erhard Blum, "Der 'Schiqquz Schomem' und die Jehud-Drachme BMC Palestine S. 181, nr. 29," *BN* 90 (1997): 13–27.

135. Christian Frevel, "Der Eine oder die Vielen? Monotheismus und materielle Kultur in der Perserzeit," in *Gott—Götter—Götzen. XIV. Europäischer Kongress für Theologie (11.-15. September 2011) in Zürich*, ed. Christoph Schwöbel, VWGT 38 (Leipzig: Evangelische Verlagsanstalt, 2013), 238–65, at 264 (emphasis in original; explanations

in parentheses by FH). For the presumable Persian era/early Hellenistic debates over images of Yhwh see also Christoph Uehlinger, "Exodus, Stierbild und biblisches Kultbildverbot. Religionsgeschichtliche Voraussetzungen eines biblisch-theologischen Spezifikums," in *Freiheit und Recht. Festschrift Frank Crüsemann*, ed. Christof Hardmeier and Rainer Kessler (Gütersloh: Mohn, 2003), 71–73.

136. For an initial orientation to the state of the discussion in older and newer scholarship, cf., e.g., Christoph Dohmen, "Bilderverbot (AT/NT)," in Dohmen, *Studien zu Bilderverbot und Bildtheologie des Alten Testaments*, SBA 51 (Stuttgart: Katholisches Bibelwerk, 2012), 73–76 (= *NBL* 1 [1991]: 296–98); Werner H. Schmidt, *Die Zehn Gebote im Rahmen alttestamentlicher Ethik*, EdF 281 (Darmstadt: Wissenschaftliche Buchgesellschaft, 1993), 59–77; Matthias Köckert, *Die Zehn Gebote*, C. H. Beck Wissen (Munich: Beck, 2007), 55–65; Frank-Lothar Hossfeld, "Das Werden des alttestamentlichen Bilderverbotes im Kontext von Archäologie, Rechtsentwicklung und Prophetie. Thesen," in *Die Sichtbarkeit des Unsichtbaren. Zur Korrelation von Text und Bild im Wirkungskreis der Bibel*, ed. Bernd Janowski and Nino M. Zchomelidse, AGWB 3 (Stuttgart: Deutsche Bibelgesellschaft, 2003), 11–22.

137. For research on the Decalogue, see now the sophisticated overview by Eckart Otto, "Exkurs: Die Literatur-, Religions- und Rechtsgeschichte der Dekaloge," in Otto, *Deuteronomium 4,44–11,32*, HTKAT 8.2 (Freiburg et al.: Herder, 2012), 684–715.

138. For traditional numberings, cf., e.g., Köckert, *Die Zehn Gebote*, 26–35.

139. Thus earlier, and pithily, Walter Zimmerli, "Das zweite Gebot" [1950], in his *Gottes Offenbarung. Gesammelte Aufsätze*, 2nd ed., TB 19 (Munich: Kaiser, 1969), 234–48, at 236–38. The subsumption of the ban on images in the prohibition of foreign gods applies, in any case, to Deut 5, but for Exod 20 it is only probable, despite the opinion, given a basis especially by Frank-Lothar Hossfeld, that the additional conjunction *waw* before *təmûnâ* ("form, figure") in Exod 20:4, in contrast to Deut 5:8, is not to be read as explicative (and thus not different in meaning from Deut 5), but as copulative. (In that case the ban on images in Exod 20:4 is marked as independent from the ban on foreign gods because the plural suffixes in v. 5a ["worship *them* // serve *them*"] would apply in retrospect only as far as "cult image *and* figure" and not to the "other gods" in v. 3.) On this, cf. Frank-Lothar Hossfeld, *Der Dekalog. Seine späten Fassungen, die originale Komposition und seine Vorstufen*, OBO 45 (Fribourg: Universitätsver-

lag; Göttingen: Vandenhoeck & Ruprecht, 1982), 21–26. But, with Rudolf Smend in his review in *TR* 79 (1982): 458–59, at 459, one should not assign too broad a meaning to this difference, because the additional *waw* in Exod 20:4 can likewise be read as explicative (matching the asyndesis in the sentence structure of Deut 5:8).

140. For the reasons for this translation of the *waw*, see the previous note.

141. For all aspects of Deut 4:1–40, see now, at length, Otto, *Deuteronomium 1,1–4,3*, 508–92; for discussion of the scholarship on the literary genesis and the postexilic dating, see 532–38 (esp. 534 on the reception of the Priestly writing).

142. For what follows, see the religious-historical and theological-historical grounding in Friedhelm Hartenstein, "Die unvergleichliche 'Gestalt' JHWHs. Israels Geschichte mit den Bildern im Licht von Dtr 4,1–40," in Janowski and Zchomelidse, *Sichtbarkeit*, 49–77.

143. When Matthias Köckert speaks of this late-Deuteronomistic focus on the making of images of Yʜwʜ in Deut 4 as Israel's "original sin," it is with a precarious religious-historical construction that he compares this with the so-called sun tablet from Sippar (see §1.1b–c above). He concludes that an anthropomorphic cult image of Yʜwʜ existed in the Jerusalem temple until the exile (see §1.1e), but his thesis, despite his emphasis on its certainty, lacks a persuasive basis. (cf. Köckert, "Entstehung," and "Kultbild"; Köckert, *Die Zehn Gebote*, 57–60.) Otto, *Deuteronomium 1,1–4,43* is also critical of Köckert (and Niehr); on 563 he writes, "But that by no means signifies that this is a polemic against a cult image of Yʜwʜ in the Jerusalem Temple....Rather, in Deuteronomy 4 the combination of a ban on foreign gods and on images in the Deuteronomistic Horeb Decalogue [i.e., in Deut 5:6–8 {FH}] is presupposed, and the ban on images is interpreted monotheistically, in the context of the post-exilic continuation of the book of Deuteronomy, whereby the ban on images, combined with the prohibition of foreign gods, in light of the presupposition that foreign gods do not exist, becomes a *ban on idols*. So the alternative, that Deuteronomy 4:15–19 is about making an image of Yʜwʜ or of foreign gods, is too simple for the post-exilic continuation in Deuteronomy 4; what is at issue here is *a ban on any kind of divine image*." (Emphasis FH)

144. The clear intertextual link between Deut 4:16–19a and the Priestly creation story (Gen 1:1—2:4a) has often been noted and evaluated (see also below at §3.2c); cf., e.g., Michael A. Fishbane, *Biblical*

Interpretation in Ancient Israel (Oxford: Oxford University Press, 1985), 321–22; Otto, *Deuteronomium 1,1–4,43*, 564–66.

145. The expansion is given in italics above (vv. 17–18). On this, see, e.g., Christoph Dohmen, *Das Bilderverbot. Seine Entstehung und seine Entwicklung im Alten Testament*, BBB 62 (Frankfurt: Athenaeum, 2d ed. 1987), 223–30, with the summary on 229–30 (addition of the relative clauses about the three cosmological regions in both Decalogues *with reference to Deuteronomy 4* by a/the later "Pentateuchal redactor").

146. On this, see Hossfeld, *Dekalog*, 272–73; Silvia Schroer, *In Israel gab es Bilder. Nachrichten von darstellender Kunst im Alten Testament*, OBO 74 (Fribourg: Universitätsverlag; Göttingen: Vandenhoeck & Ruprecht, 1987), 304–14; Dohmen, *Bilderverbot*, 41–49; Dohmen, art. psl, *TDOT* 12:30–38 (= Dohmen, *Studien zum Bilderverbot*, 50–58); *Ges*[18], 1065–66.

147. In the polemic sense (for idols or similar objects), e.g., Deut 4:28; Isa 2:8; 17:8; 37:19; Jer 25:6–7, 14; 32:20. [Translator's note: The Hebrew word is not polemic in itself and in most English translations is simply "work" {so NAB, NRSV, etc.} or "works" {AV}. But the author here translates *Machwerk* = "concoction," "lousy job," etc.]

148. This is frequently called a *dativus commodi* (e.g., by Hossfeld, *Dekalog*, 272). For clarification we refer to the fundamental semantic study by Ernst Jenni regarding the following aspects of the *lamed dativum*, which are apposite for its usage in the formulations of the ban on images: (a) "effecting possession," (b) specified by "make, produce," and finally, (c) "referential identity between the giver and the recipient" = reflexive; the relevant passages are listed in Rubric 322 (all instances with the verb *ʿśh*), at 3224 in Ernst Jenni, *Die hebräischen Präpositionen 3: Die Präposition Lamed* (Stuttgart: Kohlhammer, 2000), 90; for the classifying criteria listed above, see 3, 84. For an extrabiblical example of analogous usage of *ʿśh + l* see lines 24–25 of the Moabite Mesha inscription from the 9th century BCE (KAI 181): "*Make for yourselves*, each one of you, a cistern in [your] house" (Manfred Weippert, *Historisches Textbuch zum Alten Testament*, GAT 10 [Göttingen: Vandenhoeck & Ruprecht, 2010], 247; emphasis FH).

149. Thus the broad scholarly consensus on dating; cf., besides the works of Hossfeld, Otto, and Köckert mentioned above, Christoph Levin, "Der Dekalog am Sinai," in Levin, *Fortschreibungen. Gesammelte Studien zum Alten Testament*, BZAW 316 (Berlin: de Gruyter, 2003), 60–80, according to whom the ban on images was not yet part of the "original

Decalogue [*Urdekalog*]" in Exod 20 (64n11, concerning Zimmerli's structural analysis [see n. 139 above], which did not yet conclude to "the likely literary-critical consequences" of an identification as a "subsequent insertion").

150. German "Brennspiegel," literally "burning glass." The English "magnifying glass" is less precise.

151. Eckart Otto, "Der Dekalog als Brennspiegel israelitischer Rechtsgeschichte," in *Alttestamentlicher Glaube und biblische Theologie. FS Horst Dietrich Preuss*, ed. Jutta Hausmann and Hans-Jürgen Zobel (Stuttgart: Kohlhammer, 1992), 59–68.

152. Werner H. Schmidt, *Alttestamentlicher Glaube*, 8th ed. (Neukirchen-Vluyn: Neukirchener Verlag, 1996), 78; Cf. Schmidt, *Zehn Gebote*, 63: "as to the chronological beginnings of the ban on images we must withhold judgment."

153. On this, cf., e.g., Hans Jochen Boecker, *Recht und Gesetz im Alten Testament und im Alten Orient*, 2nd ed. (Neukirchen-Vluyn: Neukirchener Verlag, 1984), 116–65; Frank Crüsemann, *The Torah: Theology and History of Old Testament Law* (Minneapolis: Fortress, 2003), 109–328; Eckart Otto, "Recht im antiken Israel," in *Die Rechtskulturen der Antike. Vom Alten Orient bis zum Römischen Reich*, ed. Ulrich Manthe (Munich: Beck, 2003), 151–90, esp. 160–69 (overview).

154. Cf., classically, Jörn Halbe, *Das Privilegrecht Jahwes Ex 34,10–26. Gestalt und Wesen, Herkunft und Wirken in vordeuteronomischer Zeit*, FRLANT 114 (Göttingen: Vandenhoeck & Ruprecht, 1975); similarly Eckart Otto, *Theologische Ethik des Alten Testaments*, Theologische Wissenschaft 3/2 (Stuttgart: Kohlhammer, 1994), 2–3, 211, 213–14, 232–33.

155. Cf. Alexandra Grund, *Die Entstehung des Sabbats. Seine Bedeutung für Israels Zeitkonzept und Erinnerungskultur*, FAT 75 (Tübingen: Mohr Siebeck, 2011), 51–63.

156. See Shimon Gesundheit, *Three Times a Year: Studies on Festival Legislation in the Pentateuch*, FAT 82 (Tübingen: Mohr Siebeck, 2012), 11–43, who regards Exod 34:18–26 as a midrash-style resumption of the festal calendar from Exod 23:14–19 and sees in Exod 34:11–26 both deuteronomistic and Priestly influence. (For recent redaction-historical hypotheses positing a postexilic beginning, cf. Gesundheit, *Three Times a Year*, 42n87.)

157. Thus previously, and accurately, Bruno Baentsch, *Exodus–Leviticus–Numeri*, HK I/2 (Göttingen: Vandenhoeck & Ruprecht,

1903), 186, who adopts the view of a deuteronomistic redactor (in possession of an older model in v. 23): "The fact that Yahweh has spoken from heaven, thus showing himself to be a heavenly, supernatural God, appears as the basis for the prohibition of apostasy and service to idols given in v. 23. On this cf. the extended theological reasoning in Deut 4:12, 15ff.; v. 22b is in a sense the quintessence thereof." For a still more pointed presentation, see Eckart Otto, *Theologische Ethik*, 231, who locates the opening of the Book of the Covenant in Exod 22:22–23 as "linking to Exod 19:3b–8 and Deuteronomy 4, within the horizon of the Pentateuch redaction" and sees the verse, from a literary-critical point of view, as "inseparable" from the frame of the Book of the Covenant.

158. Differently the attempt by Dohmen, *Bilderverbot*, 176–80, to reconstruct an ancient and primitive form of a pre-Decalogue ban on images from Exod 20:23b (p. 271), and at the same time to find in this text, together with v. 24, "the original cultic-law introduction to the Book of the Covenant" (p. 179). In doing so he postulates an originally singular prohibition behind the plural forms in v. 23b, without any basis in the textual tradition (Dohmen, *Bilderverbot*, 162–63). It seems much more probable, however (with Hossfeld, *Dekalog*, 180) that we have in Exod 20:23 (together with v. 22) a "well-constructed reformulation of the ban on images" that is close to the later polemic against them.

159. See previously the analysis by Halbe, *Privilegrecht*, 122–26, 215–19; see further Hossfeld, *Dekalog*, 210, for the accommodation of the "law of privilege" to the Decalogue by the deuteronomistic redactor, who relates it to Exod 34:1, 4aα,b, (9b), 11b, 17, 27*; cf. Hossfeld, *Dekalog*, 268, on v. 17: "Guided by the model of the Decalogue, a deuteronomistic redactor inserts the ban here; it is therefore to be regarded as an isolated prohibition. The making of cast idols is forbidden by means of a reworking of Exod 32:31 and Deut 9:12 (cf. Lev 19:4)."

160. Cf., e.g., the analysis by Karl Elliger, *Leviticus*, HAT I/4 (Tübingen: Mohr, 1966), 245; for Leviticus 19 as a whole, see Otto, *Theologische Ethik*, 243–48.

161. For analysis, see Elliger, *Leviticus*, 363–64 (deliberate reference to Lev 19:4 with repeated ʾĕlîlîm) and Hossfeld, *Dekalog*, 268: "In Lev 26:1 the terminology of the ban on images (cf. Lev 19:4) has absorbed the ban on foreign gods. With a unique differentiation, various cultic objects are presented and rendered abhorrent. YHWH is set over against these nothings. The ban belongs to the late polemic against idols."

162. For late theology of the Sabbath (in the Holiness Code and other postexilic texts), cf. Friedhelm Hartenstein, "Der Sabbat als Zeichen und heilige Zeit. Zur Theologie des Ruhetages im Alten Testament," in *Das Fest: Jenseits des Alltags*, ed. Martin Ebner et al., Jahrbuch für Biblische Theologie 18 (Neukirchen-Vluyn: Neukirchener Verlag, 2004), 103–31, at 126–31.

163. Georg Braulik, *Deuteronomium II: 16,18–34,12*, NEB 28 (Würzburg: Echter Verlag, 1992), 202.

164. For this location, see the analysis by Walter Groß, *Richter*, HTK. AT 10 (Freiburg et al.: Herder, 2009), 754–64.

165. Cf. Hossfeld, *Dekalog*, 268: "Deuteronomy 27:15, a recognized secondary framing formula….In comparison with the Decalogue's ban on images the *dativus commodi* is missing here….The cursing clause evaluates in the style of the *tô ʿēbâ* [abomination] laws and explains with reference to Hos 13:2. We have here a newer, late-Deuteronomistic formulation of the ban on images." Dohmen's evaluation of the text, likewise as postexilic and redactional (*Bilderverbot*, 231–35) is somewhat different: Deut 27:15 is thus to be "of levitical provenience" and to lie "on the same line…as the redaction of Lev 19:4; 26:1" (p. 235; brackets tr.).

166. So also the summary by Hossfeld, *Dekalog*, 269: "The isolated appearances of the ban on images presuppose the Decalogue in its deuteronomistic redaction."

167. Cf. the summary on the origins of the Decalogue in Hossfeld, *Dekalog*, 283.

168. For an introduction to the latest state of research on the redaction- and composition-criticism as well as proposals for dating the various layers of Deutero-Isaiah (Odil Hannes Steck, Reinhard G. Kratz, Jürgen van Oorschot, et al.), cf. Jürgen Werlitz, *Redaktion*, 15–91, and also Konrad Schmid, *The Old Testament: A Literary History*, trans. Linda M. Maloney (Minneapolis: Fortress, 2012), 131–36.

169. On these marks of identity in emerging Judaism, cf. Klaus Grünwaldt, *Exil und Identität. Beschneidung, Passa und Sabbat in der Priesterschrift*, BBB 85 (Frankfurt: Hain, 1992).

170. Cf. Christina Ehring, *Rückkehr*.

171. On this, see Ehring, *Rückkehr*, 156–63, esp. 159–61 (on *kābôd* as a Deutero-Isaianic contrasting parallel to the return of the cult image of Marduk in Babylonian sources).

172. For *kābôd* in the Priestly writing, cf. Wagner, *Gottes Herrlichkeit*, 52–122; for the more or less contemporary conception in the Book

of Ezekiel, see Ehring, *Rückkehr*, 191–203; Wagner, *Gottes Herrlichkeit*, 238–85.

173. Cf. Ehring, *Rückkehr*, 206: "Both Ezekiel and Deutero-Isaiah separate themselves from the Babylonian practice of representing the return of the deity to its home location as the return of its cult image in that they retain, out of all the elements of the visible form of the divinity, only the aspect of the brilliance that emanates from it (כבוד); this was also a component of the pre-exilic Jerusalem conception of Yhwh as a king enthroned on Zion."

174. Cf. Hartenstein, *Unzugänglichkeit*, 66–68 (on the connection between Yhwh's garment and "glory"); 69–76 (on the Mesopotamian parallels of the "terrifying brilliance"); 78–107 (on the motif of the *kābōd* that fills the cosmos and the temple in the Jerusalem cultic tradition, beginning with Isa 6).

175. More fully on what follows: Ehring, *Rückkehr*, 220–62; Hartenstein, "Exklusiver und inklusiver Monotheismus," 194–219; 201–3.

176. Translation (altered) from NRSV in light of Ehring, *Rückkehr*, 227.

177. According to Herodotus, *Histories* I, 183, Xerxes is supposed to have undertaken a punitive action against the cult of Marduk in 484 BCE (cf. Herodotus, *The Histories*, trans. Tom Holland [New York: Viking Penguin, 2013], 90).

178. Cf. Ehring, *Rückkehr*, 252–55; Friedhelm Hartenstein, "'…dass erfüllt ist ihr Frondienst' (Isa 40,3). Die Geschichtshermeneutik Deuterojesajas im Licht der Rezeption von Jesaja 6 in Jesaja 40,1–11*," in Hartenstein, *Das Archiv des verborgenen Gottes: Studien zur Unheilsprophetie Jesajas und zur Zionstheologie der Psalmen in assyrischer Zeit*, Biblisch-theologische Studien 74 (Neukirchen-Vluyn: Neukirchener Theologie, 2011), 97–125.

179. Cf. Werlitz, *Redaktion*, 40–53; 221–37; Ehring, *Rückkehr*, 262–67. For a proposal for a different set of layers for the idol passages, cf. also Petry, *Entgrenzung*, 105–240.

180. Thus also Werlitz, *Redaktion*, 221–35, esp. 226–27, according to whom "the idol-texts belong, in fact, to the oldest material in Isaiah 40–55" and were written in Babylon: "Yhwh's uniqueness, his aniconic worship, guaranteed his otherness and thus also that they were finished with what was foreign and appeared to be superior. The God who did not allow himself to be pressed into an image is vastly superior to the God who is 'only' image" (235).

181. Cf. Jörg Jeremias, *Theologie*, 271, according to whom for Deutero-Isaiah "the uniquely effective creator is as a matter of course also the unique lord of history." Cf. also Hartenstein, "Frondienst"; also his "Yнwн's Ways and New Creation in Deutero-Isaiah," in *Remembering and Forgetting in Early Second Temple Judah*, ed. Ehud Ben Zvi and Christoph Levin, FAT 85 (Tübingen: Mohr Siebeck, 2012), 73–89.

182. For an extensive treatment of this idea in Isa 40:12–31, see Hartenstein, "JHWH, Erschaffer des Himmels," 400–404.

183. On this, see, at length, Berlejung, *Theologie der Bilder*, 80–171 (production of Mesopotamian cult images); 370–75 (on Isa 40:18–20 against the Mesopotamian background she has portrayed).

184. NRSV translation altered to match the author's.—tr.

185. See Matthias Albani, *Der eine Gott und die himmlischen Heerscharen. Zur Begründung des Monotheismus bei Deuterojesaja im Horizont der Astralisierung des Gottesverständnisses im Alten Orient*, ABG 1 (Leipzig: Evangelische Verlagsanstalt, 2000), 124–56.

186. For the "implicit cosmology" of the older Jerusalem psalms (Pss 24:7–10; 93; 29; 46*; 48*) [the asterisks signify that only part of the texts presumably dates back to the preexilic period], cf. Hartenstein, *Unzugänglichkeit*, 42–62.

187. For the cosmological and royal-symbolic implications of these verses, cf. Hartenstein, *Angesicht*, 164–70.

188. On this, see the excursus in Albani, *Der eine Gott*, 186–230: "Zur Bedeutung des Himmelsheeres in vorexilischer Zeit" (On the meaning of the host of heaven in the preexilic period).

189. On this, cf. also Friedhelm Hartenstein, "Weltbild und Bilderverbot. Kosmologische Implikationen des biblischen Monotheismus," in *Die Welt als Bild*, ed. Christoph Markschies and Johannes Zachhuber, AKG 107 (Berlin: de Gruyter, 2008), 15–37.

190. The remarks in this section follow, in part, Friedhelm Hartenstein, "Vom Sehen und Schauen Gottes. Überlegungen zu einer theologischen Ästhetik aus der Sicht des Alten Testaments," in *Ästhetik*, ed. Elisabeth Gräb-Schmidt and Reiner Preul, Marburger Jahrbuch Theologie 22 (Leipzig: Evangelische Verlagsanstalt, 2010), 16–37, at 27–31.

191. Important for what follows is, on the one hand, Jörg Jeremias, *Der Prophet Hosea*, ATD 24/1 (Göttingen: Vandenhoeck & Ruprecht, 1983); Jeremias, *Theologie*, 136–46; on the other hand, Henrik Pfeiffer, *Das Heiligtum von Bethel im Spiegel des Hoseabuches*, FRLANT 183 (Göttingen: Vandenhoeck & Ruprecht, 1999), to whose literary-critical

and redaction-critical analysis Christoph Uehlinger also refers ("Exodus, Stierbild," 58–63) in regard to the long-enduring reflections on God and images echoed in the Book of Hosea.

192. Cf. Reinhard G. Kratz, "Erkenntnis Gottes im Hoseabuch," *ZTK* 94 (1997): 1–24; Jeremias, *Theologie*, 137.

193. Cf. the analyses of these three passages in Pfeiffer, *Heiligtum*, 101–71.

194. Thus with Helmut Utzschneider, *Hosea—Prophet vor dem Ende. Zum Verhältnis von Geschichte und Institution in der alttestamentlichen Prophetie*, OBO 31 (Fribourg: Universitätsverlag; Göttingen: Vandenhoeck & Ruprecht, 1980), 107. For the following translations of text-critically difficult passages, cf. Jörg Jeremias, *Der Prophet Hosea*, 102, 127, 158–59; and Henrik Pfeiffer, *Heiligtum*, 130 (on Hos 8:4–6), 101 (on Hos 10:5–6), and 164–65 (on Hos 13:1–2).

195. This concept of image, almost always used pejoratively ("idol"), wavers in meaning because of the homophony of the two verb roots of *ʿṣb*: "image/bind" (*ʿṣb* I), and "grieve/annoy" (*ʿṣb* II); see Ges[18], 999. On that homophony, see Schroer, *Bilder*, 315–20; Berlejung, *Theologie der Bilder*, 305–6.

196. In Hos 8:4b, I join Pfeiffer, *Heiligtum*, 158–64, in supposing a first, image-critical redaction; his positioning of it as predeuteronomic is illuminating (164). It could well be contemporary with the basic layer of Exod 32 (see below), toward the end of the 7th century BCE. In that case the *dativus commodi*, "make for oneself," attested here for the first time and antecedent to the ban on images (see above, §2.3a) is revealing. Jeremias, *Hosea*, 107, assigns the half-verse to the prophet (critique of idolatry in light of the first commandment, something that can scarcely be maintained today). Pfeiffer (164) and Jeremias (108) agree in assigning v. 6a to postexilic polemic against imagery (see §2.2b above).

197. (Brackets in the translation represent the author's text as it differs from NRSV.) For Jeremias (*Hosea*, 105–8), Hos 8:5–6 belongs entirely to the basic material of the Book of Hosea; for Pfeiffer (*Heiligtum*, 101–29), only in part. According to Uehlinger, as regards Pfeiffer's analysis of the "less sophisticated possibilities from a literary point of view," we should give preference to an integral reading of the text (Uehlinger, "Exodus, Stierbild," 60, with n71). It may already be looking back at the conquest of Samaria (after 722/720 BCE), and with the key word *kābôd* evoking a cultic concept of the divine presence *that has already been separated from the image* (cf. the later usage in Deutero-Isaiah, "P,"

and Ezekiel. See §2.4a above). For the *kābôd* of the calf in Hos 8:5, cf. the similar reflections by Utzschneider, *Hosea*, 117–18, who interprets the concept as the "powerful and protecting presence" of God, the disappearance of which is lamented by the people in Hos 8:5.

198. According to Jeremias (*Hosea*, 158–67), within Hos 13:1–2 only v. 2bα is secondary (late polemic against idols, like Hos 8:6a). For Pfeiffer (*Heiligtum*, 164–71), the whole of v. 2 is due to a double redactional reworking: on the one hand, regarding v. 2a he points to the expression "they made a *cast image for themselves*" as alluding to Deut 9:12; 2 Kgs 17:16; Ps 106:19, and to Exod 32:4, 8; Deut 9:16; Neh 9:18, in light of the ban on images (*dativus commodi*); on the other hand he sees "all of them the work of artisans" as in the context of late anti-idol polemics such as Pss 115:4; 135:15 (see §2.2b.2 above). The direct plays on Hos 8:4–6 (silver and ʿ *ăṣabîm*, Pfeiffer, *Heiligtum*, 170–71) in Hos 13:2a would be exegesis within the Book of Hosea, and *təbûnâ*, "skill/understanding," finally, would indicate that this first redaction belongs to the postexilic period because "the production of idols rests on *their own* artistic skill" (171, emphasis in original). To me it appears that only the elements of the text that are underscored above can definitely be postexilic expansion, part of the second redaction. Still, we should pay attention to Othmar Keel's statement ("Warum," 276) that cultic kissing, as in Hos 13:2bβ, is "not a common *topos* of polemic against idols." It is attested elsewhere only for Baʿal in 1 Kgs 19:18; for religious-historical parallels, cf. Berlejung, "Kultische Küsse," n38. The situation in Hos 13:2 is complex.

199. Keel, "Warum," 255.

200. Keel, "Warum," 280.

201. Cf. Othmar Keel, *Das Recht der Bilder gesehen zu werden. Drei Fallstudien zur Methode der Interpretation altorientalischer Bilder*, OBO 122 (Fribourg: Universitätsverlag; Göttingen: Vandenhoeck & Ruprecht, 1992), 169–93 (on bull symbolism in Syria and the Levant); Klaus Koenen, *Bethel. Geschichte, Kult und Theologie*, OBO 192 (Fribourg: Universitätsverlag; Göttingen: Vandenhoeck & Ruprecht, 2003), 95–132 (on the calf at Bethel).

202. It is possible here, with reservations, to point also to the extra-biblical *Onomasticon*, where "at a particular period we can observe a clustering of *ba ʿal* elements in the vicinity of Samaria" (Fritz Stolz, *Einführung*, 127); Jeffrey H. Tigay, *You Shall Have No Other Gods: Israelite Religion in the Light of Hebrew Inscriptions*, HSS 31 (Atlanta: Scholars

Press, 1986), 65–66. Here we should note that the word was also used as an epithet for YHWH.

203. For the analysis of the narrative presupposed here, whose genesis is again the subject of controversy, cf. Erik Aurelius, *Der Fürbitter Israels. Eine Studie zum Mosebild im Alten Testament*, CB.OT 27 (Stockholm: Almqvist & Wiksell, 1988), 76–77 (7th c. BCE, "between the fall of Samaria and that of Jerusalem" [77]), as well as the thorough study by Michael Konkel, *Sünde und Vergebung. Eine Rekonstruktion der Redaktionsgeschichte der hinteren Sinaiperikope (Exodus 32–34) vor dem Hintergrund der aktuellen Pentateuchmodelle*, FAT 58 (Tübingen: Mohr Siebeck, 2008). According to Konkel, the core of Exodus 32* is predeuteronomistic. (His different assignments of texts in Exod 32–34 to separate layers are most easily grasped in the table on 246–48.) For discussion of the historical location of the fundamental narrative in Exod 32, cf. Konkel, *Sünde und Vergebung*, 279–82: 7th c. BCE (between 722 and 701 BCE). Similarly Jeremias, *Theologie*, 213–18.

204. According to Konkel, *Sünde und Vergebung*, 246, the much-discussed acclamation in Exod 32:4b–5a (also in 1 Kgs 12:28), is a later insertion in light of Deuteronomistic History ("on a level with the late-deuteronomistic section 32:7–15a," Moses's petition). For him the exposition of the basic narrative is made up of the verses here discussed, Exod 32:1–4a, plus vv. 5b–6.

205. On the level of the overall narrative in the Book of Exodus this very probably represents a perverted replication of the cultic meals that Israel had previously celebrated before YHWH at the foot of the mountain (Exod 18:12; 24:1, 9–11).

206. Jean-Luc Marion, "Idol und Bild," in *Phänomenologie des Idols*, ed. Bernhard Casper, Alber Broschur Philosophie (Freiburg and Munich: Alber, 1981), 107–32. See further also Paul Ricoeur, *Freud and Philosophy: An Essay on Interpretation*, trans. Denis Savage (New Haven, CT: Yale University Press, 1970), on the "inevitable ambiguity" of the "signs of the sacred" (531). "An idol is the reification of the horizon into a thing, the fall of the sign into a supernatural and supracultural object....For if the Wholly Other draws near, it does so in the signs of the sacred; but symbols soon turn into idols. Thus the cultural object of our human sphere is split in two, half becoming profane, the other half sacred....Thus the idols must die—so that symbols may live" (530–31). For the problem of the "freezing" of the image/in the image, cf. also Michael Moxter, "All at Once? Simultaneität, Bild, Repräsentation," in

Präsenz im Entzug. Ambivalenzen des Bildes, ed. Philipp Stoellger and Thomas Klie, HUT 58 (Tübingen: Mohr Siebeck, 2011), 129–44.

207. The focus on desire in the interpretation of Exod 32 presented here is favored not least by the unusual continuation of the event in which Moses, in the wake of God's condemnation, pulverizes the golden calf image and gives the dust to the people to drink (Exod 32:20; there is a distant analogy in Num 5:11–31). The "absorption into oneself" of the thing desired is thus accomplished as a demonstration of its nothingness.

208. Marion, "Idol und Bild," 114–16.

209. Wilhelm Martin Leberecht de Wette, *Beiträge zur Einleitung in das Alte Testament* (Halle: Schimmelpfennig und Compagnie, 1806).

210. Thus Otto Kaiser, "Pentateuch und Deuteronomistisches Geschichtswerk," in Kaiser, *Studien zur Literaturgeschichte des Alten Testaments*, FB 90 (Würzburg: Echter Verlag, 2000), 70–133, at 127.

211. On this, cf. the overview of research by Michael Pietsch, "Steine, Bilder, Texte. Überlegungen zum Verhältnis von Archäologie und biblischer Exegese für eine Rekonstruktion der Religionsgeschichte Israels am Beispiel der josianischen Reform," *VF* 53 (2008): 51–62.

212. For the minimalist position, cf. Christoph Levin, "Josia im Deuteronomistischen Geschichtswerk," in his *Fortschreibungen*, 198–216, according to which the text reads like a "Cloaca maxima" (203) of all the cultic atrocities described with horror by the deuteronomists; it should be granted no historical authority beyond its late deuteronomistic context of origin.

213. For such a cautious attempt, cf. Christof Hardmeier, "König Joschija in der Klimax des DtrG (2Reg 22f.) und das vordtr Dokument einer Kultreform am Residenzort (23,4–15*). Quellenkritik, Vorstufenrekonstruktion und Geschichtstheologie in 2Reg 22f.," in *Erzählte Geschichte. Beiträge zur narrativen Kultur im Alten Israel*, ed. Rüdiger Lux, BTSt 40 (Neukirchen-Vluyn: Neukirchener Verlag, 2000), 81–145.

214. Cf. two contrary arguments, that of Christoph Uehlinger, "Gab es eine joschijanische Kultreform? Plädoyer für ein begründetes Minimum," in *Jeremia und die 'deuteronomistische Bewegung,'* ed. Walter Groß, BBB 98 (Weinheim: Beltz Athenäum, 1995), 57–89, and that of Herbert Niehr, "Die Reform des Joschija. Methodische, historische und religionsgeschichtliche Aspekte," in the same volume, 33–55. According to Uehlinger, who agrees very closely with the literary-historical analysis of Hardmeier (see n. 213 above), there are certainly reasons, based

Notes

on the archaeological finds from Iron Age IIC, for supposing that there were (religiously motivated) reforming actions, while Niehr excludes the idea because he finds no corresponding points of reference in the archaeological "primary sources" (though he does agree that there was an increasing concentration of Judahite state governance in Jerusalem in the 7th c. BCE).

215. Michael Pietsch, *Die Kultreform Josias*, FAT 86 (Tübingen: Mohr Siebeck, 2013).

216. Cf. previously Levin, "Josia," 198–99.

217. Cf. the widely accepted religious-historical thesis of Manfred Weippert, "Synkretismus und Monotheismus. Religionsinterne Konfliktbewältigung im alten Israel," in Weippert, *JHWH und die anderen Götter. Studien zur Religionsgeschichte des antiken Israel in ihrem syrisch-palästinischen Kontext*, FAT 18 (Tübingen: Mohr Siebeck, 1997), 1–24.

218. For Deut 16:21, cf. Christian Frevel, *Aschera und der Ausschließlichkeitsanspruch YHWHs. Beiträge zu literarischen, religionsgeschichtlichen und ikonographischen Aspekten der Ascheradiskussion*, BBB 94/1 (Weinheim: Beltz Athenäum, 1995), 1:164–210, esp. 189–90.

219. Cf. Pietsch, *Kultreform*, 310–12, 322–23, 484.

220. Cf. the detailed religious- and tradition-critical studies on the individual aspects of the catalogue of reforms in 2 Kgs 23:4–20: Pietsch, *Kultreform*, 206–442.

221. Hermann Spieckermann, *Juda unter Assur in der Sargonidenzeit*, FRLANT 129 (Göttingen: Vandenhoeck & Ruprecht, 1982), 245–56.

222. Steven W. Holloway, *Aššur Is King! Aššur Is King! Religion in the Exercise of Power in the Neo-Assyrian Empire*, CHANE 10 (Leiden and Boston: Brill, 2002).

223. Cf. Othmar Keel and Christoph Uehlinger, *Gods, Goddesses, and Images of God in Ancient Israel*, trans. Thomas H. Trapp (Minneapolis: Fortress, 1998), 283–372.

224. On this see, e.g., Fritz Stolz, *Einführung*, 175–77; Jeremias, *Theologie*, 197–98.

225. Cf. n. 231 below.

226. For this extensively discussed problem based on inscriptional findings and iconography, see, e.g., Keel and Uehlinger, *Gods, Goddesses*, 210–47; Frevel, *Aschera* 2:854–80; Jörg Jeremias and Friedhelm Hartenstein, "'JHWH und seine Aschera.' 'Offizielle Religion' und 'Volksreligion' zur Zeit der klassischen Propheten," in *Religionsgeschichte Israels. Formale und materiale Aspekte*, ed. Bernd Janowski and Matthias Köckert,

VWGT 15 (Gütersloh: Kaiser; Gütersloher Verlagshaus, 1999), 79–138; Zeev Meshel et al., *Kuntillet 'Ajrud (Ḥorvat Teman): An Iron Age II Religious Site on the Judah-Sinai Border* (Jerusalem: Israel Exploration Society, 2012), 358–64, bibliography by Nira Naveh. Critical with regard to the interpretation of Asherah in the finds at Kuntillet 'Ajrud are, e.g., André Lemaire, *The Birth of Monotheism: The Rise and Disappearance of Yahwism* (Washington, DC: Biblical Archaeology Society, 2007); Benjamin Sass, "On Epigraphic Hebrew *'ŠR* and **'ŠRH*, and on Biblical Asherah," *Transeuphratène* 46 (2014): 47–66, 189–90.

227. Cf. Frevel, *Aschera* 1:538–45; 2:927–28; Pietsch, *Kultreform*, 322–23, both rightly reticent in regard to the posited "original" character of the cultic object referred to in 2 Kgs 21:7.

228. For a critical evaluation of this thesis, see Frevel, *Aschera* 2:690–94.

229. Pietsch, *Kultreform*, 323. Emphasis in the original.

230. On this, see again Keel, "Warum," 262–67, 280; Keel, *Geschichte Jerusalems* 1, 264–332.

231. Pietsch, *Kultreform* (see n. 215 above), 484. Emphasis in the original; brackets FH.

232. For this "cultic reform," see Keel, "Warum," 273–74 (with a reliance in principle on its historicity, at any rate as far as the image of the bronze serpent is concerned).

233. On this, see Keel, *Recht der Bilder*, 195–266 ("polyvalence of the serpent").

234. Cf. Yitṣhaḳ Magen, *Mount Gerizim Excavations II: A Temple City*, JSP 8 (Jerusalem: Israel Antiquities Authority, 2008), 157, fig. 283 (one individual copper serpent from the grounds of the Hellenistic temple of Yʜwʜ on Mount Gerizim).

235. Cf. fig. 5 above. It is not altogether clear whether it was always the case that a single massebah served as the central cultic symbol in Arad; for a time, at least, there is evidence of two steles in the sanctuary, though according to Jens Kamlah of Tübingen (per e-mail) it is probable that only one was set up for cultic use while the other may have been stored behind a curtain (as a sacred object no longer in use but still stored in the holy place?).

236. For "attention" as a conscious and unconscious mode of physical perception between observation and response, see Bernhard Waldenfels, *Phänomenologie der Aufmerksamkeit*, stw 1734 (Frankfurt: Suhrkamp, 2004).

237. See §2.2b above, with nn. 134–35.

238. Cf. Martin Leuenberger, *Segen und Segenstheologien*; for an overview, see Leuenberger, "Segen im Alten Testament," in *Segen*, ed. Martin Leuenberger, Themen der Theologie 10 (Tübingen: Mohr Siebeck, 2015), 49–75.

239. See Paul Ricoeur, *The Rule of Metaphor: The Creation of Meaning in Language*, trans. Robert Czerny with Kathleen McLaughlin and John Costello, SJ (London: Routledge, 2003); George Lakoff and Mark Johnson, *Metaphors We Live By* (Chicago: University of Chicago Press, 2003 [1980]). Important introductions to theory of metaphors include Anselm Haverkamp, ed., *Theorie der Metapher*, Studienausgabe (Darmstadt: Wissenschaftliche Buchgesellschaft, 1996); Gerhard Kurz, *Metapher, Allegorie, Symbol*, 5th ed., KVR 1486 (Göttingen: Vandenhoeck & Ruprecht, 2004 [1982]).

240. For the relationship and differentiation of metaphors and symbols as two kinds of signs on *one* axis of the semantics of "double-meaning," such that the symbol is characterized by its ineffable anchoring in the concrete, see Paul Ricoeur, "Metaphor and Symbol," in his *Interpretation Theory: Discourse and the Surplus of Meaning* (Fort Worth, TX: TCU Press, 1976), 45–69.

241. On this, see the well-known and frequently adopted cultural-studies definition of religious symbolism as formative for a society's "perception of reality" by Clifford Geertz, "Religion as a Cultural System," in his *The Interpretation of Cultures: Selected Essays* (New York: Basic Books, 2017), 93–135, at 97. According to Geertz, religion is "(1) a system of symbols which acts to (2) establish powerful, pervasive, and long-lasting moods and motivations in men by (3) formulating conceptions of a general order of existence and (4) clothing these conceptions with such an aura of factuality that (5) the moods and motivations seem uniquely realistic."

242. I have recently attempted to demonstrate this for the Psalms: Friedhelm Hartenstein, "Iconicity of the Psalms," *HBAI* 5 (2016): 326–49; cf. esp. 327–30 ("Linguistic and Non-Linguistic Symbols").

243. Cf. Friedhelm Hartenstein, "Präzise Mehrdeutigkeit. Zur Multiperspektivität von Text und Auslegung am Beispiel von Ps 23," in *Anknüpfung und Aufbruch. Hermeneutische, ästhetische und politische Perspektiven der Theologie*, ed. Cornelia Richter, Marburger Theologische Studien 110 (Leipzig: Evangelische Verlagsanstalt, 2011), 13–24.

244. Cf. Friedhelm Hartenstein, "Gott als Horizont des Menschen. Nachprophetische Anthropologie in Psalm 51 und 139," in *Die unwiderstehliche Wahrheit. FS Arndt Meinhold*, ed. Rüdiger Lux and Ernst-Joachim Waschke, ABG 23 (Leipzig: Evangelische Verlagsanstalt, 2006), 491–512.

245. Paul Ricoeur, *The Symbolism of Evil*, trans. Emerson Buchanan (Boston, Beacon Press, 1969), 11: "We have never ceased to find meanings in the sky."

246. Cf. Hartenstein, "Personalität Gottes," 39–46, esp. 44–46, on the corresponding biblical statements as "limit expressions" or limit conceptuality, i.e., as linguistic inventions shaped in the sense of (later) analogical thought on the margins of the unsayable.

247. For what follows, cf. esp. Hartenstein, "Vom Sehen und Schauen Gottes."

248. See a fuller analysis of this world of symbolic concepts in the Psalms modeled on an audience with the king-god in terms of Ps 27 in Hartenstein, *Angesicht*.

249. For death symbolism in the Psalms, cf. Bernd Janowski, *Arguing with God: A Theological Anthropology of the Psalms*, trans. Armin Siedlecki (Louisville, KY: Westminster John Knox, 2013), "'My Life Has Touched the Underworld' (Ps 88:3/4)," 211–47.

250. On this, see the detailed work of Bernd Janowski, *Arguing with God*, 14–35 ("The Language of Human Beings"); for the concept of "mutual modeling," see Janowski, "'Dem Löwen gleich, gierig nach Raub' (Ps 17,12). Zum Feindbild in den Psalmen" (in the appendix: "Reflexionen über den Feind") in his *Die rettende Gerechtigkeit*, 49–77, at 63n56.

251. For this fundamental hermeneutical perspective on the significance of the Bible in the present time, cf. Friedhelm Hartenstein, "Personalität Gottes," 19–25.

252. Martin Luther, "Preface to the Psalter" (1528), *WA DB* 10:1, 98 = *LW* 35:253–57, at 257.

253. For this much-cited dictum of the Egyptologist Henri Frankfort, see n. 48 above.

254. For analysis of Exod 33:18–23, cf. Hartenstein, *Angesicht*, 277–83; for an interpretation of v. 20, cf. Christoph Dohmen, "'Nicht sieht mich der Mensch und lebt!' (Ex 33,20). Aspekte der Gottesschau im Alten Testament," in Baldermann et al., *Die Macht der Bilder*, 31–51;

Jeremias, *Theologie*, 106, 219; for a literary-historical location in scholarship, cf. Aurelius, *Fürbitter*, 103–4; Konkel, *Sünde*, 177.

255. For what follows, cf. Hartenstein, "'Gestalt,'" and "Vom Sehen und Schauen Gottes," 33–36; see also Friedhelm Hartenstein "'Der vom Sinai': Atopie und Topologie der Theophanie JHWHs als bildhermeneutische Herausforderung," lecture delivered on November 9, 2012, to the conference on *Entzogene Bilder. Die Sinaitheophanie zwischen Bilderverbot und Bilderstiftung (Ex 19—24 und Ex 32—34).* (Withdrawn images: The Sinai theophany between the ban on images and the endowment of images [Exod 19—24 and Exod 32—34]).

256. Cf., as representative, Hans-Joachim Kraus, "Hören und Sehen in der althebräischen Tradition," in his *Biblisch-theologische Aufsätze* (Neukirchen-Vluyn: Neukirchener Verlag, 1972), 84–101.

257. Cf. Hartenstein, "'Gestalt,'" 59–67.

258. On this, cf. Hartenstein, "Wolkendunkel"; Reinhard Müller, *Jahwe als Wettergott. Studien zur althebräischen Kultlyrik anhand ausgewählter Psalmen*, BZAW 387 (Berlin: de Gruyter, 2008).

259. See further, from a phenomenological perspective, Bernhard Waldenfels, "Das Unsichtbare dieser Welt oder: Was sich dem Blick entzieht," in *Die Sichtbarkeit des Unsichtbaren*, ed. Rudolf Bernet and Antje Kapust (Munich: Fink, 2009), 11–26.

260. Here we may mention Georges Didi-Huberman, *Vor einem Bild* (Munich: Hanser, 2000; trans. of *Devant l'image*, trans. Reinold Werner [Paris: Minuit, 1990]); Knut Ebeling, "Maurice Blanchot," in *Bildtheorien aus Frankreich. Ein Handbuch*, ed. Kathrin Busch and Iris Därmann, Eikones (Munich: Fink, 2011), 73–84.

261. Exod 20:18 (traditionally regarded as "Elohistic") belongs literarily also to a late redactional layer within the Sinai theophany.

262. For Exod 33:20 as the latest addition to Exod 33:18–23, cf. Hartenstein, *Angesicht*, 281–83.

263. Cf., in this sense, on Gen 22 Friedhelm Hartenstein, "Die Verborgenheit des rettenden Gottes. Exegetische und theologische Bemerkungen zu Genesis 22," in *Isaaks Opferung (Gen 22) in den Konfessionen und Medien der frühen Neuzeit*, ed. Johann Anselm Steiger and Ulrich Heinen, AKG 101 (Berlin: de Gruyter, 2006), 1–22; Jeremias, *Theologie*, 78–79.

264. On this, see the essays in Gottfried Boehm, Gabriele Brandstetter, and Achatz von Müller, eds., *Figur und Figuration. Studien zu Wahrnehmung und Wissen, Bild und Text* (Munich: Fink, 2007).

265. On this, see Gottfried Boehm, "Die Wiederkehr der Bilder," in *Was ist ein Bild?*, ed. Gottfried Boehm, 2nd ed., Bild und Text (Munich: Fink, 1995), 11–38, and with regard to the Old Testament, see Friedhelm Hartenstein, *Angesicht*, 34–39. For the figure and its perception as a figuration, see Gottfried Boehm, "Die ikonische Figuration," in Boehm et al., *Figur und Figuration*, 35–52, esp. 51–52.

266. See Gottfried Boehm, "Die ikonische Figuration," 36–37: "[The *appearance of the figure* is] a movement worthy of consideration that allows absence to intrude into the present. Where there was nothing at all, visual traces configure themselves into visibility....Figuration shares with the image (on every presentation) the boldness of an act that makes the hiatus between invisibility and visibility the locus of a genesis, of the appearance of something. That chasm cannot be bridged in principle but only in an individual act of configuration. Always but once, since images do not exist in and for themselves; rather, they make themselves concrete, they require a genesis, that is, the time that makes them to be and to appear as what they are on each occasion....If we speak of figuration and the meaning it generates, this means that something absent, something that is not yet, transitions into a visual present. For theological interpretation of figures this was the figural fulfillment of a promise." What seems fascinating here is the possibility of translating these basic considerations derived from artistic actions and those of the reception of images to the question of the image character of language in the Old Testament in light of the critique of images.

267. Boehm, "Die ikonische Figuration," 52.

268. Cf. Friedrich Wilhelm Graf, *Missbrauchte Götter. Zum Menschenbilderstreit in der Moderne* (Munich: Beck, 2009), 83–132 ("Ebenbilder" [likenesses; copies]).

269. Cf., still, Odil Hannes Steck, *Der Schöpfungsbericht der Priesterschrift. Studien zur literarkritischen und überlieferungsgeschichtlichen Problematik von Genesis 1,1–2,4a*, 2nd ed., FRLANT 115 (Göttingen: Vandenhoeck & Ruprecht, 1981).

270. Cf. the excellent description of the state of the problem by Walter Groß, "Gen 1,26.27; 9,6: Statue oder Ebenbild Gottes? Aufgabe und Würde des Menschen nach dem hebräischen und griechischen Wortlaut," in *Menschenwürde*, ed. Ingo Baldermann et al., JBT 15 (Neukirchen-Vluyn: Neukirchener Verlag, 2001), 11–38; see further Klaus Koch, *Imago Dei—Die Würde des Menschen im biblischen Text: vorgelegt in der Sitzung vom 7. Juli 2000* (Hamburg: Joachim Jungius-

Gesellschaft der Wissenschaften in Kommission bei Verlag Vandenhoeck & Ruprecht, 2000).

271. On this, cf. Dominik Bonatz, "Was ist ein Bild im Alten Ori-
ent? Aspekte bildlicher Darstellung aus altorientalischer Sicht," in
Bild—Macht—Geschichte. Visuelle Kommunikation im Alten Orient, ed.
Marlies Heinz and Dominik Bonatz (Berlin: Reimer, 2002), 9–20.

272. Bonatz, Bild, 13.

273. For these points, see more precisely Bernd Janowski, "Die leben-
dige Statue Gottes. Zur Anthropologie der priesterlichen Urgeschichte,"
in his Die Welt als Schöpfung. Beiträge zur Theologie des Alten Testaments
4 (Neukirchen-Vluyn: Neukirchener Verlag, 2008), 140–71.

274. Janowski, "Statue," 150. Emphasis in the original.

275. For the semantics, tradition history, and theological aspects of
rādâ, see Bernd Janowski, "Herrschaft über die Tiere. Gen 1,26–28 und
die Semantik von רדה," in his Die rettende Gerechtigkeit, 33–48; in detail:
Ute Neumann-Gorsolke, Herrschen in den Grenzen der Schöpfung. Ein
Beitrag zur alttestamentlichen Anthropologie am Beispiel von Psalm 8,
Genesis 1 und verwandten Texten, WMANT 101 (Neukirchen-Vluyn:
Neukirchener Verlag, 2004), 207–27; for kābaš, see Neumann-Gorsolke,
Herrschen in den Grenzen, 274–300.

276. On this, see Neumann-Gorsolke, Herrschen, 300–315, esp. 315:
"This anthropological guideline is part of creation: the human being,
image of God, rules within creation as responsible sovereign and preserves the structures that support life—though within the limits that
the integrity of the world as a whole with all its creatures as well as the
stigmatizing of violence (Gen 6!) establish."

277. On this, see also the critical further studies and interpretations
by Annette Schellenberg, Der Mensch, das Bild Gottes? Zum Gedanken
der Sonderstellung des Menschen im Alten Testament und in weiteren
altorientalischen Quellen, ATNT 101 (Zürich: Theologischer Verlag
Zürich, 2011); see also the review by Bernd Janowski, JAOS 136 (2016):
189–92.

278. On this, see, e.g., Bernd Janowski, Sühne als Heilsgeschehen. Studien zur Sühnetheologie der Priesterschrift und zur Wurzel KPR im Alten
Orient und im Alten Testament, WMANT 55 (Neukirchen-Vluyn: Neukirchener Verlag, 1982), 309–12 (Excursus VI: "Tempel und Schöpfung
in der Priesterschrift").

279. Bernd Janowski, "Statue," 153. Emphasis in original; Hebrew
transliterated.

280. Rüdiger Lux, "Das Bild Gottes und die Götterbilder im Alten Testament," *ZTK* 110 (2013): 133–57.

281. Lux, "Das Bild Gottes," 154.

282. Cf., e.g., Gerhard Bodendorfer, "Menschenrechte und Menschenwürde in der rabbinischen Literatur," in Ingo Baldermann et al., *Menschenwürde* (see n. 270), 67–92.

283. On this, cf. Bernd Janowski, "Der eine Gott der beiden Testamente. Grundfragen einer Biblischen Theologie," in his *Die rettende Gerechtigkeit*, 249–84; Bernd Janowski, "Die kontrastive Einheit der Schrift. Zur Hermeneutik des biblischen Kanons," in *Kanonhermeneutik. Vom Lesen und Verstehen der christlichen Bibel*, ed. Bernd Janowski, Theologie interdisziplinär 1 (Neukirchen-Vluyn: Neukirchener Verlag, 2007), 27–46.

284. Gottfried Boehm, "Repräsentation—Präsentation—Präsenz. Auf den Spuren des homo pictor," in Gottfried Boehm, *Homo Pictor* (2001), 3–13, at 13. Emphasis in the original.

III. Systematic Perspectives

1. Cf. Jean-Luc Nancy, *The Ground of the Image* (from the French, *Au fond des images*), trans. Jeff Fort, Perspectives in Continental Philosophy 51 (New York: Fordham University Press, 2005), 2. The footnotes in this book are numbered separately in the principal sections, and references to literature already cited also concern only those works cited in the particular section. When there is reference in parentheses to other parts of section III, this will be without repetition of the Roman numeral, but such reference will be made in cases of allusions to section II.

2. This estimation follows the theoretical constructions of Luhmann and Waldenfels. Cf. only Niklas Luhmann, *Theory of Society*, trans. Rhodes Barrett, 2 vols. (Stanford, CA: Stanford University Press, 2012–13), 1:23–26, and Bernhard Waldenfels, *Hyperphänomene: Modi hyperbolischer Erfahrung* (Berlin: Suhrkamp, 2012), 358.

3. Cf. Klaus Koch, *Imago Dei. Die Würde des Menschen im biblischen Text: vorgelegt in der Sitzung vom 7. Juli 2000* (Hamburg: Joachim Jungius-Gesellschaft der Wissenschaften in Kommission bei Verlag Vandenhoeck & Ruprecht, 2000), 17–18.

4. Cf. George Orwell, *Nineteen Eighty-Four* (many editions).

5. Cf. Koch, *Imago Dei*, 19ff.

6. Cf. Alain Besançon, *The Forbidden Image: An Intellectual History of Iconoclasm*, trans. Jane Marie Todd (Chicago: University of Chicago Press, 2000), 3, 57–62, at 61.

7. Ernst H. Kantorowicz, *The King's Two Bodies: A Study in Mediaeval Political Theology* (Princeton, NJ: Princeton University Press, 2016), 314–17, 407–10.

8. Kantorowicz, *The King's Two Bodies*, 419–37.

9. For the connection between the practice described by Kantorowicz and a qualified concept of representation, cf. Horst Bredekamp, *Thomas Hobbes. Der Leviathan. Das Urbild des modernen Staates und seine Gegenbilder, 1651–2001* (Berlin: Akademie Verlag, 2006), 100, 106.

10. Cf. Kantorowicz, *The King's Two Bodies*, 424–25.

11. Kantorowicz, *The King's Two Bodies*, 419–20.

12. For the connection between the theological discussion of the real presence of the body of Christ in the Lord's Supper and the changes in the character of political relationships of representation, cf. Kantorowicz, *The King's Two Bodies*, 88ff., 101ff., 194ff.

13. Kantorowicz, *The King's Two Bodies*, 92.

14. Thomas Aquinas, *Summa theologiae* III, q. 73, art. 5. Cf. Joseph Imorde, *Präsenz und Repräsentanz, oder, Die Kunst, den Leib Christi auszustellen: (das vierzigstündige Gebet von den Anfängen bis in das Pontifikat Innocenz X)* (Emsdetten et al.: Edition Imorde, 1997), 17–18.

15. Jan Assmann, *The Price of Monotheism*, trans. Robert Savage (Stanford, CA: Stanford University Press, 2010), 30; cf. Klaus Müller, "'Bilderverbot' oder: wie ein theologisches Missverständnis zum philosophischen Mythos wird," in *Die Zehn Gebote: Ein widersprüchliches Erbe?* ed. Hans Joas. Schriften des Deutschen Hygiene-Museums Dresden (Cologne: Böhlau, 2006), 33–46, at 36.

16. Talmud *Sefaria* 3.9, *Mishnah Avodah Zarah*, at https://www.sefaria .org/Mishnah_Avodah_Zarah.3.1?ven=The_Mishna_with_Obadiah _Bartenura_by_Rabbi_Shraga_Silverstein&lang=bi. Cf. Astrid Deuber-Mankowsky, "Repräsentationskritik und Bilderverbot," in *Babylon: Beiträge zur jüdischen Gegenwart* 22 (Frankfurt: Neue Kritik, 2007), 109–17, at 115.

17. Friedrich Nietzsche, *Beyond Good and Evil: Prelude to a Philosophy of the Future*, trans. Helen Zimmern (New York: Macmillan, 1907), 3.

18. Hans Belting, *An Anthropology of Images: Picture, Medium, Body*, trans. Thomas Dunlap (Princeton, NJ: Princeton University Press, 2011), 114.

19. Andreas Bodenstein von Karlstadt, "Von Abthuung der Bilder und dass kein Bedtler unter den Christen sein soll" (1522), in *Flugschriften der frühen Reformationsbewegung (1518–1524)*, vol. 1, ed. Adolf Laube, Annerose Schneider, and Sigrid Looss (Vaduz: Topos; Berlin: Akademie-Verlag, 1983), 105–27, at 111–12.

20. Because Karlstadt was concerned only with images in worship, it is no self-contradiction that an image adorns the title page of "Von Abthuung der Bilder."

21. John Calvin, *Institutes* I/11,2: "The majesty of God is defiled by an absurd and indecorous fiction when he, who is incorporeal is assimilated to corporeal matter…." Translation by Henry Beveridge at http://www.ccel.org/ccel/calvin/institutes.

22. Cf. Irene Dingel, "'Dass wir Gott in keiner Weise verbilden.' Die Bilderfrage zwischen Calvinismus und Luthertum," in *Gott im Wort— Gott im Bild. Bilderlosigkeit als Bedingung des Monotheismus?*, ed. Andreas Wagner et al. (Neukirchen: Neukirchener Verlag, 2005).

23. Cf. Eusebius of Caesaria, *Letter to Constantia*, MPG 20, 1545–49.

24. Belting, *Anthropology of Images*, 115.

25. Epiphanius of Salamis, Letter to John of Jerusalem (= Jerome, CSEL 54, 411). My description follows that of Klaus Wessel, "Dogma und Lehre in der Orthodoxen Kirche," *HDTG* 1, ed. Carl Andresen (Göttingen: Vandenhoeck & Ruprecht, 1982), 284–405, at 289.

26. Epiphanius of Salamis, Fragments 12, 14, 22. See Karl Holl, "Die Schriften des Epiphanios gegen die Bilderverehrung," in his *Gesammelte Aufsätze* 2 (Tübingen: Mohr, 1928), 351–87, at 359, 361, and cf. Wessel, "Dogma und Lehre."

27. Gregory Nazianzus, *Oratio in Pascha II*, as found in Wessel, "Dogma und Lehre," 290.

28. MPG 40, 167B, as cited in Wessel, "Dogma und Lehre," 289.

29. Cf. Fragments 24 and 26 in Epiphanius of Salamis, *Schriften des Epiphanios gegen die Bilderverehrung*, ed. Karl Holl; cf. Wessel, "Dogma und Lehre," 289–90.

30. Plato, *Phaedrus* 250b.

31. Cf. Plato, *Laws* V, 597a.

32. *Laws* VII, 514c.

33. Cf. Hans Blumenberg, *Theorie der Lebenswelt*, ed. Manfred Sommer (Berlin: Suhrkamp, 2010), 166; cf. his *Höhlenausgänge* (Frankfurt: Suhrkamp, 1989), 113, 116.

34. Cf. Wolfram Hogrebe, "Bild," *Historisches Wörterbuch der Philosophie* 1:913–19; cf. also Besançon, *Image*, 29.

35. Cf. Hans Blumenberg, *Ästhetische und metaphorologische Schriften*, ed. Anselm Haverkamp (Frankfurt: Suhrkamp, 2001), 57.

36. Cf. Hogrebe, "Bild," 913.

37. Cf. Hans Blumenberg, *Paradigms for a Metaphorology*, trans. Robert Savage (Ithaca, NY: Cornell University Press, 2010). Johann Kreuzer offers a friendlier interpretation of Plato (although reading Plato by way of Augustine). He sees the logical place of the image as a material phenomenon that secures awareness of what it images (Kreuzer, "Was heißt es, sich als Bild zu verstehen? Von Augustinus zu Eckhart," in *Denken mit dem Bild. Philosophische Einsätze des Bildbegriffs, von Platon bis Hegel*, ed. Johannes Grave and Arno Schubbach [Munich: Fink, 2010], 75–98, at 79).

38. Cf. Besançon, *Image*, 29.

39. René Descartes, *Meditations on First Philosophy, with Selections from the Objections and Replies*, Latin and English ed., trans. and ed. John Cottingham (Cambridge: Cambridge University Press, 2013).

40. Thomas Aquinas had already defined this as something that can form *aliquod idolum rei absentis* (*ST* Ia, q. 85,2; Cf. Aquinas, *De veritate* I, a. 11).

41. Cf. Paul Ricoeur, *Fallible Man*, trans. Charles A. Kelbley, rev. ed. (New York: Fordham University Press, 1986), 1–3, 25, 34–35.

42. Cf. Augustine, *De doctrina christiana* I, 4.4.

43. Friedrich Schiller, *Mary Stuart*, trans. Joseph Mellish (Project Gutenberg, 2004), act I, scene 6, p. 22.

44. Gustav Seibt pointed to this text in the context of a German debate on the cross as "blasphemy against God and worship of images" ("Ich könnte an ein Kreuz glauben," *Süddeutsche Zeitung*, 17 May 2010).

45. Paul argued with the ban on images, to which later distinctions between original sin (*peccatum originale*) and actual sins (*peccatum actuale*) could link, when he wrote, "Claiming to be wise, they became fools; and they exchanged the glory of the immortal God for images resembling a mortal human being or birds or four-footed animals or reptiles. Therefore God gave them up...to impurity, to the degrading of their bodies among themselves" (Rom 1:22–24).

46. Quoted from Peter Jezler et al., "Warum ein Bilderstreit? Der Kampf gegen die 'Götzen' in Zürich als Beispiel," in *Bilderstreit. Kulturwandel in Zwinglis Reformation*, ed. Hans-Dietrich Altendorf and Peter

Jezler (Zürich: Theologischer Verlag, 1984), 83–102, at 88. The biblical counterpart to such concerns is found in the allegorical figure of Oholibah, whose sexual lust for Chaldeans with turbans and girdled loins was aroused by wall paintings (in vermillion!) according to Ezek 23.

47. Cf. Claus Westermann, "Exkurs. Zur Auslegungsgeschichte von Gen 1,26-27," in his *Genesis 1—11*, BKAT I/1 (Neukirchen-Vluyn: Neukirchener Verlag, 1974), 203–14, at 207; for more recent research (with literature), see above at §II.3.2c.

48. Johann Andreas Quenstedt, *Theologia didactio-polemica sive Systema Theologicum* (Wittenberg: Quenstedius, 1685 [1691]), II/7 (cf. *The Nature and Character of Theology: An Introduction to the Thought of J. A. Quenstedt*, ed. and trans. Luther Poellot [St. Louis: Concordia Publishing, 1986]), quoted by H. Schmid, *Die Dogmatik der evangelischlutherischen Kirche. Dargestellt und aus den Quellen belegt*, new ed. H. G. Pöhlmann, 9th ed. (Gütersloh: Gütersloher Verlagshaus, 1979), 156.

49. Corresponding to the much-cited remark of Friedrich Christof Oetinger; cf. Oetinger, *Biblisches und Emblematisches Wörterbuch* (Hildesheim: Olms, 1776; repr. 1969), 407.

50. I am being careful in writing "seems" because this potential has not been exploited precisely where it was most appropriate. A "sympathy for embodiment" found a place in Christology and in the doctrine of the Eucharist, but it did not leave its mark in anthropology.

51. Cf. Schleiermacher's argument regarding docetism and Ebionitism as the two natural heresies of Christianity related to the uniqueness of the Redeemer: Friedrich D. E. Schleiermacher, *Der christliche Glaube nach den Grundsätzen der evangelischen Kirche im Zusammenhange dargestellt*, 2nd ed. (Berlin: G. Reimer, 1830/31), §25, in *Friedrich Schleiermacher Kritische Gesamtausgabe* vol. 1, 13.1, ed. Rolf Schäfer (New York: de Gruyter, 2003), 169–72.

52. Cf. Belting, *Anthropology of Images*, 63.

53. Cf. Belting, *Anthropology of Images*, 22–25.

54. Cf. Belting, *Anthropology of Images*, 57–58.

55. One revealing example is found in the works of John Coplans, collected in his book *A Body* (New York: PowerHouse Books, 2002). In Coplans's work the pose can become a farce; the body is cut apart in the picture and the human face and head are never displayed, as if they were not part of the body.

56. Cf. Belting, *Anthropology of Images*, 95.

57. Belting, *Anthropology of Images*, 95.

58. Belting, *Anthropology of Images*, 96.

59. "Under his opposite." That, at any rate, was the perspective of Martin Noth, *History of Israel* (London: SCM, 1983 [1960]), and Gerhard von Rad, *Theology of the Old Testament*, vol. 2, *The Theology of Israel's Prophetic Traditions*, trans. D. M. G. Stalker (Louisville, KY: Westminster John Knox, 1962), 99–112. Even when the idea of a genuine deuteronomistic theology (constituted by this ex-post interpretation) is called into question and the pre-exilic prophetic announcement of the divine judgment is regarded as having a historical core, the formative power of the exile for the Old Testament text collection is not to be denied.

60. The latter is supported by Micha Brumlik, *Schrift, Wort und Ikone. Wege aus dem Bilderverbot*, 2nd ed. (Hamburg: Philo, 2006), 37ff., in interpreting 2 Chr 34 and 2 Kgs 22—23. Brumlik proceeds from the impression that critical scholarship has shown these biblical texts to be historically reliable (cf. Brumlik, *Schrift*, 38, 40). For the actual complex relationships, cf. §II.2.4b.2 above and Michael Pietsch, *Die Kultreform Josias. Studien zur Religionsgeschichte Israels in der späten Königszeit* (Tübingen: Mohr Siebeck, 2013).

61. Assmann, *Price of Monotheism*, 8–11.

62. Assmann, *Price of Monotheism*, 87.

63. Gerhard von Rad, *Old Testament Theology*, vol. 1, *The Theology of Israel's Historical Traditions*, trans. D. M. G. Stalker (Louisville, KY: Westminster John Knox, 1962) proposed that Exod 22:19 ("Whoever sacrifices to any God, other than the LORD alone, shall be devoted to destruction") is the oldest version of the first commandment. He thought that such a coefficient of divisive intolerance was typical of the YHWH cult from the beginning and expressed in the term "a jealous God" (Exod 20:5; 34:14; Deut 6:14). "This intolerant claim to exclusive worship is something unique in the history of religion, for in antiquity the cults were on easy terms with one another and left devotees a free hand to ensure a blessing for themselves from other gods as well" (*OTT* 1:208). For doubts about deriving "monotheistic" intolerance from ancient roots (see §II above), cf. also Friedhelm Hartenstein, "Monotheismus und Intoleranz. Überlegungen aus alttestamentlicher Sicht," *Glaube und Lernen* 26 (2011): 13–25.

64. Sigmund Freud, *Moses and Monotheism*, trans. Katherine Jones (New York: Vintage, 1967).

65. Cf. Jan Assmann, "Monotheismus und die Sprache der Gewalt," in Assmann, *Das Gewaltpotential des Monotheismus und der dreieinige Gott*, QD 216, ed. Peter Walter (Freiburg: Herder, 2005), 18–38.

66. Cf. Jan Assmann, *Monotheismus und Kosmotheismus. Ägyptische Formen eines "Denkens des Einen" und ihre europäische Rezeptionsgeschichte*. Sitzungsberichte der Heidelberger Akademie der Wissenschaften, Philosophisch-Historische Klasse 1993, 2 (Heidelberg: 1993).

67. Cf. Assmann, *Price of Monotheism*, 137.

68. Cf. G. W. F. Hegel, *The Phenomenology of Spirit*, trans. Michael Inwood (Oxford: Oxford University Press, 2018), 216–28, 233–37.

69. According to Assmann, Akhenaten failed as an enlightener, but only because he, like the French Revolution, tried to stage the rule of reason as a religious foundation; cf. Assmann, *Monotheismus und Kosmotheismus*, 34.

70. The word is formed from *eikōn* (image) and *klaein* (break).

71. Cf. also Jochen Hörisch, *Der Sinn und die Sinne. Eine Geschichte der Medien* (Frankfurt: Eichborn, 2001), 49.

72. Hermann Cohen is the outstanding representative of a corresponding interpretation; cf. his *Religion of Reason: Out of the Sources of Judaism*, trans. Simon Kaplan (New York: F. Ungar, 1972).

73. Midrash Rabbah Genesis (Noach, 38, 13, at https://archive.org/stream/RabbaGenesis/midrashrabbahgen027557mbp_djvu.txt). Cf. Bruno Latour and Peter Weibel, ed., *Iconoclash: Beyond the Image Wars in Science, Religion and Art* (Karlsruhe: ZKM; London: MIT Press, 2002), 38.

74. Cf. Eckard Nordhofen, "Bilderverbot und jüdische Aufklärung," *Zeitschrift für Didaktik der Philosophie* (ZDP) 1 (1993): 44–54.

75. In Nordhofen, ed., *Bilderverbot. Die Sichtbarkeit des Unsichtbaren* (Paderborn: Schöningh, 2001), 16–17.

76. Sigmund Freud, *Moses and Monotheism*, 131–76, at 144.

77. Cf. Nordhofen, *Bilderverbot*, 10.

78. Nordhofen, "Die Konkurrenz der Gottesmedien," in *Christusbild. Icon und Ikone. Wege zu Theorie und Theologie des Bildes*, ed. Peter Hofmann and Andreas Matena (Paderborn et al.: Schöningh, 2010), 15–30, at 17.

79. The problem has already been described with precision by Karl-Heinz Bernhardt, *Gott und Bild. Ein Beitrag zur Begründung und Deutung des Bilderverbotes im Alten Testament* (Berlin: Evangelische Verlagsanstalt, 1956), 109.

Notes

80. The reference is to a German fable about a race between a hedgehog and a rabbit, somewhat similar to *The Tortoise and the Hare*. Instead of running the race, the hedgehog places his (similar-looking) wife at the goal, and as the rabbit approaches, she shouts, "Ick bün all hier" = "I'm already here." The "race" is repeated 73 times with the same result.

81. Emmanuel Lévinas, "Reality and Its Shadow" (1948), republished in his *Unforeseen History*, trans. Nidra Poller (Urbana: University of Illinois Press, 2004), 76–91, at 89.

82. Emmanuel Lévinas, *Otherwise Than Being, or, Beyond Essence*, trans. Alphonso Lingis (Pittsburgh: Duquesne University Press, 1998)

83. *Eis theos, en te theoioi kai anthrōpoisi megistos/outi demas thētoisin homoios oude noēma* (Zenophanes of Colophon, fr. 15–16, 23); Cf. http://www.westcotthort.com/books/Hort_-_Clement_of_Alexandria_-_Miscellanies_Book_VII_(1902).pdf (pt. II, n. 98).

84. Besançon, *Image*, 19–20.

85. Against Besançon, who allows the dogmatic perspectives of the church fathers to enter into his presentation of Zenophanes (cf. Besançon, *Image*, 20).

86. Cf. Parmenides, *On Nature*, fr. 8, at http://parmenides.com/about_parmenides/ParmenidesPoem.html?page=12.

87. Pseudo-Dionysius Areopagitica, *De divinis nominibus* (On Divine Names), trans. John Parker (1897), I. Available at http://www.sacred-texts.com/chr/dio/dio04.htm. Cf. Willi Oelmüller, "Das Bilderverbot aus einer philosophischen Perspektive der negativen Theologie heute," in Nordhofen, *Bilderverbot*, 149–72, at 151.

88. Formulated to reflect canon 2 of the Fourth Lateran Council; on this, see Eberhard Jüngel, *God as the Mystery of the World: On the Foundation of the Theology of the Crucified One in the Dispute between Theism and Atheism*, trans. Darrell L. Guder (Grand Rapids: Eerdmans, 1983), 283, citing Erich Przywara. The Council's text read, "Between the Creator and the creature so great a likeness cannot be noted without the necessity of noting a greater dissimilarity between them" (Denzinger, *The Sources of Catholic Dogma*, trans. Roy J. Deferrari [St. Louis: Herder, 1957], §432, p. 171).

89. Nicholas of Cusa, *De docta ignorantia* I, 26. Translated by Jasper Hopkins as *On Learned Ignorance* (Minneapolis: Banning Press, 1981), 45. Online at http://jasper-hopkins.info/DI-I-12-2000.pdf.

90. Cf. Moses Maimonides, *The Guide for the Perplexed* (12th c.), trans. Michael Friedländer, 2nd rev. ed. (New York: Dover Publications, 1961), XLIX.

91. For a brief presentation, cf. Christoph Asmuth, *Bilder über Bilder—Bilder ohne Bilder. Eine neue Theorie der Bildlichkeit* (Darmstadt: Wissenschaftliche Buchgesellschaft, 2001), 58ff.

92. Cf. Johann Kreuzer, "Was heißt es, sich als Bild zu verstehen? Von Augustinus zu Eckhart," in *Denken mit dem Bild. Philosophische Einsätze des Bildbegriffs von Platon bis Hegel*, ed. Johannes Grave and Arno Schubbach (Paderborn and Munich: Fink, 2010), 75–98, at 85.

93. All these play a role in the Bible: the scene at the burning bush, the garden of Gethsemane, the Acts of the Apostles, the ark of the covenant, etc.

94. Cf. Emmanuel Lévinas, "La trace de l'autre," *Tijdschrift voor Filosofie* 25 (1963): 605–23.

95. Cf. Willi Oelmüller, "Das Bilderverbot" (2001), 154ff. For the connection between humanity as image of God and the concept of image, cf. also Michael Moxter, "Der Mensch als Darstellung Gottes," in *Theologie zwischen Pragmatismus und Existenzdenken. FS Hermann Deuser*, ed. Gesche Linde, MTSt 90 (Marburg: Elwert, 2006), 271–84.

96. Immanuel Kant, *Critique of Pure Reason*, trans. F. Max Müller (New York: Macmillan, 1896), 115–16.

97. Immanuel Kant, *Groundwork of the Metaphysics of Morals*, trans. Thomas Kingsmill Abbott (LaVergne, TN: BN Publishing, 2010), 99.

98. Cf. Immanuel Kant, *Critique of Judgment*, trans. Nicholas Walker, Oxford World Classics ed. (Oxford: Oxford University Press, 2007 [1952]), pt. 1, bk. 2, "Analytic of the Sublime," 75–164.

99. Kant, *Critique of Judgment*, 104–5.

100. Kant, *Critique of Judgment*, 104.

101. Cf. Gottfried Boehm, "Die Bilderfrage," in *Was ist ein Bild?*, ed. Gottfried Boehm, 2nd ed., Bild und Text (Munich: Fink, 1995), 325–43, at 340–43.

102. Søren Kierkegaard, *Practice in Christianity No. III*, Kierkegaard's Writings 20, ed. and trans. Howard V. Hong and Edna H. Hong (Princeton, NJ: Princeton University Press, 1991), 254–55.

103. Cf. Hörisch, *Sinn*; Assmann, *Price of Monotheism*, 104.

104. Heinrich Heine spoke of a "portable fatherland" of Jewish existence (see his *Sämtliche Werke* 13, ed. Hans Kaufmann [Munich: Kindler, 1964], 128).

105. Nordhofen, "Konkurrenz," 25.

106. For this connection, see Paul Tillich, *Systematic Theology*, vol. 1, *Being and God* (Chicago: University of Chicago Press, 1951), 118–25 ("The Mediums of Revelation").

107. Thus for the Reformed theologian Jürgen Moltmann "the cross of Christ is the source of a permanent iconoclasm of the christological icons of the church and the portraits of Jesus in Christianity; and the theology of the cross is a kind of iconoclasm of the Christological images and titles of the church. It is iconoclasm for Jesus' sake and is justified and regulated by the recollection of his cross" (Moltmann, *The Crucified God. The Cross of Christ as Ground and Critique of Christian Theology* [Minneapolis: Fortress, 2015], 120).

108. For a critical evaluation ("Triumph eines Zeiches über die Bilder"), cf. Hans Belting, *Das echte Bild. Bildfragen als Glaubensfragen* (Munich: Beck, 2006), 143.

109. Paradigmatic in this regard is Augustine's definition, *omnis imago est similis ei, cuius imago est* (every image is like that of which it is an image), which depends on a relationship between the three concepts of *imago* (image), *aequalitas* (equality), and *similitudo* (similarity or likeness) (*De gen. ad lit. lib. imperf.* 16; CSEL 28/1, 497–98). The state of being an image lies between indispensable similarity and unattainable sameness—an argument already articulated by Plato when he points to the contradiction that a fully conceived image of Cratylus would not be an image but a second Cratylus, a twin. Tradition has repeatedly adopted Augustine's definition: so we find it again in the work of David Hollaz, who defines the moment of similarity to God under the logic *quia imaginis est, repraesentare rem cujus est imago. Hoc autem sine similitudine fieri nequit* (Insofar as its nature is that of an image, it represents the thing of which it is the image. But without similarity this is impossible) and thus makes convergence with the prototype the decisive meaning of *imago* (*Examen theologiae acroamaticae* [1701], 462, quoted in Schmid/ Pöhlmann, *Dogmatik*, 152). This background still shapes Wolfhart Pannenberg's concept of image in his *Systematic Theology*, trans. Geoffrey W. Bromiley, vol. 2 (Grand Rapids: Eerdmans, 1994), 203–4.

110. Cf. Regina E. G. Schymiczek, *Höllenbrut und Himmelswächter. Mittelalterliche Wasserspeier an Kirchen und Kathedralen* (Regensburg: Schnell und Steiner, 2006). I am grateful to V. Leppin for this reference. We should also recall the lions and dragon serpents of the Ishtar Gate from Babylon (from the period of Nebuchadnezzar II), which were

buried beneath the earth. Among the images and inscriptions of kings in the ancient Near East that marked the presence of the ruler there is a relief with the image of the Babylonian king Nabonidus (555–538 BCE), discovered several years ago in the Sela' region in Jordan (in the territory of ancient Edom); it was carved very high up on an unapproachable cliff face (cf. Othmar Keel, *Die Geschichte Jerusalems und die Entstehung des Monotheismus*, OLB IV/1.2 [Göttingen: Vandenhoeck & Ruprecht, 2007], 848–49; cf. Keel, *Jerusalem and the One God: A Religious History*, ed. Brent A. Strawn, trans. Morven McLean [Minneapolis: Fortress, 2017], 129). I am grateful to Friedhelm Hartenstein for this reference.

111. Boehm, "Die Bilderfrage," 328.

112. Hannah Arendt also emphasizes in her interpretation of the ban on images that the Hebrew God can be heard but not seen: "*The invisibility of truth in the Hebrew religion is as axiomatic as its ineffability in Greek philosophy.*" (Hannah Arendt, *The Life of the Mind* [2 vols. in 1], ed. Mary McCarthy [New York: Harcourt, 1977], 119. Emphasis in original).

113. Jean Calvin, *Institutio christianae religionis* 1:11.

114. Gerhard von Rad, *Old Testament Theology* 1:213.

115. Cf. Henri Crouzel, "Bild Gottes II. Alte Kirche," *TRE* VI, ed. Gerhard Müller et al. (Berlin: de Gruyter, 1980), 499–502, at 499.

116. Cf. Eberhard Jüngel, "*Quae supra nos, nihil ad nos*. Eine Kurzformel der Lehre vom verborgenen Gott. Im Anschluss an Luther interpretiert" (1972), in Jüngel, *Entsprechungen: Gott, Wahrheit, Mensch* (Tübingen: Mohr Siebeck, 2002), 202–51, at 248; see also his *God as the Mystery of the World* (Grand Rapids: Eerdmans, 1983).

117. In this connection, cf. Michael Moxter, "Die verborgene Kirche und das Unsichtbare der Gemeinschaft," in *Grenzgänge der Gemeinschaft. Eine interdisziplinäre Begegnung zwischen sozial-politischer und theologisch-religiöser Perspektive*, ed. Elisabeth Gräb-Schmidt and Fernando Giuseppe Menga, Dogmatik in der Moderne 17 (Tübingen: Mohr Siebeck, 2016).

118. *Non ille digne Theologus dicitur, qui invisibilia Dei per ea, quae factu sunt, intellecta conspicit…Sed qui visibilia et posteriora Dei per passiones et crucem conspecta intelligit.* Martin Luther, "The Heidelberg Disputation" (1518), 19–20, in *The Book of Concord: The Confessions of the Lutheran Church*, at https://bookofconcord.org/sources-and-context/heidelberg-disputation/.

119. "Sihe, das ist der echte gottisdienst, datzu man keyner glocken, keiner kirchen…keyniß gemelds noch bildiß…bedarff. Denn das sind alliß menschen fundle und auffsetz, die gott nit acht, und den rechten gottisdienst mit yhrem gleyssen vordunckeln." Martin Luther, "Sermon for Christmas Eve; Titus 2:11–15," from his Church Postil of 1522, at http://sermons.martinluther.us/sermons14.html.

120. "The True and False Views of Christ's Sufferings," *The Sermons of Martin Luther* II, 183, at http://www.sacred-texts.com/chr/luther/chrsuff.htm.

121. Luther, "Christ's Sufferings," trans. adapted by MM.

122. Luther, "Christ's Sufferings," trans. adapted by MM.

123. Luther, "Christ's Sufferings."

124. Martin Luther, "Against the Heavenly Prophets in the Matter of Images and Sacraments" (1525), *LW* 40, at http://www.angelfire.com/poetry/luther/temporary/againsten.html.

125. Martin Luther, "Die Dritte Predigt, auff den Ostertag" (1533), *WA* 37:63.25–26. Translation by Ilmari Karimies, "Christ's Victory over Hell and Ours Too. Luther's 'Torgau Sermon' on Christ's Descent into Hell," German-Nordic colloquium "Love and Death, Dying and Empathy" 10.06.–13.06.10, University of Heidelberg, p. 4. Available at https://researchportal.helsinki.fi/en/activities/german-nordic-colloquium-love-and-death-dying-and-empathy.

126. Martin Luther, "Lectures on Genesis" (1535–45), *LW* 2 (St. Louis, MO: Concordia, 1960), on Gen 8:21, "*For the imagination of man's heart is evil from his youth.*" The similarity of *pingere* (paint) and *fingere* (imagine) sticks in the mind.

127. Martin Luther, "Lectures on Jonah" (1525), *LW* 19 (1974), 54.

128. Therefore the assertion that in his opposition to Karlstadt's removal of pictures from the church, Luther's concern was first of all to remove images from people's hearts is unpersuasive. Thus Dominik Burkard, "Bildersturm? Die Reformation(en) und die Bilder," in *Bilder-Streit. Theologie auf Augenhöhe*, ed. Erich Garhammer (Würzburg: 2007), 115–40, at 130. It is only against the background of such (mis-)interpretations that one may assert that "hostility to images was simply characteristic of the Reformation" (Burkard, "Bildersturm?," 120).

129. Cf. Martin Luther, "A Sermon on Preparation for Death" (1519), in *WA* 2:685–97, at 687, 691–92.

130. Martin Luther, "Sermon for Maundy Thursday" (1540), *WA* 49:72–78, at 74–75, lines 39–40.

131. Cf. Walther von Loewenich, "Bilder VI. Reformatorische und nachreformatorische Zeit," *TRE* VI, 546–57.

132. Martin Luther, "Preface to the Wittenberg Hymnal," *LW* 53 (Philadelphia: Fortress, 1999), 316.

133. Cf. Alfons Reckermann, "Kunst/Kunstwerk II," *HWP* 4, 1365–78, at 1367.

134. Martin Luther, "Preface to the Psalter," *LW* 35, 256–57.

135. This is especially true when there is a warning against confusing such self-determination with abstract autonomy or "human self-fulfillment by human powers alone" (as, e.g., by Wolfhart Pannenberg, *Contemporary Anthropology in Theological Perspective*, trans. Matthew J. O'Connell [London: T&T Clark, 1985], 58). Such reservation arises primarily from the conviction that one should think of being/becoming the image of God as a process of "self-realization" (59).

136. In this regard some part company with Pannenberg: Eberhard Jüngel, "Der Gott entsprechende Mensch. Bemerkungen zur Gottebenbildlichkeit des Menschen als Grundfigur theologischer Anthropologie," in his *Entsprechungen: Gott, Wahrheit, Mensch: theologische Erörterungen* (Munich: Kaiser, 1980), 290–317, at 294–95; also Ulrich Barth, "Kreativität und Kreatürlichkeit," in his *Gott als Projekt der Vernunft* (Tübingen: Mohr Siebeck, 2005), 173–92, at 190. Traditional reservations about the modern terminology of self-determination and self-directedness are retained by Wilfried Härle, "Menschwürde: konkret und grundsätzlich," in *Menschenwürde*, ed. Wilfried Härle and Reiner Preul, MJbT XVII (Marburg: Elwert, 2005), 135–66, at 138, 155–56.

137. Gerhard Ebeling, *Dogmatik des christlichen Glaubens*, vol. 1 (Tübingen: Mohr, 1979), 390.

138. Cf. Ralf Meyer-Hansen, *Apostaten der Natur. Die Differenzanthropologie Helmut Plessners als Herausforderung für die theologische Rede vom Menschen*, RPT 73 (Tübingen: Mohr Siebeck, 2013), 351.

139. Belting, *Anthropology of Images*, 57.

140. Cf. Ernst Cassirer, *The Philosophy of Symbolic Forms*, vol. 1, *Language*, trans. Ralph Manheim (New Haven, CT: Yale University Press, 1955), 107.

141. Cf. Gottfried Boehm, "Die Wiederkehr der Bilder," in his *Was Ist ein Bild?* 11–38, at 16, 35. The point of Boehm's reception of the concept of figuration is that time reveals itself in the image. Cf. his "Die ikonische Figuration," in *Figur und Figuration*, ed. Gottfried Boehm et al. (Munich: Fink, 2007), 33–52, at 50–51.

142. Paul Klee, "Schöpferische Konfession," in his *Kunst-Lehre*, ed. Günther Regel (Leipzig: Reclam, 1987), 60–66, at 60.

143. Martin Heidegger, "…dichterisch wohnet der Mensch…" (1951), in Heidegger, *Vorträge und Aufsätze*, pt. 2, 3rd ed. (Pfullingen: Neske, 1967), 74.

144. Cf. Thomas Nagel, *The View from Nowhere* (New York: Oxford University Press, 1986).

145. Cf. Jean-Luc Marion, *The Crossing of the Visible*, trans. of *La Croisée du visible* by James K. A. Smith (Stanford, CA: Stanford University Press, 2004).

146. Cf. Philipp Stoellger and Thomas Klie, eds., *Präsenz im Entzug. Ambivalenzen des Bildes*, Tagungen des Instituts für Bildtheorie [Institute for Iconicity] der Theologischen Fakultät der Universität Rostock im Herbst 2008 und Frühling 2009 (Tübingen: Mohr Siebeck, 2003).

147. Cf. Luca Giuliani, *Image and Myth: A History of Pictorial Narration in Greek Art*, trans. Joseph O'Donnell (Chicago: University of Chicago Press, 2013),

148. William J. T. Mitchell, *Iconology, Image, Text, Ideology* (Chicago: University of Chicago Press, 1986), 39.

149. Cf. Petra Bahr, *Darstellung des Undarstellbaren. Religionstheoretische Studien zum Darstellungsbegriff bei A. G. Baumgarten und I. Kant* (Tübingen: Mohr Siebeck, 2004).

150. Boehm, "Die Bilderfrage," 328ff. Cf. also Nancy, *Ground of the Image*, 31.

151. Think, e.g., of Sergio Leone's film *Once Upon a Time in America* or Quentin Tarantino's *Kill Bill*.

152. On this, cf. Jean-Luc Nancy, "Image and Violence," in his *Ground of the Image*, 15–26, at 20–21. This context plays a central role in Augustine's assessment of *curiositas*, and the pleasure in spectacle that appears in the arena and in the theater (cf. *Confessions* VI/8). That Augustine regards it undialectically as a lust for the senses is one of the limitations of his theology.

153. Georg Franck, *Ökonomie der Aufmerksamkeit: Ein Entwurf* (Munich: Hanser, 2015).

154. Belting, *Anthropology of Images*, 19–20.

155. There are exceptions: the new media create images simultaneously with the event or thing itself so that, for example, attendees at major sports events can see themselves on the large or small screen. Surprisingly, the directors always change the camera image at the very

moment when viewers are discovering themselves in the picture, as if the innocence of images can be preserved even today only in distance.

156. Theodor W. Adorno already saw that; cf. his *Aesthetic Theory*, ed. Gretel Adorno and Rolf Tiedemann, new trans. and ed. Robert Hullot-Kentor, Theory and History of Literature 88 (Minneapolis: University of Minnesota Press, 1997). Adorno assured a transition from the pretended physical presence of the dead to symbolic indications of their presence, giving examples in reflections on the development of sculpture. He continued, "One of the models of art may be the corpse in its transfixed and imperishable form. In that case, the reification of the formerly living would date back to primordial times, as did the revolt against death as a magical nature-bound practice" (376). Subsequently Maurice Blanchot has also influenced the discussion.

157. I am referring to the terra cotta army of the Emperor Qin Shihuangdi near Xi'an, China.

158. Cf. Belting, *Anthropology of Images*, with reference to such accounts in Polybius, Sallust, and Diodorus (117–18).

159. Cf. Hans Blumenberg, who sees the image as an anticipation of what concepts would achieve (see his *Höhlenausgänge* [Frankfurt: Suhrkamp, 1989], 26).

160. Cf. Belting, *Anthropology of Images*, 80.

161. Cf. Gottfried Boehm, "Die Wiederkehr der Bilder," 29–30.

162. Cf. Ernst Cassirer, *The Philosophy of Symbolic Forms*, vol. 2, *Mythical Thought* (1965).

163. Cf. Hans Jonas, "Homo Pictor und die Differentia des Menschen," *Zeitschrift für philosophische Forschung* 15 (1961): 161–76.

164. Jean-Paul Sartre, *The Imaginary: A Phenomenological Psychology of the Imagination*, trans. Jonathan Webber, Routledge Classics (London: Routledge, 2004).

165. Sartre, *The Imaginary*, 5–6, with reference to David Hume's *Treatise of Human Nature*, bk. 1.

166. Sartre, *The Imaginary*, pt. 1, chap. 2.

167. Sartre, *The Imaginary*, pt. 1, chap. 2.

168. Sartre, *The Imaginary*, 24.

169. Sartre, *The Imaginary*, 24.

170. Kant, *Critique of Pure Reason*, A 141.

171. Ludwig Wittgenstein, *Philosophical Investigations*, trans. G. E. M. Anscombe, dual-language ed. by P. M. S. Hacker and Joachim Schulte (Chichester: John Wiley & Sons, 2009).

Notes

172. Ludwig Wittgenstein, *Tractatus logico-philosophicus*, trans. Frank P. Ramsey and C. K. Ogden (New York: Harcourt, Brace, 1922), 29.

173. Cf. Anthony Kenny, *Wittgenstein* (Malden, MA: Blackwell, 2006), 44.

174. "The picture can represent every reality whose form it has. The spatial picture, everything spatial, the coloured, everything coloured, etc." Wittgenstein, *Tractatus*, 2.171 (p. 41).

175. Cf. Wittgenstein, *Tractatus*, 1, 1.1, 1.2, 2.223 (pp. 31, 43).

176. Wittgenstein, *Tractatus*, 2.161 (p. 41).

177. Wittgenstein, *Tractatus*, 2.17.

178. Cf. Wittgenstein, *Tractatus*, 6.52, 6.53, and 7 (pp. 187, 189).

179. Wittgenstein, *Philosophical Investigations*, 4.

180. Cf. Wittgenstein, *Lectures and Conversations on Aesthetics, Psychology, and Religious Belief*, ed. Cyril Barrett (Berkeley: University of California Press, 1967), 63.

181. "To say that God is in the picture, is not to say that it is a picture of God," as Phillips notes against a realistic misunderstanding of the picture. The latter thinks of representation as something that could be replaced by another (more accurate or more representative) picture. (Dewi Z. Phillips, "On Really Believing," in Phillips, *Wittgenstein and Religion* [New York: St. Martin's Press, 1993], 33–55, at 38.) Cf. also "Of certain pictures we say that they might just as well be replaced by another—e.g., we could, under certain circumstances, have one projection of an ellipse drawn instead of another....But in other cases, religious cases included...the whole weight may be in the picture." (Wittgenstein, *Lectures*, 71–72).

182. Thus Kant's expression in *Critique of Judgment* A 37 (V, 223).

183. Cf. Günter Wohlfart, *Der Augenblick. Zeit und ästhetische Erfahrung bei Kant, Hegel, Nietzsche und Heidegger mit einem Exkurs zu Proust* (Freiburg: Herder, 1982).

184. Boehm et al., *Figur und Figuration*, 41.

185. Boehm et al., *Figur und Figuration*, 27.

186. Boehm et al., *Figur und Figuration*, 34.

187. Cf. Michael Moxter, "All at Once? Simultaneität, Bild, Repräsentation," in *Präsenz im Entzug. Ambivalenzen des Bildes*, ed. Philipp Stoellger and Thomas Klie, HUT 58 (Tübingen: Mohr Siebeck, 2011), 129–44.

188. Cf. also *Bild und Zeit. Temporalität in Kunst und Kunsttheorie seit 1800*, ed. Thomas Kisser (Paderborn: Fink, 2011), as well as the collection

edited by this author and Markus Firchow, *Die Zeit der Bilder. Ikonische Repräsentation und Temporalität* (Tübingen: Mohr, 2018).

189. This becomes the primal experience of an encounter with the gods in Robert Walser's little story, "Das Götzenbild," in his *Sämtliche Werke in Einzelausgaben*, vol. 4, *Kleine Dichtungen*, ed. Jochen Greven (Zürich: Suhrkamp, 1985), 34. I am grateful to Friedhelm Hartenstein for this reference.

190. Frank Crüsemann also argues in this direction in "Der Gott Israels und die Religionen der Umwelt," in *Wahrheitsansprüche der Welt-religionen*, ed. Christian Danz and Friedrich Hermanni (Neukirchen-Vluyn: Neukirchener Verlag, 2006), 213–32, at 226–27.

191. Karl Barth, *Church Dogmatics*, ed. Geoffrey W. Bromiley and Thomas F. Torrance, trans. G. T. Thomson and Harold Knight, vol. I/2, *The Doctrine of the Word of God* (Edinburgh: T & T Clark, 1956), §17, "The Revelation of God as the Abolition of Religion," p. 280.

192. Paul writes similarly in Rom 1, when he uses the prophetic ridicule of idols and the deuteronomistic polemics against the erection of the image of a foreign god as paradigms for the understanding of the power of sin.

193. Cf. Belting's remarks on the epitaph of Paul Straus, a 15th-century work by Friedrich Herlin (in the Nördlingen Stadtmuseum), "Christ as Man of Sorrows," in which wheat and vine grow out of the wounds in the feet of Christ and are transformed into bread and wine, represented as a chalice with a host suspended above it; the host appears as an empty circle, the holy as a hole in the picture (cf. Belting, *Das echte Bild*, 92).

194. *Das echte Bild*, 91–92.

195. We find an interesting pointer in Louis Marin's interpretation of the picture, "The Mass of St. Anthony Abbot" (ca. 1435), attributed to the Osservanza Master, which depicts the interior of the cathedral of Siena, but at the price of the removal of all the pictures that were actually there. In place of the pictures there is the host, but it, too, remains unseen, although the Mass is celebrated in order that it may be consumed. The empty interior space, represented by the white wall of the cathedral, marks by means of absence the only place where the presence of Christ, or of God, may be expected in human guise. A comparable concept of the relationship between an empty space and the presentation of Christ is found in the Predella at Wittenberg by Lukas Cranach the Elder (here cf. the interpretation by Christian Spies, "Ikonen

des abwesenden Bildes," in *Christusbild. Icon und Ikone: Wege zu Theorie und Theologie des Bildes*, ed. Peter Hofmann and Andreas Matena
[Paderborn: Schöningh, 2010], 47–62, at 54ff.)

196. One may doubt whether we should call this double image
typical for Catholicism or Protestantism, since on the one hand it is so
color-loving and demonstrative, and on the other it seems to emphasize
difference.

197. Cf. my critical position in Michael Moxter, "Hören," in *Wörterbuch der philosophischen Metaphern*, ed. Ralf Konersmann, 3rd ed.
(Darmstadt: Wissenschaftliche Buchgesellschaft, 2011), 149–71.

198. Jacob Taubes, *Occidental Eschatology*, trans. David Ratmoko
(Stanford, CA: Stanford University Press, 2009), 16.

199. Werner H. Schmidt, *Die Zehn Gebote im Rahmen alttestamentlicher Ethik*, EdF 281 (Darmstadt: Wissenschaftliche Buchgesellschaft,
1993), 75.

200. Jürgen Ebach, "Die Einheit von Sehen und Hören. Beobach-
tungen und Überlegungen zu Bilderverbot und Sprachbildern im Alten
Testament," in *Im Zwischenreich der Bilder*, ed. Rainer-M. E. Jacobi,
Bernhard Marx, and Gerlinde Strohmaier-Wiederanders, Erkenntnis
und Glaube n.s. 35 (Leipzig: Evangelische Verlagsanstalt, 2004), 77–104,
at 94.

201. Martin Luther, sermon (on Ps 8) preached in Merseburg
(August 6, 1545), *WA* 51:11–22, at 11, line 29–33. Translation LMM.

202. "Thus the external and worldly kingdom consists only in doing
and stress that belong to seeing and fists. But the kingdom of Christ consists only in hearing, that is, that I hear the word, receive it, and believe
it....No emperor, king, or prince can rule in this way." *WA* 51, 13, lines
30–33, at 36. Translation LMM.

203. Thus the contrast between the two authors proposed by Jérôme
Cottin, *Le regard et la Parole. Une théologie protestante de l'image*
(Geneva: Labor et Fides, 1994).

204. Thus Cottin's critique.

205. Gregory the Great, CCSL 1440A, Ep. XI, at http://www
.newadvent.org/fathers/360211013.htm. My colleague in Hamburg,
Barbara Müller, to whom I am indebted for a critical reading of this part
of the text, advocates a strict translation: the images are helpful "for the
pagans"; Gregory here, as in other letters, reflects the religious-cultural
situation in the port city.

206. Still, Gregory of Nyssa (†394) could adduce in another context, in defense of images, that he had never yet looked at a picture of the sacrifice of Isaac without being moved to tears (cf. *HDTG* 1, 294).

207. Thus, the monk John of Jerusalem (ca. 764); cf. *HDTG* 1, 305.

208. Gregory of Nyssa could adduce that on behalf of images in another context: "For painting, even if it is silent, is capable of speaking from the wall and being of the greatest benefit. Likewise the mosaicist transforms the floor into a storyteller" (Gregory of Nyssa, *Oratio laudatoria Sancti ac Magni Martyris Theodori*, MPG 46, 737D–40A).

209. Gervais Dumeige, *Nicäa II* (787), Geschichte der ökumenische Konzilien 4 (Mainz: Matthias-Grünewald, 1985), 28.

210. Cf. St. John of Damascus, *Contra imaginum calumniatores orationes tres* = *Three Treatises on the Divine Images: Apologia against Those Who Decry Holy Images*, based on text in the common domain, trans. and ed. Andrew Louth (Crestwood, NY: St. Vladimir's Seminary Press, 2003). The occasion was again an iconoclastic action: Leo III and his son, who was an even more hardened opponent of images, had caused an image of Christ on the door of their palace to be replaced by a simple cross; the removal was accompanied by tumults. Patriarch Germanus, who disputed the legitimacy of the emperor's actions, was forced to resign.

211. *Three Treatises*, pt. 2, 20: *Autos ho theos protos epoiēsen eikona kai edeixen eikonas.*

212. *Three Treatises*, pt. 3, 16: *Eikōn men oun estin homoiōma kai paradeigma kai ektypōma tinos en heautō deiknuon to eikonizomenon.*

213. In analogy to the ark of the covenant, which appears as holy on account of the law that is hidden and contained within it.

214. "Not made by hands" (*axeiropoiētos*) refers to the opposition of "made by human hands" and "created by God." This opposition appears in Paul's writing in the New Testament (2 Cor 5:1) and is the counterpart to the critical conviction in Isa 44:9–11 (cf. §II.2b.2 above) that what is made by hands cannot be divine. So also Acts 19:26 identifies a core thesis of Pauline preaching: *ouk eisin theoi hoi dia cheirōn ginomenoi* (Those are not gods who came into being through [human] hands).

215. For extensive discussion, see Belting, *Das echte Bild*, 56ff.

216. This connection is strengthened by the fact that the Sudarium fell into the hands of plunderers during the so-called *Sacco di Roma* in 1527 and that they handed it around in the city's taverns; it had to be recovered and remembered in images painted by artists (cf. *Das echte*

Bild, 63ff., 126ff.). In the case of the Shroud of Turin the miraculous (surprising) discovery of the image in negative form by the unsuspecting photographer of the cloth lent it an aura of the *acheiropoetic*—and this in an era of technical reproduction.

217. Cf. Wessel, *Dogma*, 300–301, 306. The difference lay in the fact that for John of Damascus it was the *incarnate* Logos who cannot miss the ability of being depicted, but religious worship was paid not to the material colors and forms but to what was shown (in them), whereas for the emperor's religious politics the divine nature of the *logos* excluded depiction.

218. *The Sources of Catholic Dogma*, trans. Roy J. Deferrari from the 30th ed. of Henry Denzinger's *Enchiridion Symbolorum* (Fitzwilliam, NH: Loreto Publications, 1955), old numbering 302–4 (new numbers 600–603), p. 121. Available at http://patristica.net/denzinger/#n200.

219. *Heidelberger Katechismus* (1563), in *Die Bekenntnisschriften der reformierten Kirche*, ed. E. F. Karl Müller (Leipzig: Deichert, 1903), 682–719, at 710 (question 98).

220. Theodor W. Adorno and Max Horkheimer, *Dialectic of Enlightenment*, trans. John Cumming (London: Verso, 1979), 23.

221. Cf. Francis Bacon, *Novum Organum*, trans. and ed. Peter Urbach and John Gibson (Chicago: Open Court, 1994), 55–56.

222. Horkheimer and Adorno, *Dialectic*, 23–24.

223. Thus Adorno's summary on the relationship between reason and revelation in his *Critical Models: Interventions and Catchwords*, trans. Henry W. Pickford (New York: Columbia University Press, 1998), 28. Adorno's observation that an understanding of the ban on images "[leads] far beyond what this once originally meant" has been confirmed for us step by step.

224. Cf. *Luther und die Folgen für die Kunst*, exhibition at the Hamburg Kunsthalle, November 11, 1983–January 8, 1984, catalogue ed. Werner Hofmann (Munich: Prestel-Verlag, 1983), 23.

225. Cf. Martin Luther, "Confession Concerning Christ's Supper," *LW* 37, 161–372, at 371: "Images, bells, eucharistic vestments, church ornaments, altar lights, and the like I regard as things indifferent [*adiaphora*]." The quoted passage is from Martin Luther, "Eight Sermons at Wittenberg," Sermon 4 (March 12, 1522), *LW* 51, 84–88, at 86.

226. Hofmann, *Luther*, 46.

227. Thus, e.g., Christian Tümpel, "Die Reformation und die Kunst der Niederlande," in Hofmann, *Luther*, 309–21, at 314, and Eckhard

Schaar, "Calvinismus und Kunst in den nördlichen Niederlanden," in Hofmann, *Luther*, 348–74, at 348.

228. Hofmann, *Luther*, 50.

229. "For those who see it so, it is a consolation, for those who do not see it so, it is a cross." Caspar David Friedrich, "Brief an Louise Seidler, 9 May 1815," in *Caspar David Friedrich in Briefen und Bekenntnissen*, ed. Sigrid Hinz (Munich: Rogner & Bernhard, 1974), 27.

230. Hofmann, *Luther*, 47. So we should not be surprised when, now and then, a museum custodian cleans up something like Joseph Beuys's *Fettecke* (an abstract piece including butter) in the course of his or her duties. (The author refers to an actual incident that took place in Düsseldorf in 1986.) That is the price we pay for the precedence accorded the observer's perspective.

231. Cf. *Religion und Säkularisierung. Ein interdisziplinäres Handbuch*, ed. Thomas M. Schmidt and Annette Pitschmann (Stuttgart: Metzler, 2014), including Michael Moxter, "Eigenständigkeit der Moderne (Blumenberg)," 49–63.

232. See the examples in P.-K. Schuster, "Abstraktion, Agitation und Einfühlung. Formen protestantischer Kunst im 16. Jahrhundert," in Hofmann, *Luther* (see n. 224), 115–25.

233. Cf. Hofmann, *Luther*.

234. Cf. Tümpel, "Reformation," 309ff., 312.

235. Huldrich Zwingli, "Ein kurtze und christeliche inleitung" (1523), in *Sämtliche Werke* 2, ed. Emil Egli and Georg Finsler (Leipzig: Heinsius, 1908), 626–63, at 654–58; on images, 658; cf. Tümpel, "Reformation," 314.

236. Schuster, "Abstraktion," 115–125, at 116. The triptych shows the Ten Commandments on the side panels, recalling the tables of the law that Moses smashed when he saw the golden calf; cf. Belting, *Das echte Bild*, 164–65.

237. *De laudibus sanctae crucis* (= Codex Vaticanus Reginensis latinus 124). Barbara Müller pointed this work out to me.

238. Cf. Hofmann, *Luther*, 601.

239. Hofmann, *Luther*, 607.

240. Cf. Besançon's interpretation, *Image*, 362.

241. Besançon, *Image*, 364.

242. Cf. Friedrich Nietzsche, *Also Sprach Zarathustra. Ein Buch für Alle und Keinen* [1883–1885] = *Thus Spoke Zarathustra. A Book for*

Everyone and Nobody, trans. Graham Parkes, Oxford World's Classics (Oxford: Oxford University Press, 2005), 77.

243. (God is not overthrown!); cf. Kazimir Malevich, *Gott ist nicht gestürzt! Schriften zu Kunst, Kirche, Fabrik*, ed. Aage Ansgar Hansen-Löve (Munich: Hanser, 2004).

244. Cf. Paul Tillich, *The Courage to Be*, The Terry Lectures, 3rd ed. (New Haven, CT: Yale University Press, 2014), 186.

245. Cf. Lucy R. Lippard, *Ad Reinhardt* (New York: H. N. Abrams, 1981), 158: "I'm merely making the last painting which anyone can make." In interpreting this statement by Reinhardt I am following Mark C. Taylor, *Disfiguring: Art, Architecture, Religion* (Chicago: University of Chicago Press, 1992), 84–88. I owe Taylor's book many insights.

246. Taylor, *Disfiguring*, 85. Cf. Ad Reinhardt, *Art-as-Art: The Selected Writings of Ad Reinhardt*, ed. Barbara Rose (New York: Viking, 1975), 90.

247. Thus Hofmann, *Luther*, 607.

248. Cf. Belting, *Das echte Bild*, 143, 145.

249. Quoted in Taylor, *Disfiguring*, 49. My remarks follow Taylor.

250. A notable example for such negation of the image is also Robert Rauschenberg's *Erased De Kooning* (1953). Rauschenberg had acquired a sketch in chalk and charcoal as a gift, and over two months he so completely erased it that nothing remained but a trace of the depictorialization.

251. Thorsten Rodiek and Heribert Schulz, *Arnulf Rainer*, An Exhibition by the Museum and Art Society and Museum of Cultural History of Osnabrück (Osnabrück: Verlag des Museums und Kunstvereins, 1993).

252. Rodiek and Schulz, *Arnulf Rainer*, 154.

253. See, e.g., Mark C. Taylor, *Disfiguring*, 299.

254. Hofmann, *Luther*, 639.

255. Taylor, *Disfiguring*, 298.

256. Taylor, *Disfiguring*, 299.

257. Nancy, *Ground of the Image*, 28.

258. Hofmann, *Luther*, 602.

259. G. W. F. Hegel, *Aesthetics: Lectures on Fine Art*, vol. 1, trans. T. M. Knox (Oxford: Clarendon, 1975), 101, 103.

260. Cornelius Castoriadis, *Gesellschaft als imaginäre Institution. Entwurf einer politischen Philosophie* (Frankfurt: Suhrkamp, 2009), 564ff.

261. Belting, *Das echte Bild*, here introduces the section title: "Questions of Image as Questions of Faith."

262. Hörisch, *Sinn*, 53.

263. Gerhard Richter, quoted from Dietmar Elger, *Gerhard Richter: A Life in Painting*, trans. Elizabeth M. Solaro (Chicago: University of Chicago Press, 2009), 147.

264. From a sermon by P. Bahr.

265. Bruno Latour, "What Is Iconoclash? or Is there a World beyond the Image Wars?" in *Iconoclash*, 26–38, at 38.

IV. Prospect

1. Kia Vahland, "Doppelmord an Mensch und Werk: Interview with Horst Bredekamp," *Süddeutsche Zeitung* 8 (Monday, January 12, 2015): 9.

2. Horst Bredekamp, *Image Acts: A Systematic Approach to Visual Agency*, trans. Elizabeth Clegg (Boston: de Gruyter, 2018).

3. Vahland, "Doppelmord," 9.

4. Silvia Naef, *Bilder und Bilderverbot im Islam* (2007). French: *Y a-t-il une 'question de l'image' en Islam?*

5. Naef, *Bilder und Bilderverbot*, 137. The concluding sentence of the book follows: "This results in a new, perhaps also somewhat provocative question: Is the 'ban on images' in Islam not basically a question—or even an invention—of the West?" In view of current conflicts one will not be inclined simply to agree. Instead, at this very point there is need for a more elevated discussion.

6. Naef, *Bilder und Bilderverbot*, 27.

7. Naef, *Bilder und Bilderverbot*, 11–32 on the texts of the tradition; 131–37 on the present situation.

8. Vahland, "Doppelmord," 9.

9. Vahland, "Doppelmord," 9.

10. Cf. Jan Assmann, *The Price of Monotheism* (2010), 15; 57–84, refining his *Moses the Egyptian: The Memory of Egypt in Western Monotheism* (1997). Cf. also his "What's Wrong with Images?" in *Idol Anxiety*, ed. Josh Ellenbogen and Aaron Tugendhaft (Stanford, CA: Stanford University Press, 2011), 19–31. For discussion of Assmann's monotheism thesis, cf. the documentation of critical comments in the appendix to his *Die Mosaische Unterscheidung: oder der Preis des Monotheismus* (Munich: Hanser, 2010), 193–286 (not reproduced in the English edition), and

Friedhelm Hartenstein, "Monotheismus und Intoleranz. Überlegungen aus alttestamentlicher Sicht," *Glaube und Lernen* 26 (2011): 13–25.

11. For the problematic potential of such semantics, see Jan Assmann, *Monotheismus und die Sprache der Gewalt* (Vortrag im Alten Rathaus am 17. November 2004). Wiener Vorlesungen im Rathaus 116, 5th ed. (Vienna: Picus, 2009), with summary on 57: "The semantic dynamics contained in the sacred texts of the monotheistic religions flared up not in the hands of believers but in those of fundamentalists interested in political power, who made use of motifs of religious violence in order to move the masses to follow them....Hence it is important to historicize these motifs by tracing them to their original situation. We must uncover their genesis in order to restrict their application."

12. "Interpretation is not explanation of the later in terms of the earlier, what has happened as a *necessary* result of the historical conditions, but is the interpretation of what lies before us; at the same time it is a loosening and separation of the plain material to display the whole variety of its aspects, the countless threads that have become tangled together and that through the art of interpretation are separated and find their tongues again." Johann Gustav Droysen, *Rekonstruktion der ersten vollständigen Fassung der Vorlesungen (1857), Grundriß der Historik in den ersten handschriftlichen (1857/1858) und in der letzten gedruckten Fassung (1882)*, ed. Peter Leyh (Stuttgart/Bad Cannstatt: Frommann-Holzboog, 1977), 162–63. Emphasis in the original.

13. See Gottfried Boehm, "Representation, Presentation, Presence: Tracing the *Homo Pictor*," in *Iconic Power: Materiality and Meaning in Social Life*, trans. Julia Sonnevend and Dominik Bartmański, ed. Jeffrey C. Alexander, Dominik Bartmański, and Bernhard Giesen (New York: Palgrave Macmillan, 2012), 15–24, at 16–18.

14. Cf. the prose piece "Das Götzenbild" by Robert Walser from 1913 (see above, §III.6.5, n. 189), and Georges Didi-Huberman, *Confronting Images: Questioning the Ends of a Certain History of Art*, trans. John Goodman (University Park: Pennsylvania State University Press, 2005).

15. Boehm, "Representation," 23.

16. Boehm, "Representation," 20.

17. Cf. Martin Luther, *The Large Catechism*, available at https://www.ccel.org/ccel/luther/largecatechism.html.

18. Vahland, "Doppelmord," 9.

19. Gottfried Boehm, "Die Wiederkehr der Bilder," in *Was ist ein Bild?* (1995), 35.